D-DAY

EDITOR
JANE PENROSE

D-DAY

EDITOR
JANE PENROSE

CONTENTS

Foreword by Major Richard Winters

List of Contributors

Foreword by Major Richard Winters

In his book *Band of Brothers*, Stephen Ambrose tells the story of a group of citizen soldiers who became an elite company of paratroopers in the American 101st Airborne Division. They shared good and bad World War II experiences – from training in Toccoa, Georgia, to Aldbourne, England; the battles of Normandy, Market Garden, and Bastogne; and finally reaching Hitler's Eagle's Nest in Berchtesgaden, in May 1945.

This D-Day Companion has been composed by an elite group of historians who have worked to become a literary "band of brothers," sharing with the reader the input of all those involved in the most important event of our generation – D-Day, June 6, 1944, which launched the attack on Hitler's Fortress Europe.

In combat, a soldier such as I was can only tell his memories of his "field of fire." In this compelling account of D-Day you will have the opportunity to view the war through the eyes of all branches of service. This will include President Franklin D Roosevelt, Prime Minister Winston Churchill, the commanding generals – Eisenhower, Montgomery and Rommel – the planners, the tacticians, and the men on the line, Allied and German.

As I write this foreword, almost 60 years later, I find it strange the things that stick in my mind, never to be forgotten.

Captain Richard Winters,
Executive Officer, 2nd Battalion,
506th Parachute Infantry Regiment,
101 Airborne Division in Holland,
October 1944, following his second
combat jump.

In the few days before D-Day I remember the sadness of my British family, with whom I was fortunate enough to have lived. They said goodbye, knowing without being told that this was the real thing. As we went down the road in trucks, I see in memory my British "sister," Elaine, walking ahead of us and turning to wave goodbye.

At the airfield where we loaded up, I remember the feeling of relief. "At last! At last! We're going!" After all the months of training, day and night, in heat and cold, wet and tired, waiting, waiting, waiting, we could finally put it all to use.

How surprised we were to see the British men on the airfield with tears in their eyes as they watched us file to the planes. I recall their shouts of good luck – they, who had been at war much longer than we, found it hard to stand by.

In the plane with my head out the door, I could see the planes in front and behind us in V-of-V formations, nine abreast. They seemed to fill the sky. We had seen them on the airfield, but now their power filled the air.

Then, the thrill to look down at the English Channel and see the vast magnitude of ships of all sizes streaming in the same direction – ships filled with men counting on us to pave the way for them.

My mind filled with the excitement of being a vital part of the biggest invasion in history, and the tremendous responsibility I now faced of leading men in actual battle, all of us for the first time. I prayed that I was up to the challenge.

Memories of the Normandy jump, the landing, joining others to walk to our destination, Causeway #2, even the battle at Brécourt, remain clear and filled with vivid snapshots of memory.

I recall the despair of the loss of all my equipment, and the relief of replacing it with like equipment taken from the bodies of dead Germans and GIs. How good was the momentary satisfaction when I first shot one of the enemy. I sent a prayer of thanks to that soldier who had done his job of zeroing his rifle in properly.

I remember the humility I felt when "Popeye" Wynn kept saying, "I'm sorry, Lieutenant, I'm sorry!" when he was wounded.

I felt such excitement when I found those maps the Germans had left at the gun position – maps that detailed their fortifications for the whole UTAH Beach peninsula.

How shocking to learn that our whole headquarters' plane was the one we had seen go down in flames. I was now the company commander simply by having survived the jump.

After the battle, how proud I was of all our men. They had obeyed orders instantly, had moved forward deliberately, and worked together to eliminate the battery of four 105mm cannon at Causeway #2. I wished none had been wounded or lost, but I knew there would be many battles to face and we would lose more.

Perhaps one of the most poignant things I remember was days later when I finally got to the beach. In surprise, my emotions welled up at the sight of the American flag planted there. I have never looked at our flag since without that memory in my mind.

D-Day was the beginning of the end of Hitler's dream of conquering all Europe and eventually the world. At last the tide was turned and he was on the defensive. We had our feet on the Continent and refused to leave until we had liberated France, Holland, and Belgium.

After seeing D-Day through the eyes of this group of distinguished historians, you will understand and appreciate the tremendous job that was done on June 6, 1944, to give everybody the Freedom of Speech, the Freedom of Worship, the Freedom from Fear and the Freedom from Want which we now enjoy. These Four Freedoms were given as goals in the State of the Union Speech on January 6, 1941, by President Franklin Delano Roosevelt. Although we have not achieved perfection in these goals, we continue to set an example for the whole world.

Major Richard Winters, June 2003

List of Contributors

Dr Duncan Anderson is head of the Department of War Studies at the Royal Military Academy Sandhurst. He is the author of many books including *Modern Military Elites* (1993); *D Day* (1994); *The Battle for Manila* (with John Pimlott and Richard Connaughton, 1995); *The World at War* (1999); and the *Fall of the Reich* (2000). His battlefield tours conducted for both the British and American armies include Salamanca, Waterloo, the Somme, El Alamein, Normandy and the Falklands.

Ronald J Drez a Marine combat veteran of the Vietnam War, was a company commander and the recipient of two Bronze Stars and the Vietnamese Cross of Gallantry. He is the author of *Voices of D-Day: The Story of the Invasion Told by Those Who Were There* (1998); *Twenty-Five Yards of War* (2003); *Voices of Valor* (2004); and *Remember D-Day* (2004).

Carlo D'Este is a retired US Army lieutenant colonel and military historian who has written extensively about World War II. He is the author of *Decision in Normandy (2000)*; *Bitter Victory: The Battle for Sicily, 1943 (1992)*; *Fatal Decision: Anzio and the Battle for Rome (1991)*; and biographies of Generals George S. Patton and Dwight D. Eisenhower.

Dr Andrew Gordon is a Reader in Defence Studies at the UK Joint Services Command and Staff College. He is the author of *British Seapower and Procurement between the Wars* but is best known for *The Rules of the Game: Jutland and British Naval Command*, which was first published in 1996 and which won both RUSI's Westminster Medal and the Longman– History Today Book of the Year prize. He is a former officer in the Royal Naval Reserve.

Dr Christina J M Goulter is a senior lecturer, King's College, London, and teaches at the UK Joint Services Command and Staff College. Between 1994 and 1997, she was Associate Visiting Professor of Strategy at the US Naval War College, Rhode Island. Her publications include works on the Royal Air Force in World War II, including *A Forgotten Offensive: Royal Air Force Coastal Command's Anti-Shipping Campaign, 1940–45* (1995), and works on the Special Operations Executive, intelligence in World War II, and digitisation of the battlespace.

Dr David I Hall is an air warfare historian on the Higher Command and Staff Course at the Joint Services Command and Staff College, and a Lecturer at King's College, London. He has written on a number of topics in British and German military history, from Frederick the Great to more modern subjects. His most recent book is entitled *Strategy for Victory: The Development of British Tactical Air Power, 1919–1943* (Praeger, forthcoming).

Professor Russell Hart is currently Associate Professor of History at Hawai'i Pacific University, Honolulu, and was formerly Senior Lecturer at The Ohio State University. He is the co-author of *German Tanks of WWII; Weapons and Tactics of the Waffen-SS; Panzer: The Illustrated History of Germany's Armored Forces in WWII* (1999); *The German Soldier in WWII* (2000); and *Clash of Arms: How the Allies Won in Normandy* (2000).

Dr Stephen A Hart is senior lecturer in the Department of War Studies at the Royal Military Academy Sandhurst. Prior to this he lectured in the International Studies Department at the University of Surrey, and in the War Studies Department, King's College, London. He is the author of *Montgomery and the 'Colossal Cracks': The 21st Army Group in Northwest Europe 1944–45* (2000), and has co-authored – with Russell Hart – several popular histories of aspects of the German Army in World War II.

Professor Allan R Millett is Maj. Gen. Raymond E. Mason Professor of Military History, The Ohio State University. He is the author of *Their War for Korea* (2002) and co-author of *A War to be Won: Fighting the Second World War* (2000) as well as author of three other books and co-author of *For the Common Defense*, a military history of the United States in print since 1984. He is a colonel, USMCR (Ret.).

Professor   Williamson Murray is a senior fellow at the Institute of Defense Analysis Studies, Washington, DC and Professor Emeritus in History at The Ohio State University. He is the author of numerous articles and books, including A *War to be Won: Fighting the Second World War* (2001) with Dr Allan Millett. His most recent book, written with Major General Robert Scales, US Army (Ret.) is titled *The Iraq War, A Military History* (2003).

Professor Samuel J Newland is the Professor of Military Education at the US Army War College at Carlisle, Pennsylvania, where he has held the Maxwell D. Taylor Chair of the Profession of Arms and the Henry L. Stimson Chair of Military Studies. He is the author of numerous books and articles on twentieth-century military history.

Professor Dennis Showalter is Professor of History at Colorado College, and Past President of the Society for Military History. He specializes in the military history of modern Germany and the World Wars. Among his books are *Railroads and Rifles: Soldiers, Technology and the Unification of Germany* (1988); *Tannenberg: Clash of Empires* (1991); *The Wars of Frederick the Great* (1995); and *The Wars of German Unification* (2001). He is completing a book on *Men of War: Patton, Rommel, and the Twentieth Century*.

Chapter 1: Introduction

"The great crusade"

(General Dwight D Eisenhower in his address to Allied forces, June 6, 1944)
"Soldiers, sailors, and airmen of the Allied Expeditionary Force,
you are about to embark upon the great crusade
towards which we have striven these many months."

Professor Samuel J Newland

Embedded in the memories of people of every generation are key events, defining moments which will be remembered for the rest of their lives. For millions of contemporary citizens from the Western nations, the events of September 11, 2001, in New York City will be one such key memory. A previous generation however, the generation that lived through and fought World War II, witnessed many defining moments. Some of their memories tend to focus on events that have special meaning to a particular nation. For example, few Frenchmen of that generation will ever forget the 1940 Fall of France and the vivid image of German soldiers marching, daily, down the Champs Elysées to the Place de la Concorde. Citizens of the United Kingdom have an enduring memory of the Blitz of 1940, when London endured the merciless pounding by the Luftwaffe. They will not forget the "Miracle of Dunkirk," the rescue of the British Empire's soldiers from France. US citizens of the wartime generation clearly remember December 7, 1941, when, without warning, the Japanese Navy staged its surprise attack on the US fleet at Pearl Harbor, Hawai'i.

Yet, from the World War II era there is one event, one memory, that transcends national experiences and unites the Western Allies. That event is D-Day, June 6, 1944.

The invasion of German-occupied France by an Allied joint force remains an accomplishment that is undiminished by the passage of over half a century. As readers look back at that event, through this commemorative volume, it is appropriate to ponder and evaluate the significance of D-Day. In short, as we proceed into the 21st century, what should be remembered and what can be learned from this legendary operation?

THE IMPORTANCE OF SUPERIORITY

Generations which were not a part of this epic undertaking should consider that an invasion of the Continent was a decided but necessary risk. If it succeeded, it would serve as the precursor to victory over Nazi Germany. If it failed, it would have been a bitter defeat that would likely prolong the war. Defeating Hitler's regime, and the military forces that had allowed it to extend its sway over most of Europe was, to say the least, a daunting task. In early 1944, the main areas where Allied troops could clearly take comfort in their success was in the air and on the seas. By 1944, the Kriegsmarine that had menaced the sea lanes with ships like the *Graf Spee* and the *Bismarck* could not afford to put its remaining capital ships to sea. Instead, it was forced to relegate what remained of its small fleet to relatively safe harbors, in the hope that they would not be sunk. The powerful U-boat fleet, which had terrorized the North

OPPOSITE As shown by this aerial photograph the support rendered by Allied and naval fire pounded the Normandy landscape into an almost lunar configuration. When the guns fell silent, however, the Germans were still there, waiting. (US Military History Institute)

By June 6, 1944, the Luftwaffe could not even gain local superiority over battlefields on the Western Front. Its only successes were at night against the bomber streams that pounded the Reich, as is demonstrated by the rudder assembly of this ME 110 night fighter. (Author's collection)

Atlantic and threatened the sea lanes that supported Britain, was systematically being hunted down by Allied air and sea assets. U-boats were no longer the hunters, but rather the hunted. If an invasion were to occur, the German Navy could only hope to contest an Allied invasion fleet in the English Channel through raids by their fast and maneuverable E-boats, or possibly through limited operations by their rapidly diminishing U-boat fleet. By 1944, serious resistance by the German Navy was, at best, a dubious prospect.[1]

The possibility of effective resistance by the German Luftwaffe was only a little better. That proud air arm, which had ruled the skies over eastern and western Europe from 1939–42, had begun a gradual decline in 1943. By early 1944, due to the steady attrition of its pool of skilled pilots, over-dependence on outdated airframes, and an inadequate training base, the Luftwaffe had clearly lost the air war. When, rather than if, an Allied invasion force appeared off the coast of France, the Luftwaffe could hope to stage some limited sorties against the Allies, but their assistance to the German defenders overlooking the French beaches would be limited. For certain, the German combined air/land operations of the early war years were a thing of the past.

Despite this Allied superiority in the air and on the seas, a major obstacle still remained for the Western Allies and their planned invasion of Fortress Europe – the German Army. This force had risen from the ashes like the proverbial phoenix following Hitler's assumption of power in 1933, and had established itself as a leading military power in a relatively brief period of time. The German Army, which prior to 1933 was restricted by the Versailles Treaty from possessing tanks or military aircraft, had by 1940 become the foremost proponent in the use of combined arms operations, allowing it to repeatedly dominate the battlefield. Thus, in the time that elapsed between September 1, 1939, and December 5, 1941, when the Russian counterattack rolled the Germans back from the gates of Moscow, the German Army was able to amass an almost unblemished string of victories in campaigns against Poland, France, the Low Countries, Scandinavia, and Yugoslavia. By the end of 1941, victory had only eluded the Germans in their wars against Britain and the Soviet Union. At the end of 1941, the ultimate fate of the Soviet Union was still in doubt.

Even after the German debacle at Stalingrad in early 1943, the German Army was still a formidable force, as the Russians would soon learn. While still suffering from the Russian offensive that bagged the 6th Army at Stalingrad, its capabilities allowed it to conduct von Manstein's famous "backhand" response. This counterstroke sent the Russian Army reeling back in retreat, allowing the Germans to recapture the important city of Kharkov, and stabilize the front. According to some German writers, this resilience of the German Army caused Stalin to consider negotiating an end to the war. Even the German Army's much-analyzed failure in the battle at Kursk, initiated on July 5, 1943, was more of an example of Hitler's bungling and interference in military matters than of the declining capabilities of the German Wehrmacht.

Granted, starting with mid-1943, the military fortunes of the German Army began a steady decline. But, even as Germany lost terrain, troops and equipment, the amount of territory it had to defend also diminished. Less terrain to defend and occupy, increased recruiting of Germans and kindred peoples from other European nations, and the reorganization of the German wartime industry by Albert Speer meant that, as 1944 dawned, the German Army was still a formidable adversary. It may have been a wounded giant, but the giant was not yet approaching death. The army was still a military force which, even that late in the war, could and did punish its

adversaries, as would later be demonstrated in the Huertgen and the Ardennes.[2]

THE STRENGTH OF ALLIANCE

What today's readers should consider is the quandary facing the two Western Allies. That is, what was the best method to bring about the final defeat of the German Army? The Allies had the best overall foundation for vanquishing Nazi Germany – a strong alliance and a goal from which the Alliance never wavered. In fact, the most significant lesson of the World War II campaign in Europe is likely to be the power that can be and was generated by a strong alliance which holds firmly to a mutually accepted goal.

This concept was understood early in the war by the leaders of the two major democracies, Franklin D. Roosevelt and Winston S. Churchill. Early in his first year as Prime Minister, Churchill came to believe that the defeat of Nazi Germany would take the combined might of the English-speaking nations, specifically the British Empire and the "Great Republic across the seas," the United States. President Roosevelt, an anglophile, watched with great concern as the war clouds gathered over Europe in 1939. Roosevelt understood the importance of a strong bond between the two English-speaking nations, and as early as 1940 began to prepare his nation to support the British Empire, even before any type of official alliance was forged. The relationship between the two democracies became more formalized with the ABC Talks (or American–British Conversations) held in Washington between January and March, 1941. Through these talks the two nations agreed on a common goal, a goal that carried them through some of the darkest days of the war – the defeat of Nazi Germany.

Although the British–American alliance held firm throughout the war, the problem facing the two democracies was determining the best strategy to bring about the final defeat of Germany. The Allies could continue to nibble around the periphery, to weaken and attrit Germany's strength. After all, in 1942–43 battles were being won on the land-masses bordering the Mediterranean and on the Atlantic Ocean. However, the Allied goal was not merely winning battles or concluding victorious campaigns, it was the defeat and destruction of Nazi Germany. How to expeditiously accomplish this goal was important because, as a general rule, democracies do not normally exhibit the patience to pursue strategies that take a long time to bring success. Instead, they seek closure, an end to hostilities and a return to peacetime pursuits.

OPPOSITE The war on the Eastern Front exacted a heavy toll on the German Army, as is evidenced by the faces of these two Mountain Troopers at Nikopol in early March 1944. The Western Allies would soon learn that such veteran soldiers were tough adversaries. (Author's collection)

Thus, to accomplish this goal in a timely fashion, the American Army and forces drawn from the British Empire would have to conduct amphibious landings, an invasion of the continent of Europe. Once a successful landing was made, it would have to be followed by a determined drive into the heartland of Germany, which would bring about a speedy conclusion to the war and return Europe and the world to a peacetime existence. June 6, 1944, was more than just another amphibious landing, like TORCH in North Africa or HUSKY in Sicily. It was the direct path to the German heartland and the destruction of Hitler's regime.

DECISIONS AND RESOURCES

The basic question facing planners was when and where such an invasion should occur. At conferences held by the Western Allies at Casablanca, and the "Big Three" meeting at Tehran, the Allies quibbled and at times squabbled over when and where the main thrust would be aimed. Though the prospect was daunting, the leadership

Much of the design and construction of the Atlantic Wall was under the direction of Organization TODT, a unique force of engineering and construction specialists. These specialists, captured in the battle for Normandy, failed to make it out of the construction zone in time. (NYP 30046, AP Photo)

recognized that the final defeat of the German war machine would have to come through a forcible entry into the continent of Europe. This was the only logical way to destroy Germany's army and its war-making capabilities. Regardless of whether it was in the vicinity of Calais, Normandy, or in southern France, an invasion of "Fortress Europe" would certainly have to happen.

Throughout most of 1943 the Germans gave little consideration to the possibility of an immediate invasion, although construction of the Atlantic Wall continued during the same year. Rather, they were occupied with the fall of Stalingrad and subsequent operations, and the collapse of Axis units in Tunisia. These military disasters were followed by the Allied invasion of Sicily and Italy and the subsequent overthrow of Mussolini. Still, in the collective opinion of *Oberkommando der Wehrmacht* (OKW) and Adolf Hitler, invasion of the European continent was not likely, something confirmed by the fact that German units were almost totally unprepared to repulse such an event. However, as Allied power grew throughout that year and into 1944, the Germans started to recognize that an invasion of the Continent would soon be attempted.

In late 1943, the German forces began to prepare in earnest to defeat a cross-Channel invasion. Narrowing their focus to the area from Calais through to Normandy, and under the command of the charismatic Erwin Rommel, feverish preparations were initiated to make the Atlantic coast a formidable defensive system. The pace of bunker and pillbox construction accelerated, millions of mines were laid, and anti-landing-vessel devices were planted on the most likely beaches. France, which in 1942–43 had been lightly defended and had served as a reconstitution area for German troops mauled on the Eastern Front, became a hive of activity. Troop strengths were boosted and mobile reserve forces were designated and put into position to launch a counterattack in the event that an invasion occurred. Despite the military reverses of 1943 and early 1944, the German preparations to counter an Allied attack were ominous.

German preparations plus the defensive capabilities of the Wehrmacht meant that the Western Allies were not at all certain of a successful landing, even in 1944. The balance sheet shows that the military fortunes of the Western Allies to this point in the war were mixed. Since the beginning of the European conflict, Britain had fought long and hard against Nazi aggression, but with mixed results. It had, together with its French allies, lost its foothold on the Continent, but had bloodied the German nose in the Battle of Britain. British forces had lost the island of Crete but, after a long retreat, they had stopped the famed Afrika Korps at El Alamein. British forces, together with American units, had been successful at Sicily but, like their American allies, they had become bogged down in Italy due to a well-planned and executed German defense. Britain did not lack good soldiers or great commanders, but what it did lack was resources – men, the weapons of war, and secure sources of raw materials to fight the war.

In comparison, the United States, a relative newcomer to the war, had an abundance of resources, both raw materials and industries. It also had a rapidly expanding military force that drew from an ample population base. Conversely, US participation in the European war had to that point in time produced mixed results. Operation TORCH, the landings in North Africa, had been a significant accomplishment, but Kasserine Pass had been a decided embarrassment. Sicily and Salerno had again shown significant American capabilities, but Anzio had demonstrated problems with both American planning and leadership.

Although the invasion did not occur until June 1944, British and American troops began training for amphibious operations as early as 1942. Here US Rangers are shown training with British commandos. (US Army Military History Institute)

The task facing these Western Allies was exceptionally difficult. The insertion of a military force into hostile territory is one of the most hazardous operations that a commander and his headquarters can attempt, as noted by Russell Weigley in his outstanding book *Eisenhower's Lieutenants*:

"An amphibious assault is a frontal attack, with all the perils thereby implied. The assaulting troops have no room for maneuver. They cannot fall back. They have only limited ability to outflank strong points. They cannot do anything subtle."[3]

Landings of this sort require troops well trained for such an operation, the necessary transport – in this case by land and sea – and a strong base of fire support to provide cover to the invasion force. Without these factors and sound leadership, the landings could result in a Gallipoli or Dieppe, both painful and costly defeats, a fact all too obvious to the British military establishment.

Despite all of these potential problems and perils, the invasion, codenamed OVERLORD, would have to be staged and would have to be staged at a time when the Germans were feverishly preparing their coastal defenses. In short, this was the quickest, the most decisive route to victory. Even though victories in the North Atlantic and in North Africa were not without merit, the road to victory both psychologically and militarily lay in an Allied force entering the heartland of Europe, fighting its way into Germany, and destroying the German Army and the war-making capabilities of the German nation. A quick and decisive victory was important because much of Europe had suffered under German occupation for some four years. Whilst not all Germans were barbarians, the barbarity of the National Socialist regime was truly a stain on Western society that had to be removed.

LEARNING FROM OVERLORD

Looking back after 60 years, the decision to take this risk was important not only because it would lead to the destruction of Hitler's regime, but also because it holds significant lessons, particularly for military planners today. D-Day serves as a prime example of the power and synergy that can be created through a strong alliance. In modern military history there are few better examples of a strong alliance than the one that existed between the United States and Great Britain. The strength of the alliance began at the top with the unique chemistry between Franklin D. Roosevelt and Winston S. Churchill. While each clearly and consistently represented the national interests of their individual countries, through their warm mutual respect and their common goal, Churchill and Roosevelt set an excellent example for waging warfare within an alliance.

As supreme commander Eisenhower was both a commanding general and a political figure. Here "Ike" is shown on May 12, 1944 with prime ministers Mackenzie King (Canada), Winston Churchill (Great Britain), Peter Frazier (New Zealand), Sir Geoffrey Huggins (Rhodesia), and Jan Smuts (South Africa). (US Army Military History Institute)

The strength of alliance warfare can be seen at the highest military levels. General Dwight D. Eisenhower, the Supreme Allied Commander, had the support and respect of both Roosevelt and Churchill. Roosevelt sensed early on that Eisenhower held unique abilities to work within an alliance structure. Eisenhower validated this trust on numerous occasions, not least of which was working with Churchill. Though Churchill was brilliant, working with the Prime Minister could at times be challenging, due to the latter's military background and his own strong opinions on strategy. Still, mutual respect and a common goal allowed these two men to develop a solid working relationship.

As the actual planning for OVERLORD proceeded, the importance of using the talents available through a strong alliance became evident. When Dwight D. Eisenhower was appointed Supreme Allied Commander and Field Marshal Bernard L. Montgomery was named the Ground Component Commander for the invasion (as well as Commander of the British 21st Army Group), these two senior officers were able to work closely together to develop a successful plan. In

1943, earlier planners had proposed a modest force of three divisions to invade the Continent and begin the process of unraveling Hitler's "Thousand-Year Reich." Eisenhower and Montgomery found the original 1943 plan far too weak and, through their combined efforts, a robust invasion force of five divisions, supported by three airborne divisions, was structured. Though later in the war they would have their differences, in the planning and implementation phases of OVERLORD, the talents of these two senior leaders were decidedly important for the successful invasion.

The Ground Component Commander for the Normandy invasion was the British hero of El Alamein, Field Marshal Bernard L. Montgomery. The commander is shown here with his two puppies, Rommel and Hitler. (6542 Crown copyright)

The solid commitment to use the combined abilities of the two English-speaking nations could be seen throughout Eisenhower's command structure. Thus, as 1944 began, Eisenhower's aide was Lt. Col. James Gault, a member of the Scots Guards. The air commander for the Allied Expeditionary Force was Air Chief Marshal Sir Trafford Leigh-Mallory, a bona fide British hero from the Battle of Britain. As chief of Allied naval

Supreme Allied Commander Dwight D. Eisenhower is shown here at the war's end with his deputy commander Sir Arthur Tedder. (US Army Military History Institute)

forces for the invasion Eisenhower selected Admiral Sir Bertram Ramsay. From the beginning to the end OVERLORD was truly an alliance effort.

The synergy produced by the alliance went beyond that produced by the senior leadership. For example, through its geographical location and a number of excellent ports, Britain offered the prime launching platform for an invasion force. In fact, the British Isles became one immense marshaling yard for British, US, and Canadian troops. The combined power of the Royal Navy and US Navy offered the transportation assets for men and supplies, as well as the combined firepower to make the invasion a success. The combined air assets of Britain and the United States, both tactical aircraft and strategic bombers, offered the Allies mastery of the skies, day and night. Through the Allied air and sea fleets the firepower needed to support the landings was available. Fortunately, the same strength in the air and on the seas was conspicuously absent for German forces.

In retrospect, consider what this alliance and the millions of soldiers and support personnel were able to accomplish. On June 5, an armada of some 7,000 Allied ships, consisting among others of 138 warships, 221 escort vessels, 287 minesweepers, 805 cargo vessels and 495 light coastal vessels proceeded across the Channel and converged on the Normandy peninsula. Above, 1,400 troop transports, 11,590 military aircraft of various types and 3,700 fighters supported the landings. Even more impressive, on one day, June 6, 1944, Allied naval and air assets put between 150,000 and 175,000 soldiers ashore. The Allied landings were so well planned, so well supported with an admirable deception plan that, together with a little bit of pure luck, they succeeded. Only on OMAHA Beach was there a possibility that the landings might fail, and even that was erased before the day was through.

For certain, the Normandy invasion was a tribute to the bravery of Canadian, British, American, Polish, Czechoslovakian, and Free French soldiers who faced the odds and successfully completed an amphibious landing, one of the toughest types of operation for a soldier. It was a tribute to the pilots who flew the transports through a hail of fire to land three airborne divisions on the European continent, and the navy personnel that guided the landing craft toward a well-defended shore. Above all, D-Day marked the initiation of the final chapter of the great crusade to destroy National Socialist Germany, and was a prime example of the might that can be employed through a strong alliance that has mutually agreed goals and excellent leadership. Despite the passage of 60 years, this is an example that should not be ignored in the 21st century.

Chapter 2

"Remember this is an invasion"

(Prime Minister Sir Winston Churchill,
7 April 1944 at a meeting of senior OVERLORD commanders)
"Remember this is an invasion, not the creation of a fortified beachhead."

Planning and build-up

Dr Duncan Anderson

"Remember this is an invasion, not the creation of a fortified beachhead." With this admonition the British Prime Minister concluded his address to the Anglo-American High Command at St Paul's school on the afternoon of 7 April. "He was in a very weepy condition, looking old and lacking a great deal of his usual vitality," recalled General Alan Brooke, the chief of the imperial general staff (CIGS). A few rows back on the hard, high-tiered wooden benches of the St Paul's classroom, the British director of military operations, Major General John Kennedy, got the same impression. "Winston spoke without vigour. He did not look up much while he spoke … [there was] … no fire in the delivery. I thought he was going to burst into tears as he stepped down to sit beside Eisenhower and Monty and the chiefs of staff."

FEAR AND FOREBODING

D-Day lay less than eight weeks away. Two days earlier in a meeting of the Prime Minister's defence committee, Churchill had railed against the adoption of a bombing plan to support the invasion, a plan being pressed by Tedder and Eisenhower. It would cause between 80,000 and 150,000 French civilian casualties, Bomber Command spokesmen had told him. A horrendous price – more Frenchmen dead than had so far been killed by the Germans during their four-year occupation. Better by far to continue the strategic bombing of Germany than to kill Allied civilians in what might prove to be a doomed venture.

Churchill knew better than anyone the dangers inherent in amphibious operations. A little over eight weeks earlier an Anglo-American force had landed at Anzio, only 50 miles south of Rome, in an attempt to break the stalemate on the Italian front. Instead of breaking out across the peninsula, it had been penned in and almost driven back into the sea. Twenty-nine years earlier, as first lord of the admiralty, Churchill had supported yet another amphibious operation of which much had been hoped, the landing on the Gallipoli Peninsula. It, too, had gone badly wrong. Churchill had been forced to resign and for a time it seemed that his career was over.

The idea of landing on the heavily defended Channel coast of France filled Churchill with deep foreboding. One evening in February 1944, while discussing OVERLORD with his personal staff, he had suddenly said: "Why are we doing this? Why do we not land instead in a friendly territory, the territory of our oldest ally? Why do we not land in Portugal?" A minute had been sent to the chiefs of staff that it should be discussed the following morning, and all through the night planners worked on a paper outlining the possibilities of an advance through

OPPOSITE British infantry landing under fire on 6 June 1944.

Spain and across the Pyrenees. General Alan Brooke had ripped it apart intellectually – logistic costs and the problems of crossing the Pyrenees made it a plan of little feasibility – but the CIGS himself had no great enthusiasm for the cross-Channel attack. To him – and to the generation of now senior British officers who had served on the Western Front during the First World War – it smacked of a seaborne Somme.

RETURN TO THE CONTINENT

To the first generation of post-war historians it was axiomatic that Britain had begun planning a return to the Continent almost as soon as the last boats had got back from Dunkirk. Churchill had claimed this himself. But the establishment of Commandos, the development of an amphibious capability and the creation of a combined operations command did not mean Britain had begun preparing for an invasion of north-west Europe, no matter how far off in the future. The only plan for the commitment of British forces to north-west Europe drawn up at this time was a piece of optimistic fantasy, a landing on the coast of France east of Le Havre in the event of a sudden German collapse.

Unlike many other units of the US Army in Britain during the build-up to OVERLORD, the US Army Rangers trained rigorously in execises that simulated actual combat conditions. These included amphibious assaults using live ammunition, scaling cliffs hundreds of feet high on the Isle of Wight and forced marches in full kit in the Highlands of Scotland.
(IWM PL 10575)

Hitler's and Mussolini's declarations of war on 11 December 1941 brought the United States into the European conflict. Seizing the moment, on 22 December Churchill and the British chiefs of staff arrived in Washington. They stayed until 14 January 1942 for what would become known as the Arcadia Conference. The British managed to secure the American High Command's agreement to give priority to the war against Germany, though this caused difficulties for Roosevelt. While the Pearl Harbor attack had inflamed popular feeling in the United States against Japan, attitudes towards Germany and Italy were more ambivalent. A large proportion of the American population were of German or Italian descent; moreover, there was a genuine and not unfounded suspicion that Britain would seek to use American power to further its own ends. The chief of staff of the US Navy, Admiral Ernest J. King, obsessed with the war in the Pacific against Japan, strongly opposed the emphasis given to Europe. The chief of staff of the US Army, General George C. Marshall, was acutely aware that the 'Germany-first' strategy, while the most sensible policy in a purely military sense, might well be overturned by popular pressure in America. A massive American military effort devoted to Europe could be justified only if it were designed to create an invasion force that would knock Germany out at the earliest possible opportunity. As Brigadier General Eisenhower, Marshall's newly promoted assistant chief of staff at the war plans division, put it at the end of the Arcadia conference, "We've got to build up air and land forces in England and when we're strong enough, go after Germany's vitals, and we've got to do it while Russia is in the war."

OPERATION BOLERO

In the second week of April 1942, General Marshall arrived in London with a plan devised by Eisenhower and his team. A year hence, 48 divisions supported by 5,800 combat aircraft were to land on the coast of France between Étretat (north of Le Havre) and Cap Gris Nez. All this would be brought to pass by a massive logistic operation, codenamed BOLERO, after Ravel's steadily rising musical score. Harry Hopkins, Roosevelt's special advisor who had accompanied Marshall, waxed eloquent in defence of the decision to attempt a second front in 1943. It was, he said, "one of the most momentous which had ever been faced". The British appeared to greet the plan with enthusiasm. In a closed session of parliament, Churchill announced to the House that "the liberation of the continent of Europe by equal numbers of American and British troops is the main war plan of our two nations", while for foreign secretary Anthony Eden, it presented "the great picture of two English-speaking countries setting out for the redemption of Europe".

In fact, Britain's leaders knew the plan was not feasible in the time Marshall had allowed. They also had a fair idea that while the plan may have been designed as a statement of long-term intent, Marshall's immediate purpose was to prevent America drifting towards a 'Pacific-first' strategy. Brooke outlined in his diary the pressures King and MacArthur were exerting on Washington. "To counter these moves Marshall has started the European offensive plan and is going 100 per cent all out on it! It is a clever move which fits in well with present political opinion and the desire to help Russia." Churchill's response to Roosevelt was equivocal. He appeared to agree to the Marshall Plan, which would start "with an ever increasing air offensive both by night and day and more frequent and large-scale raids, in which United States troops will take part." However, there was a proviso – the United States should assist Britain in fighting Japan in the Indian Ocean. In other words, British policy would remain the same – raiding in Europe and a colonial war to defend the British Empire.

OPERATION GYMNAST

Two months later, Churchill descended on Washington with the plans of Operation GYMNAST, a scheme for an Anglo-American invasion of North Africa, by which he intended to divert American efforts from a cross-Channel invasion to a campaign in the Mediterranean. A furious Marshall attempted to block the scheme, by siding with King and recommending that the United States adopt a Pacific-first policy, but Roosevelt supported Churchill. Like the British Prime Minister, Roosevelt, a former secretary of the navy, understood to a much greater extent than the generals of America's army the dangers inherent in amphibious operations. On 18 August these apprehensions were underlined when a large-scale raid composed predominantly of Canadian forces was all but wiped out in an attack on Dieppe. The disaster was convenient in helping the British prove their case – too convenient for some revisionist historians who have argued that Dieppe was intended to be a fiasco. It wasn't; Dieppe was the product of Lord Louis Mountbatten's Combined Operations HQ at its very worst.

Thus it was that the first Anglo-American landings of the war took place on the coast of French North Africa on 8 November 1942 against sporadic resistance. A little over two months later, the British and American High Commands met at Casablanca, where the well-prepared British secured the Americans' agreement to the continuation of a Mediterranean strategy, at least so far as the invasion of Sicily was concerned. The price was the establishment of an Anglo-American planning staff in London, who were to be tasked with planning an invasion of the Continent, now scheduled for the early summer of 1944.

COSSAC

It would have been logical for the Anglo-American meeting in Casablanca to have appointed a supreme allied commander, who could then have constructed a staff. The need to maintain Anglo-American harmony, however, meant that any such appointment would be premature. Churchill, who was at this stage merely humouring the Americans, was reluctant to give a cross-Channel invasion a champion, while the Americans knew that any appointment made in early 1943 would have to go to a British officer, and they intended that it would fall to an American. The solution was to provide the still-notional

Lieutenant General Sir Frederick Morgan was appointed chief of staff to the supreme allied commander for the invasion of Europe in 1943. He was principal planning officer for Operation OVERLORD and later served as Eisenhower's deputy chief of staff to the end of the war. (IWM EA 33078)

supreme allied commander with a chief of staff, who could form a team to do all the preparatory work. This mantle fell upon Lieutenant General Frederick Morgan, the commander of British 1st Corps, who took to calling himself COSSAC (chief of staff to the supreme allied commander). It was joke, but the name stuck.

Arriving in London in early March, Morgan received a less-than-reassuring brief from General Alan Brooke. "Well, there it is" said the CIGS. "It won't work, but you must bloody well make it." Assigned space in Norfolk House in London, Morgan found an unoccupied room and established squatters' rights. He recalled that "equipment consisted of a couple of desks and chairs we found in the room, and we were lucky enough also to find a few sheets of paper and a pencil that someone had dropped on the floor." Acutely aware that Norfolk House was considered the home of lost causes – it was sufficient, he recalled, "for an individual to say that he was working in Norfolk House to cause a perceptible drop in the temperature surrounding any given conversation" – Morgan suspected that the British military and political hierarchy did not take his organisation very seriously. Within days of setting up his office, a memorandum arrived from the Prime Minister seeking COSSAC's support in redirecting the American build-up to the Mediterranean. Morgan, as chief of staff of an allied organisation, felt honour-bound to pass the memorandum on to the Americans. The unholy trans-Atlantic row that erupted did little to help Morgan's career in the British army, but did establish his credentials with the Americans as a British officer they could trust. Morgan suspected for some time that he was part of some enormous deception operation; even a visit later that summer from Henry L. Stimson, the US secretary for war, did not entirely reassure him.

The establishment of a staff took some time. Morgan found in Brigadier General Ray W. Barker a deputy who, though an American, had spent much of his leave in England, and who consequently possessed a sympathetic understanding of the British and their eccentricities. Other Americans took longer to appoint, partly the product of finding suitably qualified officers, thanks to the massive expansion of the American Army. From the Royal Navy came Commodore John Hughes-Hallet, one of the chief planners of Dieppe, while American sailors, preoccupied with the Pacific, were at first thin on the ground. Problems were also encountered with the appointment of air force officers. The 'bomber barons' – Harris for RAF's Bomber Command and Spaatz for the USAAF's Eighth Air Force – convinced that they alone could win the war, regarded COSSAC's activities with a mixture of disdain and suspicion. Morgan managed to secure Air Chief

Marshal Trafford Leigh-Mallory, a fighter pilot who was *persona non grata* with the rest of the RAF, fighters being largely confined to air defence over Britain, with bombers being the order of the day overseas. As a result, there was a long delay in producing an integrated air staff to work intimately with COSSAC.

COSSAC was tasked not merely with the preparatory work for a large-scale invasion, but with two subsidiary operations, both revamped versions of earlier schemes to rush forces to the Continent if either a Soviet or a German collapse seemed in the offing. Morgan subsumed both subsidiary operations into the process of planning the large-scale invasion, so that much time was saved. His staff also discovered hundreds of plans and thousands of files, produced earlier in the war, many by Mountbatten's Combined Operations HQ. Much of this material was now incorporated into the planning process.

The most pressing issue was to choose a site for the invasion to come ashore, a subject Combined Operations had already studied in some detail. Only two areas were feasible – the Pas de Calais and the coast of Normandy west of the Seine estuary. Setting his British staff to study the Pas de Calais, while his Americans investigated Normandy, Morgan was disappointed when the result was not more clear-cut. Both had good access routes leading inland, and both had shorelines that were a mixture of shingle and cliff, interspersed by wide sandy beaches. The Pas de Calais was closer to Germany, but Normandy offered better anchorages. It was also likely that both areas would be defended at least as heavily as Dieppe had been on 18 August 1942.

THE RATTLE CONFERENCE

Morgan was saved from his dilemma by Mountbatten, who invited him to a brain-storming session at Combined Operations training HQ at Largs in Scotland. Known as the Rattle Conference, it turned out to be a combination of intensive study and 1920s house party. Only Mountbatten could have done this. Twenty generals were present, along with 11 air marshals and air commodores, and eight admirals. Of the total number there, five were Canadians and 15 Americans. Seminar sessions chaired with rigorous enthusiasm by Mountbatten were interspersed with displays by pipe bands, and champagne suppers. Rattle did the job. The assembled company chose Normandy. Though further from Germany, it offered the opportunity of capturing two major ports from the landward side – Cherbourg and Le Havre – and made possible a strike to the west to capture the ports of Brittany. The Pas de Calais, though much closer to the ultimate objective, offered none of these advantages.

A generation after he was murdered by the IRA, controversy continues to swirl around Louis Mountbatten. Appointed to head Combined Operations in 1941, the 40-year-old naval captain found himself at the bottom of a steep learning curve. Mountbatten made mistakes at Combined Operations – the most serious was the Dieppe Operation – but his critics overlook the fact that without his combination of vigorous enthusiasm, intellectual open-mindedness and political and social connections the dead hand of British bureaucracy, assisted by inter-service rivalry, would have imposed crippling delays on preparations for amphibious operations. The inefficiency of British planning machinery was so great that it is difficult to see how an operation as complicated as OVERLORD would have come to fruition unless there had been someone like Mountbatten to set the machine in motion. (IWM F489)

Having decided where to land, the conference also discussed the related problem of how to supply the armies in the interval between coming ashore and capturing a port, and returning the port to working order. Like the tank in the World War I, many claimed credit for MULBERRY, giant artificial harbours which would be towed across the Channel. Mountbatten, Churchill and John Hughes-Hallett all discussed various aspects of the scheme from time to time, but despite wartime propaganda there was really nothing novel about the idea. As early as 1917 the War Office had drawn up plans for the construction of floating docks and breakwaters, and in the late 1930s the Royal Navy had towed an enormous dock complex the 10,000 miles from Southampton to Singapore, a voyage which was covered extensively in contemporary newsreels. It was very much an idea of its time. Churchill was an enthusiast, but it is clear that at first he was thinking of the use of artificial harbours in a much wider context, in the Mediterranean and the Far East, than in sustaining a cross-Channel invasion. In mid-August Churchill, Roosevelt and their advisors, meeting at Quebec for the Quadrant Conference, endorsed COSSAC's plan. Churchill also insisted that an enterprise of such magnitude be given a suitably portentous name. While most codenames were chosen from an approved list, it was rumoured that he himself chose OVERLORD. However, this did not mean that he had warmed to the project.

BOLERO TAKES SHAPE

While COSSAC drew up plans, Operation BOLERO shipped American forces and equipment into Britain. Attempting liaison with America's logisticians, COSSAC experienced mounting difficulties. Two problems had emerged – the actual organisation of the chain of command, and the personality of the man at the top of the organisation. The first American theatre commander in Britain, General Chaney – an officer of the USAAF and protégé of General 'Hap' Arnold, commander of the USAAF – was determined to create a massive bomber force in East Anglia. His intention was not merely to strike at Germany, but to create conditions for the establishment of an independent US Air Force, co-equal with the other services. To this end he strove to create an in-theatre logistic chain that would be under his command and would give primacy to the needs of the USAAF, without reference to the wider purposes of BOLERO. All Chaney's successors maintained and developed this chain.

From his office in the newly constructed Pentagon, which he himself had designed, the first commander of the US Army's Service of Supply (SOS), General Brehan Somervell, had watched Chaney's activities with growing dismay. It was his contention that the SOS commander-in-theatre, not the theatre commander, should control BOLERO. Securing Marshall's agreement, in May 1942 Somervell appointed General John C. H. Lee to command SOS in Britain. Lee was an old friend. In 1918 he had managed to secure a Distinguished Service Cross for Somervell, a reward that had allowed him to survive successive

The American Army's chief logistician, Somervell played a vital role in controlling and coordinating the movement of supplies to theatres around the world. In late 1944, with differences emerging between British and American objectives, Somervell used his control of the supply line to ensure that Britain continued to comply with American strategy.
(Corbis U744915ACME)

cutbacks and eventually develop a successful career. Lee was a difficult man, pompous, self-important and completely devoid of humour and self-knowledge. Like many Americans he was religious, but his religion had grown into religiosity. He believed he was a good man with good motives, that God knew this, and that God had placed him in a position – head of the largest supply organisation ever created – so that he could prosper. Lee became rich. Most saw this as the product of corruption, but Lee saw it as the working out of God's will. One of his nicknames – Jesus Christ Himself Lee – reflects his outlook.

One of Lee's first actions on arriving in Britain was to move his headquarters from London to a recently completed British complex (a War Office evacuation HQ) outside Cheltenham in Gloucestershire. The ostensible reason was to free up office space in the increasingly crowded area around Grosvenor Square, and to place his HQ at the apex of what was going to become the centre of the American build-up.

But now he was also 90 miles away from the theatre commander's HQ, which would increase his freedom of action. Lee's lifestyle soon attracted adverse comment. He acquired a private train with ten carriages and several flat cars, on which were carried five staff cars and several jeeps. His personal accommodation, beautifully fitted-out sleeping and dining cars, with kitchen and personal chef, verged on the luxurious, in stark contrast to the caravans and camp beds which were to be enjoyed by Eisenhower and Montgomery.

Until Eisenhower was appointed supreme allied commander in late 1943, Lee was the most powerful American in Britain. He developed and

General John C. H. Lee was Chief of the Services of Supply in the European theatre of operations 1942–45. He was also deputy commander of US forces from January 1944. (US Army Military History Institute)

Vast quantities of shells, guns and equipment build up in preparation for the invasion. This photograph shows packing cases filled with rifles, Bren guns, 20mm guns and Piat mortars at a bulk store house somewhere in England. (IWM BH 23144)

maintained an in-theatre administrative apparatus which not only paralleled, but exceeded that of the theatre commander. Thus there were two adjutant generals, two inspector generals, two provost marshals and so on, all with their own staff officers. The inevitable result was an overlapping of function, a conflict over jurisdiction, and confusion. When he was writing the official history of these events in the early 1950s,

Ruppenthal broke off his narrative and addressed the reader directly: "If you have found the foregoing confusing you must remember it was equally confusing for those who had to work in such an environment." It was not until Eisenhower, very much against his own better judgement, was forced to appoint Lee deputy theatre commander in January 1944, that some attempt was made to sort out the chain of command. By that time a complex of informal machinery had grown up, which when lubricated with the oil of corruption, made the wheels work.

The propaganda of the time, and popular memory thereafter, was of BOLERO disgorging ever-larger quantities of equipment and ever-larger numbers of men, until the British Isles became an armed camp. But it was only like that in the spring of 1944; for most of the time BOLERO produced a much more erratic flow. Corruption and incompetence in Lee's command was only part of the problem. There were also major difficulties with British infrastructure and manpower. German domination of the Continent meant that the ports of the south and the east – the huge Southampton–Portsmouth anchorage, and all the docks of the Thames estuary – could no longer be used for large-scale logistic movements. BOLERO was confined to four areas – the Clyde, the Mersey, the Severn and Belfast, the last of which entailed transhipment. In 1942 Britain had only about one third the port capacity she had enjoyed in 1938, a much bigger problem than shortages of shipping.

LABOUR AND SUPPLY

To the Americans, British ports were antiquated. Colonel Ross, a transport officer, was charmed by his first sight of Liverpool docks, with long lines of draught horses clattering along the quays, a sight not seen in New York since the turn of the century. British ports were also very labour-intensive, British dockers strongly unionised, and British work-practices designed to maximise workload and minimise efficiency. Thanks to conscription, the quality of the workforce had also declined. By 1942 the average age of Britain's 100,000 dockers was 52. The solution was to employ American labour battalions, but it took Lee's HQ prolonged negotiations to secure the agreement of the unions and the ministry of labour for this proposal. The sight of hundreds of black GIs unloading ships in Liverpool and Cardiff did not become common until Christmas 1943.

In the autumn of 1942, many US units in Britain preparing for Operation TORCH were without personal kit, weapons or ammunition, the product of poor loading and security at both American and British ports. A furious Eisenhower ordered Lee to "take charge personally, and

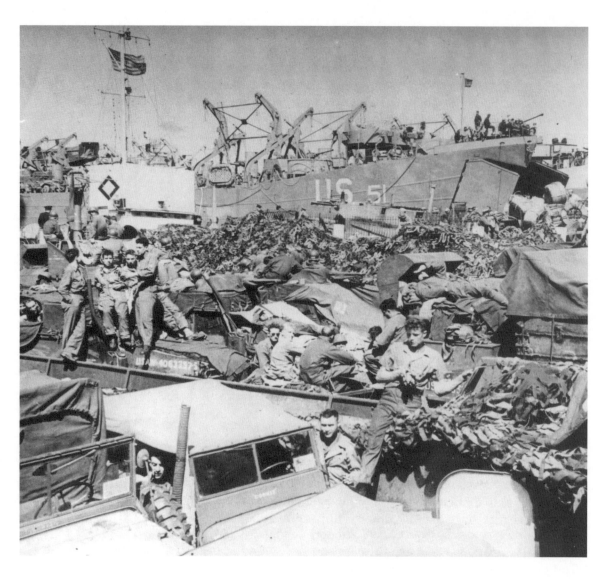

American troops and equipment waiting to load to move across to France. (IWM EA 25974)

to spare no effort or expense to accomplish the task of sorting and cataloguing supplies that have already been received". The immediate crisis was overcome by borrowing missing items, particularly ammunition, from the British. The long-term solution was the establishment of an inspection service in New York to ensure that cargoes were properly marked. On its first day in action it turned back 14,700 pieces of freight that could not be identified. In addition, a four-man logistic team was allocated to each freighter, who were familiar with the loading procedure of that particular ship. By these means the chaos in the ports was gradually brought to an end. Moves to dismiss Lee for incompetence were blocked by Somervell and Democrat friends in the Senate and Congress, and, to be fair, his organisation had only been partly responsible.

Lee's organisation had more success in creating an infrastructure to accommodate the BOLERO supplies. By early 1944 an army of 60,000 US engineering troops and 75,000 British workmen, about 30,000 more than were being employed at this time on the other side of the Channel building the Atlantic Wall, had transformed the English countryside. Nearly six and a half million square feet of covered storage and shop space was built, nearly four million by British civilian contractors and two and a half million by US engineers. An additional 13,500,000 square feet was requisitioned. In addition, SOS managed to acquire 43,500,000 square feet of open storage and hard standing, and additional facilities for the storage of 450,000 tons of ammunition, 175,000 tons of petrol, oil and lubricants, and parks for some 50,000 vehicles. Of all the depots, Lee's jewel in the crown was the giant complex at Ashchurch, just outside his headquarters at Cheltenham. Virtually all the photographs that appeared in wartime propaganda were taken at Ashchurch, which became a mandatory attraction for VIPs. By the spring of 1944 the depot had nearly two million square feet of covered storage space, and slightly more than two million square feet of open storage space. It was manned by 10,000 American soldiers and 500 British civilians, who operated 32 giant cranes, and scores of fork-lift trucks, prime-movers and tractors.

PREPARING FOR COMBAT

Nothing on the scale of BOLERO had ever been attempted before. That mistakes were made was unsurprising, and ultimately it didn't really matter that perhaps as much as a third of the materiel produced went missing. Much more serious were the shortcomings in training US combat forces for action. Britain was a small, overcrowded island, where substantial British and Canadian forces had already occupied the best training areas in the east, and in south central England. As early as the spring of 1942, officers of the first two divisions to deploy to Ulster, the 1st Armoured and the 34th Infantry, were complaining about inadequate space for training. They spent most of 1942 scattered across Tyrone and Fermanagh in battalion-size encampments, assembling and disassembling their weapons and marching. Having never trained under realistic conditions as divisions, in December 1942 they went to North Africa, and in February 1943 encountered Rommel's Afrika Korps at the Kasserine Pass. Eisenhower's conclusion of the ensuing debacle was that "they had arrived in Ulster half-trained and the situation there gave the officers and men scant opportunity for improvement".

Increasingly desperate attempts were made throughout 1943 to secure more land for realistic training, but the best the Americans could usually get was local dual-use agreements, with heavy restrictions on live firing. The US 29th Division, which was in England for 20 months before D-Day, spent much of its time on long 25-mile marches around Stonehenge. According to a divisional medical officer, in the winter of 1943–44 the 29th trudged 3,000 miles, equivalent to a march back to the United States. He complained to the divisional commander that the programme was unusually strenuous and was breaking down many soldiers. His CO agreed, but said "what else is there to do?" Generally speaking, the fighting efficiency of US divisions in Normandy related inversely to the length of time they had been in England – the longer the time, the less effective the training.

By contrast, British and Canadian divisions, with the run of Thetford and Salisbury Plain, had few problems with live firing exercises. Formations which had not yet seen overseas service, for example the 43rd Wessex Division and the 11th Armoured Division, were put through 'battle school' exercises which, although well-intentioned, inclined to encourage formulaic approaches. Deviation from the script was firmly discouraged. Training at all levels was intense, but many British and Canadian soldiers by the spring of 1944 were complaining about being over-trained. From late 1943 the British had Eighth Army formations returning, like 51st Highland Division and 7th Armoured Division. Montgomery put great faith in his veterans, and ignored warnings from Major General Richardson, the British Army's chief of psychiatry, that extended leave over Christmas and New Year 1943–44 would erode the cohesion and fighting spirit of these formations. It did, but there was nothing else Montgomery could have done.

FROM COSSAC TO SHAEF

When Eisenhower was appointed supreme allied commander in December 1943, he subsumed the COSSAC staff into Supreme Headquarters Allied Expeditionary Force (SHAEF). The projected date of the invasion was now barely four months away. There was still much be done, and new problems kept emerging. Amphibious exercises were revealing serious weaknesses in organisation, equipment and fire-support. The new land force commander, General Montgomery, deeply worried about the relatively small size of the projected beachhead, began pressing for a much larger initial landing. At the same time it became clear that the 'bomber barons' had no intention of diverting more than token air support to OVERLORD, which they regarded as an unnecessary diversion from their main effort. Air Chief Marshal Leigh-Mallory, who had been kept on to organise SHAEF's air component, became increasingly concerned about the number of casualties airborne forces might sustain. Equally serious was the prospect that the Germans would penetrate Allied security and discover the actual landing zones.

On top of all this, Allied commanders harboured growing doubts about the effectiveness of some of their formations. Britain's chief military psychiatrist was warning Montgomery that the veterans of El Alamein, Tunis, Sicily and Salerno felt they had done their bit, and that it was now time for the lads who had been at home to take some risks. Montgomery was also very conscious that he had under his command Britain's last army – shortages of manpower meant that heavy casualties could not be replaced. At the same time, Eisenhower was receiving reports that, with the exception of the 82nd and 101st Airborne Divisions and the Rangers, most American units and formations were inadequately or inappropriately trained for the task that lay ahead. As winter gave way to spring there was a sense that the odds on establishing a lodgement on the enemy coast were little better than even. Churchill shared all these concerns. It was this mood of deepening gloom that led the Prime Minister on 7 April to remind his audience that the landing was only the beginning of their problems.

Chapter 3

"The great shadow-boxing match"

(Lieutenant General Sir Frederick Morgan, in **Overture to Overlord**, 1950)
*"The great shadow-boxing match had to go on without a break.
One bogus impression in the enemy's mind had to be succeeded
by another equally bogus."*

Deception and intelligence

Dr Christina J M Goulter

"All warfare is based on deception", so said Sun Tzu back in 500 BC.[1] Like other classic theorists of war and the best senior commanders, Sun Tzu identified deception as a universal feature of warfare.[2] Indeed, throughout history, methods of deception have been employed to confer a number of advantages, chief of which are the force-multiplier effects flowing from surprise and dispersal of enemy forces. Therefore, the nations which have had the greatest interest in deception in the past have tended to be those with comparatively small forces, at least in relation to their opponents, and heading the list of expert practitioners of the art of deception has been Britain.

Throughout World War II, Britain faced serious manpower and materiel deficiencies, and therefore sought force multipliers. Even after the Americans joined the fight in December 1941, with all the industrial might that they could bring to bear, the Allies still lacked sufficient resources to prosecute decisively a simultaneous multi-theatre war (Europe, Mediterranean, Far East and Pacific). Indeed, Churchill understood the critical importance of deception when, at the Allied conference at Tehran in November–December 1943, convened in order to discuss the invasion of Europe, he said: "In wartime, truth is so precious that she should always be attended by a bodyguard of lies."[3] This gave rise to the codename for the most important deception effort of World War II: Operation BODYGUARD.

This was the overall deception plan for use against Germany during 1944. Its focus was a major deception effort to disguise the objective of Operation OVERLORD, the invasion of Europe via Normandy, and a smaller attack via southern France, codenamed Operation ANVIL. Although the Allies knew that the Germans were anticipating a cross-Channel invasion, the aim was to convince them that the invasion was not going to take place until the late summer of 1944, and that the Allies were also planning large-scale amphibious operations elsewhere in Europe, including Norway and Greece. BODYGUARD comprised two main elements. At the strategic level, the aim was to persuade the Germans to position their forces in areas which posed the least threat to Operations OVERLORD and ANVIL. At the operational level, the objective was to deceive the enemy as to the strength, timing and objectives of their two operations. This second element of BODYGUARD as it related to OVERLORD was codenamed Operation FORTITUDE, and it is recognised as not only the most ambitious and sophisticated of deception plans ever employed, but also one of the most successful. Without FORTITUDE, D-Day might still have succeeded, but the task would have been made immeasurably more difficult.

Halifaxes bombing Calais, late summer 1944, as part of ongoing FORTITUDE deception.
(Air Historical Branch (RAF), Ministry of Defence, UK)

FOREBEARS OF OPERATION FORTITUDE

Operation FORTITUDE represented the cumulative experience gained in deception measures up to that point in the war, including lessons learned from enemy efforts. From the very beginning of the war, Britain employed various means of deception: visual (camouflage and dummy constructions), false communications (Wireless Telegraphy (W/T) and radio), and what was known as 'Special Means' (Double-Cross agents). Serious efforts in deception were first made at the time of the Battle of Britain, when the country's very survival lay in the balance, and every measure to gain some sort of comparative advantage over the Luftwaffe was sought. German aircraft were misled by false airfields and ports, stocked with dummy aircraft and ships, and when radar stations on the coast were hit and partially disabled, the RAF ensured that they continued to transmit in order to make the Germans think that the installations were still viable. By the end of 1941, it was decided that Britain's deception efforts had to be coordinated, not only across the Services but also with the Western

The Big Three – the fate of the doomed Axis was sealed when Stalin, Roosevelt and Churchill met in Tehran to finalise their plans to defeat Hitler. Marshal Stalin wears the Order of the Red Star on his tunic, President Roosevelt wears a business suit and Prime Minister Churchill wears the uniform of an RAF Air Marshal. (Courtesy of the Wilfrid Laurier Centre for Military Strategic and Disarmament Studies, Wilfrid Laurier University, Canada)

Allies. A special unit, given the cover name of the London Controlling Section, was set up within the chiefs of staff structure to coordinate deception within and across theatres. Thereafter, deception became an integral part of any campaign undertaken by the Allies. The first major campaign-level deception was when Britain became embroiled in the Mediterranean, where the need for strategic, operational and tactical-level deception was always urgent.[4]

From the time of Italy's entry into the war in mid-1940, and most seriously when the Germans came into the theatre at the start of 1941, Britain was at a serious numerical disadvantage, and deception was one of the ways she sought to achieve force-multiplier effects. A special section in Middle East HQ, Cairo, was devoted solely to the deception effort. Known by its cover name as 'A-Force', its prime objective was to convince the enemy that the Allied forces in the Middle East and Mediterranean were much stronger than they actually were. Some of the efforts to simulate real units were ingenious, including dummy tanks, aircraft and ships made out of canvas, employed to mislead the enemy as to the location and size of real units. They could also be used to enable real units to move under cover of darkness and then be substituted by dummy units by daybreak, thus deceiving the enemy over Allied

Another aspect of the FORTITUDE deception was to conceal real aircraft, ships etc, in those parts of the UK being used to muster forces for D-Day. Aircraft, such as this Spitfire, were concealed under what was known as Type X camouflage netting. Camouflage netting was also used to partially cover dummy aircraft in zones deliberately exposed to Luftwaffe reconnaissance as part of the FUSAG element of the FORTITUDE deception, thereby adding to the believability of the ruse. (Air Historical Branch (RAF), Ministry of Defence, UK) dispositions and intent. By the end of 1941, 'A-Force' had considerable experience in visual deception measures. It also perfected communications deception, by simulating the level of signals traffic that could be expected from notional units. To these measures, which were aimed at deceiving the enemy in the field, were added deception measures at the strategic level, aimed at the enemy's higher command decision-making process, with a view to misleading the enemy over Allied strength within the theatre, and overall intentions. While visual and communications deception contributed to the higher-level strategic deception, this was most readily achieved through intelligence channels, specifically through

A dummy Spitfire on the corner of an airfield in south-east England as part of the FORTITUDE deception. Dummy aircraft, such as this, were first used at the time of the Battle of Britain to draw Luftwaffe attacks away from real targets. (Air Historical Branch (RAF), Ministry of Defence UK)

double agents. 'A-Force' built up a team of double agents in Cairo, who were especially valuable at the time of Allied offensives in the Western Desert, when gaining a surprise advantage was key to success. Double agents were able to mislead the enemy over Allied plans, by feeding misinformation on Allied dispositions and strengths, very often reporting directly into Rommel's HQ.[5]

The impact that deception had in the North African campaign prior to 1942 tended to be relatively short-lived, because the Allies lacked sufficient weight of forces to take full advantage of the surprise achieved. However, where deception did make a substantial difference was at the time of Operation HUSKY, the invasion of Sicily in July 1943. In this case, a strategic-level deception was required in order to convince the Germans that the Allies intended to launch into southern Europe via Greece and not Italy. In order to achieve this objective, the Special Operations Executive (SOE) was instructed to increase guerrilla activity within Greece to give the appearance of battlefield preparation prior to an invasion. Operation ANIMALS was put into effect between 21 June and 14 July, and was very successful. The German commander-in-chief for south-east Europe believed that the guerrilla operations indicated that an Allied landing in Greece was imminent, and reinforced the number of German divisions within the Balkans and Greece from nine to 26. While all the deception efforts in the Mediterranean theatre were vital, it was this type of strategic-level deception that underpinned ultimate success, and the Allies learned very important lessons from this experience.[6]

THE KEYS TO SUCCESSFUL DECEPTION
When detailed planning for D-Day got underway at the beginning of 1944, the Allied senior commanders and their planning staffs were very conscious of the fact that this operation meant everything. If the invasion failed, it was considered unlikely that the Allies could get back on the Continent again until at least mid-1945. Having already learned some very bitter experiences in amphibious warfare (most notably Dieppe and Guadalcanal in 1942), there was a general desire to over-insure against defeat this time around. This meant that every aspect of the D-Day plan was carefully considered, including guaranteeing air superiority, securing sea lines of communication (especially in the critical invasion 'funnel', but also across the Atlantic to ensure resupply and reinforcement from North America), blinding the enemy by taking out his advance warning radar stations, isolating the battlefield by bombing road and rail networks feeding the Normandy area, and silencing coastal defences. Planning staffs felt that getting all these aspects right in preparation for

D-Day and in the critical weeks that followed would give the Allied invasion forces a real chance of success, but their concerns were still such that they sought additional means of gaining a comparative advantage over the German enemy. Deception measures offered one of the best means of gaining such an advantage.

A number of effects were sought. First, the objective was to deceive the Germans into believing that the invasion, when it came, would be aimed at an area other than the one intended, thus compelling the Germans to deploy their forces in zones other than Normandy. In this case the deception aimed to reinforce the Germans' own preconceived idea that the main invasion would be aimed at the area from Calais to Boulogne, and that the Normandy assault was nothing more than a feint. The effect sought was to tie down German forces in the Calais area for at least two weeks after the Normandy landings, thus giving the Allies breathing space in which to consolidate their gains. A secondary deception effort aimed to convince the Germans that the Allies were planning a simultaneous attack in Norway (codenamed FORTITUDE North). Additionally, it was hoped that deception would have force-multiplier effects, arising in part out of the surprise created by diverting enemy forces to other locations, but also by convincing the Germans that the Allies had more expeditionary forces than was actually the case. A significant effort was devoted to convincing the Germans of the existence of a fictional US army group (the First US Army Group, or FUSAG, under General George Patton).[7]

Like any successful deception, Operation FORTITUDE depended on two critical pillars: operational security (OPSEC) and intelligence. With an operation on the scale of OVERLORD, it was going to be practically impossible to keep secret all aspects of the planning and preparation. However, measures were put in place to reduce the risk of compromise. Apart from the most senior British and American commanders, very few people were privy to the overall D-Day plan. The Soviets were involved in general discussions of the plan during the Tehran conference and were also given sight of the overall BODYGUARD deception, but the finer details were for the Western Allies only. The plan and all its elements were given a special classification, 'Bigot', and this material was distributed strictly on a 'need-to-know' basis. Generally speaking, those who took an active part in D-Day knew their destination only at the very last moment, sometimes only hours before the operation was due to start. Strict OPSEC was observed at all levels of the military, and to ensure that no information leaked from the forces mustering in the south coast ports, movement in the south of England was severely restricted in the months leading up to D-Day, with civilians being most restricted of all. A coastal strip ten to 50 miles deep was out of bounds to all but authorised personnel, and travel between Ireland and Britain was prohibited.[8]

BALANCING CONCEALMENT AND DECEPTION

Deception was not without its conundrums. Every effort had to be made to conceal real war preparations, while at the same time allowing the Germans to see dummy war materiel and supporting infrastructure as part of the FUSAG deception. This led to some of the most ingenious methods of physical deception of the war. Dummy invasion craft were constructed in east coast ports; dummy trucks and tanks lined roads and filled 'depots' in and around these same ports, and while German reconnaissance aircraft were kept as far away as possible from the real 'invasion' ports on the south coast, the Royal Air Force was instructed to allow the Luftwaffe the occasional 'look-in' over Kent and Essex to photograph FUSAG preparations. This aspect of the deception was reinforced by spoof radio and W/T signals to simulate the amount of communications traffic which could be expected to emanate from an army group size formation. This was achieved by a handful of mobile units moving around eastern England, signalling between and within

Dummy aircraft were not only quick to construct, but could be transported easily from site to site. A dummy Spitfire and its supporting stand could be packed in two carry bags. (Air Historical Branch (RAF), Ministry of Defence, UK)

non-existent divisions. While this was going on, a parallel effort was conducted as part of FORTITUDE North in Scotland, although the main focus here was on spoof W/T and radio communications, as it was acknowledged that the Germans would be unlikely to fly reconnaissance aircraft over Scotland. Therefore, with the exception of a concentration of shipping in the Firth of Forth, naval exercises offshore and a few dummy aircraft on Scottish airfields, FORTITUDE North was employed using communications means almost exclusively. Like the FUSAG deception, its intention was to convince the Germans of the existence of a fictional army, in this case, the British Fourth Army, notionally based near Edinburgh, and that this would be a major component of the expeditionary force attacking Norway.[9]

THE KEY ROLE OF INTELLIGENCE AND DOUBLE AGENTS

The factor which above all else ensured both OPSEC and the success of the deception effort as a whole was intelligence. The role that intelligence played in the success of D-Day should not be under-estimated, and it contributed in a number of ways. First, counter-espionage by MI5 had led to the imprisonment or turning of all of Germany's operatives in Britain by the time of D-Day. MI5 had set up a special branch in mid-1941 to deal specifically with counter-espionage, and its efforts were made easier as the war progressed, as the various British intelligence agencies penetrated their opposite numbers in Germany and British intelligence broke German signals ciphers (particularly significant of which was the breaking of the so-called ENIGMA codes, used by the German Services). MI5 was also approached by a number of non-British nationals wishing to work for British intelligence as agents. By the beginning of 1944, MI5 had 15 double agents, and these fed carefully crafted misinformation into the German military intelligence apparatus, known as the Abwehr. The 'Double-Cross' agents were invaluable for reinforcing the physical deception measures. The secret of their success in the overall BODYGUARD deception can be attributed to the fact that most had been working as double agents since the early part of the war and were, therefore, trusted by their Abwehr controllers. To have double agents of such long standing was not without its dangers. In order to maintain their credibility, agents had to provide just enough information to keep them in the Germans' employ. A certain amount of sensitive material had to be leaked to the Germans, typically information on size or disposition of forces, shipping movements, etc, which the Germans could corroborate using their own means.[10]

Within the 'Double-Cross' system, three agents in particular were vital to British intelligence. The most celebrated was given the codename of

'Garbo'. This was the Spanish-born Juan Pujol. Motivated by liberal ideals, he approached the British Embassy in Madrid as early as 1940, but his offer to work for British intelligence was at first rejected. He then convinced the Abwehr that he could work for them, and it was after a year of working for the Germans that MI5 and MI6 realised his value. The most notable feature of Garbo's double-cross was that he created a network of fictitious agents, numbering 24 by D-Day. The benefits of having such a fictitious network were considerable. The imaginary sub-agent could be created to meet any requirement; he had no true family or work history which could be scrutinised by the enemy (and Garbo made their existence more believable by saying to his German handler that he never divulged sub-agents' names as this would put them at risk of compromise!). One of Garbo's sub-agents was manufactured specifically to support the idea of an invasion threat to the Calais area of the French coast. This was supposedly an ex-seaman, who was 'tasked' by Garbo to report on Allied shipping around the south and south-east coasts.[11]

Among the other highly regarded double agents was the Polish officer Roman Garby-Czerniaski, codenamed 'Brutus'. He had escaped to France after the German attack on Poland in September 1939, and set up an espionage network within France. Brutus continued to supply the Allies with important information on the occupying German forces until the end of 1941, when he and his network were betrayed to the Gestapo. After a period of incarceration, Brutus managed to convince his captors that he was a genuine convert to the Nazi cause, and he was sent to Britain as a spy. On his arrival in England, he immediately informed MI5 of his mission, and was recruited as a double agent in the FORTITUDE group. Like Garbo, he set up fictitious sub-agents, and contributed to both facets of FORTITUDE (North and South). His reporting on the 'preparations' for the attack on Norway was considered by the Germans to be particularly reliable, as he said that he was able to fraternise with a Polish contingent attached to the British 52nd Lowland Division, which was carrying out real exercises in Scotland.[12]

The third double agent said to have made a vital contribution to the deception effort was a Yugoslav businessman, Dusan Popov, codenamed 'Tricycle'. He had been recruited by the Abwehr in early 1940, and was sent immediately to England. The German High Command was busy preparing plans for the invasion of Britain, and Tricycle was tasked with reporting on the nature and strength of British defences, how much war materiel was coming into the country from North America, the state of the British public's morale, and potential collaborators. However,

Tricycle had already informed the British Embassy in Belgrade about his recruitment by the Germans, and he was brought into the fledgling 'Double-Cross' system. In 1944, he fed the Abwehr very detailed misinformation about the FUSAG deception.[13]

Those who were involved in the planning and execution of FORTITUDE were to conclude that double agents were critical to its success, for while physical and communications deception were important, there was only one certain method of achieving strategic-level deception over a long period, and this was the double agent. As strategic deception is aimed at the enemy's high command, the double agent's direct feed to the Abwehr, in this case, could not be matched by any other means.[14]

TAKING THE BAIT

Having put all these various means of deception in place, the next question was whether the Germans had not only been convinced by FORTITUDE but, most importantly, had acted upon the deception. This is where intelligence again became vital. The Allies enjoyed one major advantage over the Axis nations during World War II, and this was a lead in intelligence. Most significant was the Allies' ability to read High Grade signals (the encoded military and diplomatic messages), and the chief credit for this outstanding achievement must go to the British Government Code and Cipher School (GCCS), based at Bletchley Park. Signals intelligence (or SIGINT) provided, first, a detailed knowledge of enemy strength and dispositions, and second, an insight into enemy intentions. These two facets were key to the Allies' understanding of whether or not their deception measures had succeeded. The process of breaking the so-called ENIGMA ciphers began in earnest in January 1940, with the Luftwaffe and Wehrmacht codes being broken first by the middle of that year. During December 1941, Bletchley Park broke the cipher being used by the Abwehr, and from this MI5 learned, for example, that in 1942 it controlled at least 80 per cent of the German agents based in Britain. Breaking the German naval codes took a little longer, and proved problematic again in 1942 when the Kriegsmarine modified its enciphering machine, causing nearly a year's gap in the Allies' reading of naval SIGINT, at a crucial stage in the Battle of the Atlantic. However, by 1944, the Allies' mastery of enemy signals was such that those responsible for collating and processing the intelligence derived from ENIGMA decrypts literally could not keep up with the deluge of material.[15]

What intelligence showed was that, as late as the beginning of June 1944, the Germans still had no idea of the time or place of the actual

The Government Code and
Cipher School, Bletchley Park.
(The Bletchley Park Trust)

invasion. This meant two things: first, that all German efforts in espionage and other intelligence had failed, and second, that they had swallowed most of the deception plan. The element of FORTITUDE that the Germans seemed to dismiss was the potential simultaneous attack on Norway, and this they regarded as no more than a minor diversionary attack. Therefore, no alterations were made to the force levels already committed to that area, but nor did the Germans move to France the 27 divisions allocated to defending Norway. The Germans could not afford to let Norway go without a fight, because it remained important to their strategy (including access to the North Atlantic for the German Navy, and as a supplier and trans-shipment base for vital raw materials, especially iron ore). Right up to the last minute, the German High Command was convinced that the main assault would be across the Channel, 'somewhere' in the south or south-east, with assessments ranging from Belgium to the French Bay of Biscay. At the end of April, these assessments focused more closely on Normandy and Brittany because of their port facilities, and by May attention was firmly fixed on the Calais area, with some assessments suggesting that

The 'Colossus' machine at Bletchley Park. This rudimentary computing system was used to break the German Services' High-Grade signals, encoded by the ENIGMA machine. The decrypts were referred to generically as ULTRA. (The Bletchley Park Trust)

bridgeheads would be established in Normandy and Brittany, followed by the 'real' invasion in the Calais–Boulogne sector.[16]

THE IMPACT OF FALSE INFORMATION

As the time for the real Operation OVERLORD approached, the deception effort had to be fine-tuned. Double agents deliberately fed true information about certain units alongside their usual misinformation, because the arrival in Normandy of these units would lend weight to the credibility of agents' reports. Any fine-tuning had to be very carefully coordinated with any operational activity undertaken by the Allied forces. One of the most valuable reinforcements of the FORTITUDE deception came from the work done by the Royal Air Force in the months and weeks leading up to D-Day. It was instructed to focus its interdiction of enemy rail in the northern part of France, so that for every ton of bombs dropped in the Normandy zone, two would be dropped further north, around the Pas de Calais. The proportions were the same for other target sets, including Luftwaffe airfields and coastal defences. Again, from intelligence sources, the disparity in the apparent attention given to one zone compared with the other was noted by the Germans.[17]

As with any deception effort, it was one thing to make an enemy believe the deception, it was quite another to compel him to *act* on it. In this case, how did the Germans react on D-Day and during the critical weeks that followed? Initially, Allied intelligence was disappointed. They found in the lead-up to D-Day that the Germans had not altered their Order of Battle and dispositions significantly within north-west France to reflect any concerns about an invasion targeting Calais. Some 11 infantry divisions were located either in the Normandy zone or within easy reach, and two out of three armoured panzer divisions allocated to Normandy were already in the sector, with indications that the third was en route, and that a further three panzer divisions were being released from a reserve force in order to go to Normandy. However, this did not mean that the FORTITUDE deception had failed. While the Germans were responding robustly because they did not want this 'bridgehead' to develop into anything bigger, they did not reinforce Normandy with every unit available in the region. The 1st SS Panzer Division remained in Belgium, as did regular units of the German Fifteenth Army. These dispositions showed clearly that the Germans expected an imminent threat to the Calais zone.[18]

THE LEGACY OF FORTITUDE

One of the most notable features of the FORTITUDE deception was the extent to which it continued to work, long after the real invasion. Intelligence sources and post-war interrogations of senior German commanders confirmed that the ruse had worked until mid-July. It was only then that an assessment was made by the Wehrmacht that the FUSAG threat to the Calais sector was over. However, the German intelligence assessments continued to believe in FUSAG's actual existence, and suggested that Patton's army group would be used to reinforce rather than spearhead any future attacks. One of the important reasons why FORTITUDE worked for such an extended period was that the various deception measures were continued long after the Normandy assault. For example, bombing of the Calais sector continued throughout July, and agents such as Garbo reported on "reorganisation within FUSAG".[19]

Another important reason why FORTITUDE maintained its potency was that it was also reinforced and complemented by deception carried out in other theatres, most notably the Mediterranean. As part of the overall BODYGUARD deception plan, a potential threat to the Mediterranean was kept alive through Operation ZEPPELIN, with a specific aim of keeping German reserves away from Normandy until at least the beginning of July. Although the Allies were planning an actual attack on the south of France with Operation ANVIL (later named DRAGOON), scheduled for August, it was felt that fostering the idea of an imminent attack on the area close to the Franco-Spanish border would keep German forces tied down, not only in the south of France but also, hopefully, in the Mediterranean generally. This part of Zeppelin was codenamed Operation VENDETTA, and would be conducted by the US Seventh Army, based in Algiers. Like the FORTITUDE North and South deceptions, the attacking force was also bolstered by non-existent forces. It notionally comprised 12 divisions, only four of which actually existed (three French and one American). Because the US Seventh Army's HQ was in Algiers, which was notorious as a spy capital, the deception had to be made credible by manufacturing the type of activity which could be expected at the embarkation ports in Algeria. Army vehicles and bulk stores were displayed in areas open to public view; dummy craft were floated in the harbours; large-scale exercises with landing craft were held between 9 and 11 June, and these exercises actually involved 13,000 servicemen and 2,000 vehicles being taken out to sea for three days. The exercises were made plausible also by the participation of a large number of naval vessels, including 25 destroyers and two aircraft carriers, *Victorious* and *Indomitable*, which just happened to be en route to the Far East. In addition to naval activity, Allied aircraft bombed targets in the Rhone Valley, supposedly in an attempt to interdict enemy lines of communication from the north and east of France. Finally, the borders with Morocco were closed between 11 June and 6 July, and neutral diplomats were forbidden to communicate with their governments using coded messages or the diplomatic bag. These measures deliberately paralleled those imposed in the weeks leading up to the OVERLORD landings.[20]

Although the Germans saw Allied operations in the Mediterranean at this time as nothing more than diversionary actions to draw attention away from north-west Europe, VENDETTA nevertheless succeeded in its principal aim, to keep German forces tied down in the Mediterranean, and especially to keep those forces allocated to defending southern France in southern France. Not only did VENDETTA succeed in doing this, but the Nineteenth Army assigned to the task was actually reinforced between February and March 1944, with two extra infantry divisions. Most significantly, the 9th SS Panzer Division, which was located 75 miles north of Paris, was sent south to act as a mobile reserve. Then, as OVERLORD got underway on 6 June, the Germans still had ten divisions, including two panzer divisions, allocated to southern France. Not until mid-June was one of the panzer divisions (*Das Reich*, 2nd Panzer) moved north to reinforce Normandy, and no other units followed until July.[21]

The way in which the Allied deception efforts were mutually reinforcing, both within and across theatres, is one of the most remarkable features of World War II. The coordination of the various strands of deception, which is a story in itself, demanded attention to detail as well as a grasp of the big strategic picture. Furthermore, it demanded a long-term commitment from those staffs involved. Because of the sensitivity of the subject, especially the work undertaken by double agents and other operatives, the full story of the Allied deception and intelligence work has not been told until recently. Those who were closely involved in the greatest deception to date should be acknowledged as having made a decisive contribution to the Allied victory in World War II. While it is difficult to quantify in precise terms the impact of the deception measures, they undoubtedly helped to save thousands of lives. Without FORTITUDE, the Germans would have had free rein to concentrate their forces to meet the Normandy invasion. Had this happened, it is very unlikely that the combined Allied force would have broken out of the beachhead, or, if it had broken out, progress across France would have been slow and heavily attritional. As it was, the real fight through France into Germany proved to be a very bloody contest, against an enemy who still had a few nasty surprises up its sleeve, not least of which was the major Ardennes offensive at the end of the year, and this was an enemy still able to fight on two fronts simultaneously. Against such a foe, the Allies needed all the tricks in the bag.

Chapter 4

"A very lofty perch"

(Field Marshal Montgomery, 1944)

*"The Supreme Command has to sit on a very lofty perch
and be able to take a detached view of the whole intricate problem."*

Allied high command

Dr Stephen A Hart

On 12 February 1944, the Western Allies formally established a 'combined' (multinational) 'inter-service' (joint) military headquarters to provide the high command hierarchy required to mount the Second Front – the invasion of Nazi-occupied north-west Europe, known alternatively as Operation OVERLORD. Located at Bushey Park in south-west London, this establishment – the Supreme Headquarters, Allied Expeditionary Force (SHAEF) – was the final development of the COSSAC command organisation established for OVERLORD back in 1943. A joint multinational commander – the Supreme Commander, Allied Expeditionary Force (SCAEF) – headed SHAEF and exercised overarching authority over all the forces deployed in that theatre of operations, irrespective of the service or the nationality involved.

THE RUNGS OF THE COMMAND LADDER

On 24 December 1943, 17 days after the selection had been made, US President Franklin D. Roosevelt officially announced that the SCAEF would be the American general, Dwight D. ('Ike') Eisenhower. The 53-year-old general was a highly experienced staff officer who had served during 1940–41 as a chief of staff at divisional, corps and then army level. Eisenhower, however, had little experience as a field commander, having never commanded anything larger than a battalion, and that was back in 1940. Rather, he was a skilled military administrator who possessed accomplished diplomatic skills. During 1942–43, he had commanded the multinational Allied operations mounted in French North Africa and the Mediterranean. It was in these appointments that Eisenhower's diplomatic skills helped forge an efficient Anglo-American combined inter-service command hierarchy. The effectiveness of these command organisations contributed significantly to the military victories that the Allies secured in these campaigns. Indeed, these command arrangements became the model upon which the SHAEF organisation for OVERLORD was based. Given this proven ability to work effectively with the British, it is not surprising that Roosevelt selected Eisenhower as the SCAEF.

Eisenhower's immediate subordinate at SHAEF held an intermediate position between the SCAEF and the three service chiefs who made up the next rung in the OVERLORD command hierarchy. The British air chief marshal, Sir Arthur Tedder, held this intermediate position as Deputy Supreme Allied Commander, Allied Expeditionary Forces (DSCAEF). This appointment reflected the Allies' desire to select an even number of British and American officers for the senior command appointments available within SHAEF. The choice of an air force commander for this position also reflected the importance that aerial

OPPOSITE The Supreme Commander, Allied Expeditionary Forces – US General Dwight D. Eisenhower – outlines on a large map the broad parameters of the forthcoming Operation OVERLORD, during his first press conference, held on 17 January 1944. (NAC, PA-173357)

The senior ranks of the OVERLORD command hierarchy seen together on 1 February 1944, namely SCAEF Eisenhower (front centre), DSCAEF Tedder (front left), naval C-in-C Ramsay (rear, second from left), air C-in-C Leigh-Mallory (rear, centre-right), land forces commander Montgomery (front right), SHAEF chief of staff Bedell Smith (rear right), and finally FUSA commander Bradley (rear left). (NAC, PA-129050)

operations were to play in the execution of the eventual D-Day landings. Tedder was an obvious choice for this job; he had established an effective relationship with Eisenhower in the Mediterranean during 1943, and believed that national sensibilities should not interfere with the creation of the efficient inter-Allied cooperation required to defeat the potent German armed forces. An accomplished and energetic organiser, the 54-year-old Tedder was unusual among the SHAEF establishment in that he was both a university graduate and a published author. Moreover, it was through Tedder that Eisenhower directed the strategic assets of RAF Bomber Command (led by Marshal of the RAF, Sir Arthur Harris) and the US Strategic Air Forces Europe (USSAF, led by Lt. Gen. Carl Spaatz), which had been assigned to support OVERLORD.

Below Tedder in the SHAEF hierarchy came Eisenhower's three service commanders, Admiral Ramsay, Air Chief Marshal Leigh-Mallory and General Montgomery. As Commander-in-Chief Allied Expeditionary Naval Force (C-in-C AENF), the British Admiral

Bertram H. Ramsay exercised overall control of Operation NEPTUNE, the codename allocated to the naval dimension of OVERLORD. Ramsay controlled a fleet of 1,213 warships and 4,126 landing craft – arguably the greatest naval armada ever assembled. By D-Day, the 61-year-old Ramsay had notched up 46 years' service in the Royal Navy, including a variety of naval staff positions. He had commanded the evacuation of Allied forces from Dunkirk during May–June 1940, had subsequently planned the 1942 Allied TORCH landings in North Africa, and then had served as the commander of the Eastern Task Force in Operation HUSKY, the landings on Axis-occupied Sicily. These experiences made him an obvious choice for NEPTUNE, the most ambitious amphibious assault ever mounted up to that point in history.

Alongside Ramsay in the SHAEF hierarchy came the C-in-C Allied Expeditionary Air Force (AEAF), the British air chief marshal Trafford L. Leigh-Mallory. He exercised command authority over all the tactical air assets allocated to OVERLORD, which included the 1,576 aircraft of the RAF's Second Tactical Air Force (2 TAF) and the 2,600 aircraft deployed by the US Ninth Air Force. Leigh-Mallory, however, had no formal command responsibility over the other independent aerial commands that would assist the preparation for, and execution of, the D-Day landings. These commands comprised not just Harris and Spaatz's strategic bombers, but also the RAF's Coastal Command and Air Defence of Great Britain. To secure the support of these commands for OVERLORD, Leigh-Mallory cooperated with DSCAEF Tedder, who at least exercised 'operational direction' over the strategic bombers.

The service chief who completed this rung in the SHAEF command hierarchy was the British general Bernard L. Montgomery ('Monty'). The general commanded the British 21st Army Group, under whose control served all the British and Canadian military formations that had been assigned to OVERLORD. For the D-Day landings and the immediate campaign thereafter, however, Eisenhower delegated his authority of operational control and coordination over all ground forces to Montgomery. The British general, therefore, was in effect a theatre land forces commander just as Ramsay and Leigh-Mallory were theatre naval and air commanders, respectively. For these battles, therefore, Montgomery's 21st Army Group controlled all ground forces deployed in theatre, irrespective of their nationality, including Lt. Gen. Omar N. Bradley's First US Army (FUSA). In theory, the FUSA had a status within the 21st Army Group identical to that of the British and Canadian army commands serving in that group.

Eisenhower, however, had always intended that Montgomery would only temporarily act as land forces commander. For, unlike with the campaign's aerial and naval dimensions, the Allies had realised during the planning for D-Day that eventually the US ground forces deployed in theatre would exceed those of the British. As soon as the operational situation made it feasible, the Americans intended to deploy a second army and thus create an American army group with force strengths that exceeded the total British troops deployed in France. This situation would make it difficult for American commanders to accept orders from a British land forces commander. Actual events broadly conformed to this vision, and thus, by late August 1944, SHAEF deployed in theatre two entire American army groups – Bradley's 12th and Devers' 6th – in addition to Montgomery's Anglo-Canadian 21st Army Group. How could Montgomery, a 'mere' army group commander, also exercise command over army group commanders Bradley and Devers, especially when more American forces were deployed in theatre than British ones?

Consequently, on 1 September 1944, Eisenhower took over from Montgomery as land forces commander, while continuing as SCAEF.

Senior ground commanders involved in the north-west Europe campaign pose for the cameras during a medal ceremony at Geldrop, Holland, in March 1945. From left to right, front row: 21st Army Group Commander Montgomery, SCAEF Eisenhower, Omar Bradley (First US Army Group); (rear row) GOC-in-C First Canadian Army Henry Crerar, Lt. Gen. W. H. Simpson (US Ninth Army), and Second (British) Army commander 'Bimbo' Dempsey.

This decision, which Eisenhower had always intended to make, tarnished his relationship with the rather myopic Montgomery who, having just secured a tremendous victory in Normandy, saw the move solely as an undeserved 'demotion'. This development brought to a head the serious frictions that had simmered below the service in the 'Ike'–'Monty' relationship from long before D-Day. Tactless and vain, the operationally cautious Montgomery was determined to protect British national interests within the wider alliance, and this alienated him from many of the American commanders with whom he had to cooperate.

These three service commanders' immediate subordinates formed the next rung down in the OVERLORD command hierarchy. Under Ramsay served the British Rear Admiral Philip L. Vian and the American Rear Admiral Alan G. Kirk, who respectively commanded the Eastern and Western Naval Task Forces. The 50-year-old Vian had

The British Rear Admiral Philip L. Vian (centre rear) commanded the Eastern Naval Task Force on D-Day, which covered the three Anglo-Canadian beaches, GOLD, JUNO and SWORD. The 50-year-old Vian, seen here with Montgomery and Dempsey on 12 April during Exercise TROUSERS, had previously served in the Allied amphibious assault on Sicily in HUSKY. (NAC, PA-140708) joined the Royal Navy in 1907, and went on to command with distinction the 4th Destroyer Flotilla during 1939–41, before serving as one of the four British naval commanders involved in Operation HUSKY. The 56-year-old Kirk had previously served as Commander, Amphibious Force, US Atlantic Fleet and then went on to serve as a naval commander in the Allied landings in Sicily. Both commanders, therefore, were eminently qualified to serve as the principal formation commanders during NEPTUNE.

Under Leigh-Mallory there served two highly experienced subordinates, through which his control of the OVERLORD tactical air forces would be exercised. Air Chief Marshal Sir Arthur Coningham commanded the 2 TAF, while the American Lt. Gen., Lewis H. Brereton commanded the US Ninth Air Force. A former World War I pilot, Brereton had commanded the American air forces deployed in the Mediterranean. 'Mary' Coningham – his sobriquet was a distortion of 'Maori', a take on his New Zealand nationality – had led the British tactical air forces deployed to support the ground operations conducted in North Africa, Sicily and Italy during 1942–44. Coningham and Brereton were more experienced in the control of tactical air forces than Leigh-Mallory, and this caused their working relationships with their superior to be imbued with significant tension.

Under Montgomery in the 21st Army Group served his subordinate army commanders. On D-Day itself, the spearheads of Bradley's FUSA and Lt. Gen. Miles C. ('Bimbo') Dempsey's Second (British) Army assaulted the German coastal defences. Unusually for the dogmatic, forceful and tactless Montgomery, he exercised some sensitivity to the nuances of inter-Allied cooperation when dealing with Bradley. Rather than treating the FUSA like any other part of his 21st Army Group, Montgomery eschewed giving Bradley formal directions and instead sought merely to influence the American's conduct of operations. Such persuasion was not even always successful, with Montgomery noting on 27 June 1944, that, although he had encouraged Bradley to thrust toward Coutances simultaneously with completing the capture of Cherbourg, the American had not wanted to take this risk. In this way, Bradley enjoyed a freedom to exercise his initiative that Montgomery's tendency to 'over-control' his subordinates denied to the other senior British and Canadian commanders serving in the 21st Army Group.

This tendency toward over-control was more evident in Montgomery's relationship with Dempsey, his other subordinate D-Day army commander. Dempsey was one of the 'Monty men' – subordinates that the general had picked out as commanders of potential who needed to be developed. Montgomery and Dempsey had worked extremely well

together during the campaign in Italy, and in north-west Europe their particularly close professional relationship – which was based entirely on verbal orders – contributed significantly to the combat effectiveness of the 21st Army Group. Indeed, some commentators felt that the two understood each other's thinking so well that a 'symbiosis' existed in their collective decision-making, with each feeding off the other. An introverted commander who stoically tolerated Montgomery's frequent interference, Dempsey shunned publicity and focused his imperturbable energy on executing his professional duties. The self-effacing Dempsey, therefore, provided the perfect foil for the egotistical, publicity-seeking Montgomery.

Air and ground commanders hold a planning conference at Amblie in Normandy on 4 August 1944. Those involved include (from right to left) the C-in-C AEAF, Trafford Leigh-Mallory, the C-in-C 21st Army Group, Bernard Montgomery, the 2 TAF commander, 'Mary' Coningham, and the commander of the newly operational First Canadian Army, General Henry D.G. Crerar. (NAC, PA-129122)

SHAEF ORGANISATION
Below these six commanders the respective service chains of command flowed down to the lowest tactical level, but constraints of space preclude a discussion of these lower command levels. There was, moreover, in addition to this operational command hierarchy, another

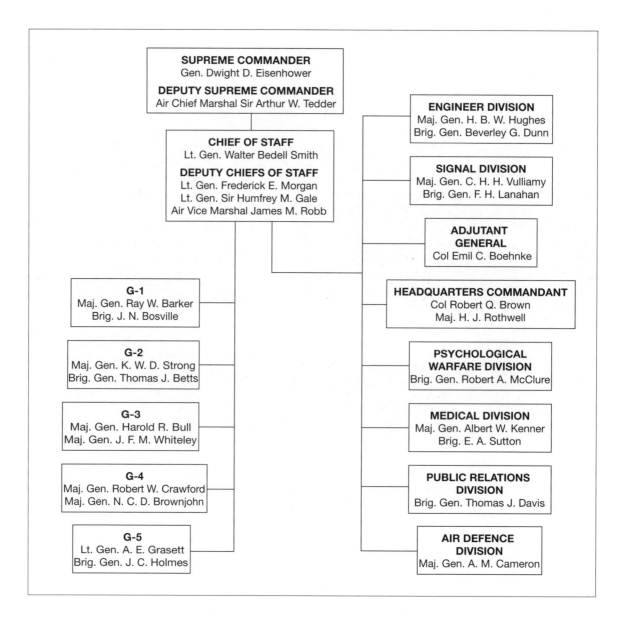

SUPREME COMMANDER Gen. Dwight D. Eisenhower **DEPUTY SUPREME COMMANDER** Air Chief Marshal Sir Arthur W. Tedder	**ENGINEER DIVISION** Maj. Gen. H. B. W. Hughes Brig. Gen. Beverley G. Dunn
CHIEF OF STAFF Lt. Gen. Walter Bedell Smith **DEPUTY CHIEFS OF STAFF** Lt. Gen. Frederick E. Morgan Lt. Gen. Sir Humfrey M. Gale Air Vice Marshal James M. Robb	**SIGNAL DIVISION** Maj. Gen. C. H. H. Vulliamy Brig. Gen. F. H. Lanahan
	ADJUTANT GENERAL Col Emil C. Boehnke
G-1 Maj. Gen. Ray W. Barker Brig. J. N. Bosville	**HEADQUARTERS COMMANDANT** Col Robert Q. Brown Maj. H. J. Rothwell
G-2 Maj. Gen. K. W. D. Strong Brig. Gen. Thomas J. Betts	**PSYCHOLOGICAL WARFARE DIVISION** Brig. Gen. Robert A. McClure
G-3 Maj. Gen. Harold R. Bull Maj. Gen. J. F. M. Whiteley	**MEDICAL DIVISION** Maj. Gen. Albert W. Kenner Brig. E. A. Sutton
G-4 Maj. Gen. Robert W. Crawford Maj. Gen. N. C. D. Brownjohn	**PUBLIC RELATIONS DIVISION** Brig. Gen. Thomas J. Davis
G-5 Lt. Gen. A. E. Grasett Brig. Gen. J. C. Holmes	**AIR DEFENCE DIVISION** Maj. Gen. A. M. Cameron

The structure of SHAEF headquarters.

chain of command that flowed down from Eisenhower – that of the SHAEF headquarters itself. SHAEF was divided into five subordinate staff branches and eight specialist divisions. Eisenhower's trusted chief of staff, Lt. Gen. Walter Bedell Smith, directed the daily functioning of SHAEF. Three British deputy chiefs of staff assisted Bedell Smith – Lt. Gen. Frederick E. Morgan, who had headed COSSAC back in 1943, Lt. Gen. Sir Humfrey Gale, the chief administrative officer, and Air Vice Marshal James M. Robb, the air deputy chief of staff.

The principal operational nerve centres within SHAEF were the G-3 Branch, which focused on planning and the execution of operations, and the G-2 Branch, which dealt with intelligence matters. The American Maj. Gen., Harold R. Bull, headed G-3, while the British Maj. Gen., Kenneth W. D. Strong, directed G-2. The main administrative departments within SHAEF were Maj. Gen. Ray W. Barker's G-1 (Personnel) Branch, Maj. Gen. Robert W. Crawford's G-4 (Supply) Branch, and Lt. Gen. A. E. Grasett's G-5 (Civil Affairs) Branch. In addition, the principal SHAEF specialist departments included Brig. Gen. Robert A. McClure's Psychological Warfare Division and Brig. Gen. Thomas J. Davis' Public Relations Division. Between these various operational and administrative sections, the SHAEF headquarters employed a staff of 4,900 by early July 1944.

ORIGINS OF THE OVERLORD HIGH COMMAND

Having described the high command hierarchy for OVERLORD, this chapter will now explore how this structure was established. It was back at the December 1941 'Arcadia' Conference that the Americans and British had established an integrated high command structure that was to endure until VE-Day. The service chiefs from both nations met regularly as the Combined Chiefs of Staff (CCOS) to formulate the Western Allies' strategic conduct of the war.

During 1942–44, the CCOS comprised seven officers: Fleet Admiral William D. Leahy (chief of staff to the commander-in-chief, President Roosevelt); General of the Army George C. Marshall (US Army chief of staff); Admiral Ernest J. King (commander-in-chief, US Fleet); General Henry H. Arnold (commanding general, US Army Air Forces); Field Marshal Alan Brooke (chief of the imperial general staff (CIGS)); Admiral of the Fleet Sir Andrew B. Cunningham (first sea lord); and Marshal of the RAF Sir Charles Portal (chief of the air staff). By 1944, it had become the practice of the CCOS to delegate overall command of all Allied ground, naval and air forces, irrespective of nationality, in a given theatre of operations, to a supreme allied commander who exercised his authority through a combined inter-service headquarters. As head of the Allied Force Headquarters (AFHQ) in the Mediterranean during 1943, Eisenhower had been the first such commander.

Throughout 1943, the thorny issue of the form, timing, and command of the Second Front had dominated Allied strategy. Despite experiencing major disagreements, the British and Americans nevertheless agreed at the January 1943 Casablanca Conference to begin preparations for the Second Front. Consequently, the CCOS ordered the creation of a combined inter-service headquarters staff for this operation, and began

In the front row, from left to right, Canadian Prime Minister W. L. Mackenzie King, US President Franklin D. Roosevelt, and British Prime Minister Winston Churchill sit in front of members of the British and American chiefs of staff at the August 1943 'Quadrant' Conference at Quebec. The latter include, from left to right, General Henry H. Arnold, Marshal of the RAF Sir Charles Portal, General Alan Brooke, Admiral Ernest J. King, General Sir John Dill, General George C. Marshall, Admiral Sir Dudley Pound, and Admiral William D. Leahy. (NAC, PA-183423)

the process by which the SCAEF would be appointed. While the latter process unfolded, Lt. Gen. Morgan led this new combined headquarters as chief of staff to the supreme allied commander (designate) (COSSAC), by which name the headquarters itself became known. During the rest of 1943, COSSAC undertook the preliminary planning required for OVERLORD. Eventually, on 16 January 1944, the newly appointed SCAEF – plus a small staff brought over from AFHQ – arrived in England and absorbed COSSAC, thus creating a headquarters organisation that, on 12 February, was officially designated as SHAEF. It was on this date that the SCAEF received his formal CCOS directive, which, in addition to defining the various command roles involved in OVERLORD, ordered him "to enter the continent of Europe and … undertake operations aimed at … the destruction of [Germany's] armed forces". Given that D-Day was at that time slated for May 1944, the year-long delay experienced in appointing the SCAEF and then issuing his directive left SHAEF scant

time to complete the complex preparations required for a successful execution of the landings.

The sensitivities of the Anglo-American strategic relationship shed much light on the delay experienced in selecting the SCAEF. Both nations concurred that the nation furnishing the greater number of troops for the Second Front should also provide the SCAEF. In early 1943, Allied planners believed that this would be Britain, and consequently British Prime Minister Winston Churchill favoured CIGS Brooke as SCAEF. As the year progressed, however, it became apparent that the Americans would contribute the greater military force and this swung discussion in favour of an American SCAEF. At the August 1943 Quebec Conference, Roosevelt and Churchill agreed to appoint an American SCAEF, which the former indicated would be US Army chief of staff, General Marshall. Finding himself unable to contemplate Marshall's absence from Washington and the CCOS, however, Roosevelt prevaricated, until on 7 December 1943 he selected as SCAEF the obvious best alternative to Marshall – Dwight Eisenhower. At the same time as appointing Eisenhower, moreover, the CCOS also announced the selection of Tedder as DSCAEF. The British air chief marshal had worked closely with Eisenhower as C-in-C Air Forces in the Mediterranean, and thus the pair were expected to swiftly renew their effective working relationship. A similar long-term relationship was also renewed in January 1944, when – on Eisenhower's insistence – his former chief of staff, Bedell Smith, assumed this same position within SHAEF.

Eisenhower's three subordinate service chiefs, however, had been selected long before his arrival in England. Back in June 1942, the CCOS – at Churchill's insistence – had appointed Admiral Ramsay to command the naval forces earmarked for the planned landings, a position he took over in July 1943, after returning from service in Operation HUSKY. By then, General Sir Bernard Paget, the C-in-C UK Home Forces, had already taken command of the 21st Army Group. Next, in August 1943 the Allies announced that Leigh-Mallory would be the C-in-C AEAF. Given that the CCOS then believed that the main air support required for D-Day would be the achievement of air superiority over the beachheads, it seemed appropriate to appoint a commander with extensive experience in fighter operations. Finally, on the day that Eisenhower was officially announced as SCAEF, the British declared that Montgomery would replace Paget as C-in-C 21st Army Group. Consequently, Eisenhower arrived in England in mid-January 1944 to find his team of three service chiefs already in place.

In addition to Prime Minister Winston Churchill, General Montgomery (both seated), and Army Commander Dempsey (centre rear), this shot – taken in Normandy on 22 July 1944 – shows five corps commanders: Lt. Gen. G Bucknall (left), Lt. Gen. Neil Ritchie (second from left), Lt. Gen. Richard O'Connor (left of Dempsey), Lt. Gen. John Crocker (right of Dempsey), and Lt. Gen. Guy Simonds (second from right). (IWM, B7883)

Half of the final appointments to the next rung in the OVERLORD command hierarchy – these service chiefs' immediate subordinates – were made after Eisenhower's arrival as SCAEF. Thus, while the CCOS had selected Kirk back in November 1943, Vian was only promoted to command the new Eastern Task Force in late January 1944, after the invasion plan was enlarged to a five-division assault. Similarly, while the Allies had chosen Brereton back in October 1943, Coningham only took charge of the 2 TAF in late January 1944. Repeating the pattern, while the Americans had selected Bradley to command the FUSA back in September 1943, the War Office only replaced General Anderson as the commander of the Second (British) Army with Dempsey in late January 1944. Montgomery had insisted on this move, not just because he and Dempsey had a proven ability to work together effectively in the field, but also because the unassuming Dempsey would not covet the publicity that D-Day would generate – publicity that Montgomery craved.

HIGH COMMAND AND THE SUCCESS OF D-DAY

Having examined the nature and genesis of the command hierarchy established for OVERLORD, it is now germane to discuss the contribution that this organisation made toward the eventual success of D-Day. It should first be noted that the smooth running of a multinational joint military headquarters is inherently difficult. There are countless potential sources of friction – misunderstandings, confusion, disagreements, and ineffective cooperation. Given this, it has to be stated that, in general, the level of inter-Allied and inter-service cooperation achieved during OVERLORD was of a high order. Notwithstanding this achievement, however, some tensions did still permeate these bilateral working relationships, whether based upon disagreements over national agendas, policy decisions, or personality issues.

Three significant factors behind the smooth running of this command hierarchy were Eisenhower's determination to subordinate national interests to the needs of the alliance; the considerable diplomatic skills he brought to bear on his duties; and his realisation that the SCAEF's principal roles were to coordinate the work of his three highly experienced service subordinates and to deal with wider political issues. Indeed, while tactfully coordinating his service chiefs' efforts, Eisenhower rightly avoided trying to micro-manage them. To this end, he delegated to these subordinates the detailed operational planning required for the invasion, in which tasks they were assisted by the preparatory work already done by COSSAC. In turn, these service chiefs – having set out the broad parameters of their respective plans – delegated the more detailed planning down to their immediate subordinates. The strengths evident in Eisenhower's command style – realism, diplomacy, flexibility and willingness to cooperate – were particularly important in sustaining a reasonable relationship with the egotistical and tactless Montgomery, who remained utterly scathing about the SCAEF's abilities as a field commander. Indeed, Eisenhower's collaborative flexibility drew from some of his American subordinates the jibe: "Ike is the best commander the British have".

Eisenhower ably used his full authority to provide support to the efforts undertaken by these subordinates. Most crucially, he gave his full backing to Montgomery's adverse assessment of the original COSSAC ground plan. Eisenhower did not allow the arrogance inherent in Montgomery's appreciation to distract him from the merit of the general's arguments. Both were correct to describe the original COSSAC assault plan, with three divisions attacking on relatively narrow frontage, as seriously flawed. That Montgomery insisted on a broad-front, five-divisional assault, backed up by elements of three airborne

The Anglo-Canadian command team for D-Day: Winston Churchill (second from right), CIGS Field Marshal Alan Brooke (second from left), C-in-C 21st Army Group Montgomery (right), First Canadian Army Commander Crerar (left) and GOC II Canadian Corps, Lt. Gen. Guy G. Simonds (centre). (NAC, PA-143952)

divisions – and that Eisenhower supported this demand – represented one of the most important contributions that the 'Ike'–'Monty' command team made to the eventual success of the D-Day landings. Furthermore, to buy extra time during which the additional forces required for the expanded assault could be assembled, Eisenhower sensibly took the difficult decision to postpone the invasion until 1 June 1944.

Eisenhower's most significant contribution to the success of OVERLORD, however, was his historic decision to launch D-Day despite the bad weather. During mid-May 1944, as the preparations for

the invasion neared completion, Eisenhower sought to finalise the day on which the invasion would be launched. Research indicated that there were only three days during the first half of June – the 5th, 6th and 7th – during which the correct combination of moon, tidal, daylight, and weather conditions would exist. Eisenhower thus set D-Day for 5 June, and as the eve of this momentous day arrived, the assault forces embarked aboard over 4,000 troop-carrying vessels. By then, however, it was clear that the bad weather the following day would seriously compromise the aerial support arranged for the landings. After hearing the views of his service chiefs, Eisenhower took the monumental decision to postpone the attack for 24 hours, thus condemning 130,000 expectant soldiers to an unpleasant night aboard their assault vessels.

The weather on 5 June was poor, as expected, and that evening the SCAEF chaired a crucial meeting to decide whether to attack the next day. The meteorologists predicted that the weather would improve somewhat during 6 June, but conditions would remain marginal. Tedder and Leigh-Mallory were wary about launching the attack in such conditions, but Montgomery insisted that they should initiate the invasion. Eisenhower was well aware that another 24-hour delay would undermine the morale of the embarked troops, then still being tossed about in the heavy swell experienced across all the harbours of southern England. With what must have been an appalling weight of responsibility resting on his shoulders, Eisenhower calmly weighed the options and decided that the risks involved in postponing the invasion were greater than those associated with mounting it: D-Day would go ahead on 6 June. Eisenhower had made what was the most significant decision of the entire Normandy campaign.

With the benefit of hindsight, his decision was clearly the correct one. By assaulting the Normandy coast in poor weather, the Allies achieved as much surprise as could be secured in the circumstances. The fact that the Germans were caught somewhat off-guard exerted a positive contribution toward the overall success of D-Day that far outweighed the difficulties experienced in executing a difficult amphibious assault in such adverse conditions. Indeed, despite the bad weather, on 6 June the D-Day landings unfolded broadly as expected – except on OMAHA Beach. Consequently, none of the key commanders – Montgomery (aboard HMS *Faulknor*), Kirk and Bradley (on the USS *Augusta*), Vian (aboard HMS *Scylla*) and Dempsey (on HMS *Hilary*) – had to make major interventions into their subordinates' conduct of the landings. Indeed, this fact testifies to the effectiveness of the vast amount of preparatory staff work conducted on the orders of these senior commanders, in the months preceding 6 June 1944.

INTERNAL TENSIONS

Sadly, the previously effective 'Ike'–'Monty' command partnership became increasingly strained as the Normandy campaign unfolded. Montgomery's operational caution, irritating arrogance, and determination to protect British national interests within the wider Allied alliance, grated away at not just the SCAEF but also many of the

The British and American High Command remained suspicious of General Charles de Gaulle, leader of the French Committee of National Liberation (the 'Free French'), largely because Roosevelt refused to accept him as the legitimate French government-in-exile. Consequently, he was largely excluded from the Allied decision-making process during OVERLORD. Indeed, General de Gaulle did not arrive in Normandy until 14 June. (NAC, PA-115159)

latter's American subordinates. On 30 June 1944, for example, when FUSA Commander Bradley took tea with Montgomery, he experienced once again the British commander's tactless egoism. When Montgomery discovered that Bradley's aide-de-camp was a major, he queried why a lowly 'dog's body' and 'whipping boy' should enjoy such a lofty position. "I would not have an ADC who is more than a captain," Monty crowed. Indeed, the charm and diplomacy of Montgomery's chief of staff, Francis W. ('Freddie') de Guingand was needed regularly to ensure that Anglo-American ground cooperation remained reasonably effective despite these tensions.

The one area of inter-service cooperation that did not quite reach the high standards achieved elsewhere in OVERLORD was that of the support provided by Allied strategic air forces. The main reasons behind these difficulties were structural, in that these command relationships remained an unhappy compromise between conflicting interests. In early 1944, Eisenhower had requested that parts of Harris' Bomber Command and Spaatz's USAAF be placed under the control of SHAEF to support OVERLORD. Given that the strategic bomber offensive against Germany was crucial to the overall Allied war effort, the British Government refused to accept this arrangement. In addition, Harris and Spaatz remained adamant that they did not want C-in-C AEAF Leigh-Mallory to control the strategic forces assigned to OVERLORD, as the latter's main experience had been with fighter operations. In mid-April 1944, however, after months of wrangling so bitter that Eisenhower had threatened to resign, a compromise was finally agreed. The SCAEF would have the authority of 'operational direction' over the strategic bombers assigned to support OVERLORD, but the command of these units would remain with Harris and Spaatz for the continuing strategic offensive against German industry.

To support the preparations for D-Day, these strategic forces carried out the vital missions of destroying German air force assets, transportation routes and communication links throughout north-west Europe. Given the difficulties in the relationship between the 'strategic bomber barons' and Leigh-Mallory, Eisenhower increasingly relied on Tedder to exercise operational direction over these strategic air assets, thereby inadvertently further diminishing the authority of the C-in-C AEAF. After D-Day, as the Normandy campaign developed, SHAEF increasingly desired that these strategic bombers should mount missions in direct support of unfolding ground operations, tasks that to Harris represented a fundamental misuse of his forces. Often, it was only the combined pressure mounted by Tedder and Montgomery in support of Leigh-Mallory's requests that eventually secured the effective support of such assets for offensives such as CHARNWOOD, GOODWOOD and TOTALIZE during July–August 1944.

The command role of the hard-pressed Leigh-Mallory was further complicated by the fact that his two highly experienced subordinates – Coningham and Brereton – knew more about the provision of tactical air support to ground formations than he did. Coningham also found that his professional relationship with Montgomery became strained as the campaign unfolded. The air chief marshal had believed the general's disingenuous propaganda that he would swiftly strike deep into the interior of Normandy to secure sites for airfields from which 2 TAF squadrons could operate. Montgomery, however, had no intention of allowing this issue – which to him was no shibboleth – to distort the unfolding of his finely tuned 'master plan' for the campaign,

The commander of the Second (British) Army, Lt. Gen. Miles C. 'Bimbo' Dempsey (centre), is seen here in Normandy on 11 July 1994 with (left) Lt. Gen. Richard N. O'Connor (British VIII Corps) and Lt. Gen. Neil M. Ritchie (XII Corps). (IWM, B6956)

and this disagreement increasingly marred the otherwise effective working partnership that the two commanders had established.

Given the tensions inevitable in a military enterprise conducted on such a vast scale as D-Day, the multinational joint cooperation implemented by this OVERLORD High Command organisation was generally very effective. Perhaps the only exception to this was the air dimension, where intractable structural problems somewhat hampered the efficiency of this cooperation. Though inter-Allied tensions remained evident during these operations, these seldom reached a severity that had a negative effect on the conduct of the campaign – and this itself was no mean achievement. Indeed, the OVERLORD command system contributed so significantly to the success that the Allies eventually secured over Hitler's Nazi Reich, that a modern multinational joint headquarters can still find useful precedents in these structures with which to enhance the efficiency of its own organisation.

Chapter 5

"Throw
them back"

(Field Marshal Erwin Rommel, 1944)
*"If we do not succeed in our mission to close the seas to the Allies,
or in the first 48 hours, to throw them back, their invasion will be successful."*

German planning
and command

Professor Dennis Showalter

For Adolf Hitler, World War II was a war to the finish – planned, initiated, and executed with the intention of obtaining European dominance and world hegemony. Any compromises would be no more than tactical concessions. There could be no peace in 1940 just as there would be no surrender in 1945. The limitations of Nazi Germany's military power relative to these ambitions became apparent almost as soon as the armistice of Compiègne was signed in 1918. The Luftwaffe's inability to achieve the air supremacy over Britain necessary for an invasion left unanswered the question of whether the planned German landings in Britain, or Operation SEALION, with its dependence on river barges and four-footed horsepower, had any real chance of succeeding. There also remained the U-boats, as yet few in number and poorly organized, but with at least some potential to starve out the island kingdom. There also remained a Mediterranean option that might break British morale by demonstrating Britain's relative impotence. Instead, Hitler's own ideological and strategic predispositions led him to focus increasingly on Russia as the key to victory, both in its own context and as a means of forcing Britain out of the war more rapidly than a death of a thousand cuts, whether inflicted in the Mediterranean basin or over the home island.

This focus meant a shift to the defensive in the West. At the end of 1941, Hitler ordered the construction of a line of fortifications along the Atlantic Coast. He intended this as the main position securing the conquered Continent and Germany's western provinces. Initially, no comprehensive plans for the system were developed. In strategic terms, however, by 1942 it was clear to the newly created High Command West that the Allies would eventually strike north-west Europe in force. The only question was when and where the blow would fall.

German planners were not influenced by the Gallipoli legacy that shaped so much British and US thinking on the subject of amphibious operations during the inter-war years. The German perspective was just the opposite. From late 1939 to early 1942, every landing made under modern conditions had succeeded. Not the strength of the land forces involved, but sea and air superiority were the crucial factors. In their presence, an assault from the sea could prevail even if initial casualties were high. There was little doubt in Wehrmacht circles that the Anglo-American alliance could achieve that superiority almost at will. The newly created High Command West began by deploying whatever divisions were available to cover directly what seemed the most vulnerable ports and landing sites. It was a wing-and-a-prayer proposition, but point defense seemed the most promising response to

OPPOSITE Adolf Hitler in a characteristic public pose. His inspirational image endured in Germany until the end of the war. (National Archives of Canada)

German experience in Norway and Crete that indicated not merely the first hours but the first minutes of an invasion could be crucial. The concept seemed validated on August 19, 1942, when a division-scale assault with heavy air and naval support was decisively broken on the beaches of Dieppe. Terrain favored the defenders at crucial points and fortune smiled that day on the men who fought under the swastika. The Germans nevertheless won their victory with military pocket-change, and Dieppe generated a new optimism among the senior officers who contemplated the burned-out Churchill tanks.

OPPOSITE Gerd von Rundstedt. (IWM 211 244 ER)

ALLOCATION OF GERMAN DEFENSIVE POWER

As Hitler's initial vision of kicking in Russia's front door drowned in blood on the Eastern Front, France increasingly became a rest-and-recuperation zone for burned-out front-line units. Even the West's supreme commander as of March 1942, Field Marshal Gerd von

BELOW Stalingrad was an absolute disaster for the Germans, and had a profound impact on men and materiel. (Yakov Ryumkin)

Rundstedt, had received his appointment after being removed from his army group in Russia. A few weeks in France to absorb equipment and replacements, to forget the war as far as possible, was a dream that ran a close third to a long furlough or a million-mark wound. The "hero-thieves" of the replacement service staged comb-out after comb-out in the formations that watched the coasts. In 1942 and 1943, just about anyone who wanted to fight, who was able to fight, or who could conceivably be made to fight, was transferred eastward. Their replacements were the lame and the halt, the elderly and the invalid. The Germans who remained increasingly saw themselves as garrison troops rather than a combat force – and wished to stay garrison troops as long and as comfortably as possible. But Dieppe suggested that, given enough concrete and barbed wire, the Wehrmacht's leftovers might be able to make "Fortress Europe" a reality.

Some historians of World War II have argued that the US-initiated plans for a full-scale landing in the spring of 1943 would have caught the Wehrmacht at its lowest ebb. German fixed defenses in the West were still embryonic. At sea, the Allies were supreme. In the air they could count on a significant margin of superiority. The disaster at Stalingrad and the preparations for Kursk reduced the German army in the West to a shell, primarily concerned with rebuilding shattered divisions, providing cadres for new ones, and conducting training courses at all levels. For a good part of 1943, High Command West had fewer combat-ready divisions than it possessed in 1942. *Ostlegionen*, battalions recruited from Russia's Asian communities or from prisoners of war, filled out its orders of battle. High Command West was also absorbed in implementing Hitler's September 1942 order to increase the coastal defenses by no fewer than 15,000 strong points. The archives include far more correspondence on details of the Führer's blockhouse projects than on proposals for repelling a full-scale cross-Channel invasion.

The Allies' Mediterranean initiatives also helped attract High Command West's attention southward. In the immediate aftermath of Operation TORCH, concern developed over the possibility of an Allied movement into Spain. The invasions of Sicily and Italy and the German occupation of Vichy France increased the stresses on already-overstretched field forces. The growth of demands for forced labor from a conquered Europe converted what had at first been compliance, to sullenness and hostility, then to opposition and resistance. During 1943, in short, the Germans in the West had so many immediate priorities that concern for a D-Day-type operation moved towards the bottom of the list by default.

ANTICIPATION OF THE NORMANDY INVASION

It did not disappear. The case for a 1943 invasion of north-east Europe appears plausible because of distractions themselves largely the product of Anglo-American initiatives in the Mediterranean. Without Operation TORCH and its consequences, High Command West would have been correspondingly free to concentrate on preparing for a major landing mounted from Britain. D-Day was an operation that could be undertaken only once. Britain's moral and material capital was nearly exhausted. Failure, to say nothing of disaster, would have had incalculably negative consequences for the war effort of the island kingdom. The US was powerful enough to bear and recover from the physical consequences of defeat on Europe's beaches. The psychological impact was a different story entirely. June 1944 in England invites comparison in US military history with July 1863 in Pennsylvania. Both occasions generated a sense of participation in something Hegel might have called a world-historical event. Seen in this light, the cross-Channel invasion was more than a military operation – too much more to risk its launching in anything but the most favorable circumstances possible.

As High Command West coped with the challenges generated by the Russian and Mediterranean theaters, the Atlantic Wall began taking on

German minefield. The German army's sophisticated use of anti-tank and anti-personnel mines inflicted heavy Allied casualties on D-Day and throughout the European campaign. (NARA)

a life of its own. By mid-1943, particularly around the major ports, the Wall looked authentic, with trenches, ditches, and minefields, machine-gun nests, concrete strong points, and heavy artillery emplaced in what, even to men who knew better, seemed impregnable bunkers. By June 1943, over 8,000 permanent installations were operable. By November, over 2,300 anti-tank guns and 2,700 guns larger than 75mm were in place. The building program, however, tailed off in the final months of the year. Allied air raids drew away skilled workers. German firms that had obtained sweetheart contracts or low-balled their bids produced unsatisfactory work or failed to meet commitments.

Nor were the commanders on the spot exactly sure what to do with the system in place. The defense of Western Europe, originally regarded as a joint-service undertaking, had by late 1943 become an army responsibility. The Kriegsmarine, defeated in the U-boat campaign, its remaining surface vessels penned in harbor, could expect to do little more than conduct coast-defense operations with a mixed bag of small craft. The Luftwaffe's attention had shifted to the Eastern Front and, increasingly, to the Reich itself. Staff and operational assignments to Air Fleet 3, responsible for Western Europe, were viewed as either dead ends or rest cures.

On October 25, 1943, von Rundstedt submitted a comprehensive memorandum describing the challenges and requirements of a sector that in the next year could expect to become a major theater of operations. He sarcastically informed Wehrmacht chief Wilhelm Keitel that he would be very glad if Hitler read this report despite his busy schedule. Otherwise the Führer might accuse his generals of failing to keep him informed should things go wrong, as he had done in December 1941. And there was a great deal to go wrong in the sectors allotted to High Command West. The Field Marshal's report pulled no punches. Von Rundstedt expected an invasion no earlier than the spring of 1944, but probably not much later. He believed the Allies would land first in the Pas de Calais, then in Normandy and Brittany. Admittedly this would put them against the best-defended sector of the Atlantic Coast. On the other hand, these invasion sites offered the easiest passages, the shortest supply lines, and the closest distances to Germany's frontiers. The Allies already had as many divisions available for such an operation as von Rundstedt could muster in his entire expanded theater. Most of them were first-class assault troops: young, sound of wind and limb, and equipped with the best American and British industry could provide. Anglo-American air and naval supremacy meant that they could also count on the advantage of tactical surprise by stifling German reconnaissance.

DEFENDING THE COAST

Von Rundstedt argued that the Atlantic Wall ordered by Hitler as the main battle line bore no comparison to the fixed defenses of World War I, with which the Führer and the Field Marshal were both familiar. Front-line trenches, pillboxes, and strong points were only half of a successful fortification system. Depth was also necessary: fall-back positions in the rear areas, mobile artillery, and enough troops for counterattacks to seal off the inevitable breakthroughs. High Command West at this stage not only lacked anything resembling an effective mobile reserve. It lacked enough static troops to do more than observe and patrol much of the endangered area.

These weaknesses, paradoxically, made the Atlantic Wall more important than ever. Abandoning the coast without a fight would sacrifice the advantage of the Channel as a moat. It would mean the loss of a heavy investment in fortifications and their armament. Above all, it would require the conduct of a mobile battle in north-east France, against an enemy whose strong point was a capacity for mobile warfare. Therefore, von Rundstedt argued, the coast line must be defended to the last. Experience in both world wars showed that landings in force would, nevertheless, succeed. But a combination of local counterattacks to disrupt initial successes, supplemented once the Allied *schwerpunkt* became apparent by the concentrated blows of a massed reserve, provided the window of an opportunity for defeating the invasion, or at least so bloodying the Anglo-Americans' noses that they might reconsider their military and political options.

Hitler read von Rundstedt's complex document with a level of attention by this time unusual. Instead of responding by insisting on the importance of will power, a Führer Directive of November 3, 1943, he accepted most of von Rundstedt's basic propositions. For two and a half years the Reich's energies had been directed against Asiatic Bolshevism. Now, an even greater danger had emerged: the Anglo-Saxon invasion. In the East, space could be traded for time. Not so in the West. An Allied breakout from a successful landing would have prompt and incalculable consequences for the Reich. No longer could the West be stripped for the sake of other theaters. Instead, its defenses must be strengthened by every means possible. In October, 1943, the western theater had only 256 tanks of all kinds – no more than a token against the thousands available to the Allies. Its half-dozen mobile divisions were skeletons or embryos. Now the General Staff and the Inspector-General of Panzer Troops were instructed to provide sufficient mobility for the formations responsible for defending northeast Europe. Divisions must be created or re-equipped. Mark IV tanks and assault guns would replace older

models. The supply of anti-tank, infantry, and artillery weapons must be increased. Similar directives went to the navy, the army, and the Waffen SS. At the same time, High Command West was ordered to reduce the garrisons of less-threatened areas and improve the counterattack capacity of even static formations by improving their mobility through internal resources.

VON RUNDSTEDT AND ROMMEL: OIL AND WATER

Hitler believed, even more than von Rundstedt, that victory in the West would ultimately depend on a full-strength counterattack against any major landing. The enemy must be thrown into the sea at all costs. Was von Rundstedt, a man of advanced years and fixed opinions, the general to perform that mission? Later in the month the Führer played a trump card by sending Field Marshal Erwin Rommel to inspect the Western theater's defenses. The entire staff of Rommel's Army Group B, over 200 officers and men, accompanied their chief. Under Hitler's personal command, Rommel and his men were to prepare plans and suggestions for the best ways of meeting an Allied invasion.

This decision arguably reflected Hitler's long-standing practice of establishing parallel systems for solving difficult problems, rather than any specific lack of confidence in von Rundstedt. Although not one of Rommel's chief admirers, von Rundstedt was nevertheless familiar enough with that process, and pleased enough with the Führer's new-found interest in the West, that he offered the newcomer full cooperation. Rommel, for his part, recognized the awkwardness of his position and took pains to avoid stepping on his senior's toes. But these men, the army's senior and junior field marshals, were like oil and water. Von Rundstedt had been to the circus and seen the clowns. He tended to let situations develop before he acted, all the while commenting on those developments with an irony that could alternately inspire admiration or fury in his associates. Rommel was a driver, accustomed to seeing every situation as an emergency, making snap decisions, and making those decisions work.

The problem was exacerbated because both men were respected and admired by their subordinates. Each possessed charisma: von Rundstedt, the "last Prussian," patrician, dignified; Rommel, the front-line commander who could still talk like a first sergeant and paid little attention to formalities. The old pro and the new broom – small wonder that within weeks even senior officers were uncertain as to who was in command. It was von Rundstedt who broke the ice. On December 30 he made a formal proposal to place Army Group B under High Command West, with direct responsibility for the region most exposed to invasion. On January 15, Rommel was assigned command of the garrison of the Netherlands and of the Fifteenth and Seventeenth Armies in the Pas de Calais and Normandy.

The solution was by no means an inevitable recipe for disaster. Von Rundstedt's command style, like that of most of his old-army contemporaries, was based on the delegation of authority. His responsibilities as theater commander had been so extended by recent Allied initiatives that he could not hope to supervise directly every area under threat. And if, as was frequently murmured behind closed General Staff doors, Rommel was no more than a good corps commander, his tactical record was nevertheless sufficiently distinguished to make him a solid choice to command Western Europe's most likely hotspot.

Rommel oversees the construction of beach obstacles during a tour of Normandy in March 1944. (Military History Institute)

ROMMEL'S TACTICS

Rommel applied the energy that had made him famous into strengthening and vitalizing the Atlantic Wall. He estimated that no fewer than fifty million mines would be needed to establish a viable belt around the coast! Such an astronomical number was, of course, unattainable. Nevertheless, between October 1943 and May 1944 the number of anti-tank and anti-personnel mines in place had risen from two million to six and a half million. Rommel also oversaw the introduction of underwater obstacles at the most likely landing sites. These ranged from angled wooden stakes to steel Belgian anti-tank barriers transplanted from their original sites on the German border. By mid-May, over 500,000 of these passive defenses had been installed, many of them with mines attached. Behind the coast the Field Marshal planted "Rommel's asparagus," pointed stakes driven into the ground, sometimes with explosives strapped to the ends, on terrain deemed suitable for paratroops or glider landings.

Rommel also brought new vigor to the construction and renovation of manned defenses. He was shocked to find that many of the gun positions and machine-gun emplacements were open, offering no significant protection from air strikes or naval gunfire. Engineers and workers from the *Organization Todt* began bringing as many heavy weapons as possible under bomb-proof protection. Camouflage and camouflage discipline improved sharply. Local commanders assisted by assigning troops to the construction efforts which included establishing dummy positions in hopes of deceiving the by-now ubiquitous Allied reconnaissance aircraft.

On paper and in reality the results were impressive. In 1944 the Germans laid over four million land mines – well over double the

Beach obstacles at low tide. Note the land mine on top of the one in the foreground, intended to disable landing craft. (NARA)

number that had been put in place since 1940. Between January and May, over 5,000 new permanent fortifications were erected – no small number even though the figures included the Mediterranean coast as well. In the Pas de Calais sector, 93 of 132 heavy guns had been put under concrete, as were 27 of the 47 heavy guns in Normandy.

Rommel's ideal was to keep the Allies from coming ashore at all. The most difficult phase of a landing was its beginning: the movement from ship to shore. The Germans should take every possible advantage of this fact. Passive defenses, mines and offshore obstacles, must complement the fire of artillery, anti-tank guns, and automatic weapons covering the landing sites. Infantry should be deployed as close to the beaches as possible. But the heart of Rommel's tactics was his proposal to deploy the panzer formations so close to the coast that their artillery could supplement the forward defenses, while combined-arms battle groups prepared to engage the enemy in the invasion's first hours. Without the immediate help of mechanized reserves, the field marshal insisted, the German divisions holding the coastline could not expect to maintain their positions. The Allies were certain to get ashore somewhere. If left undisturbed, they would flank the defenders out of their fixed defenses and roll up the Atlantic Wall like a rug.

Rommel's approach offered the advantage of employing the panzer divisions in ways grown familiar to their officers in recent years: counter-punching a tactically vulnerable enemy, with dash and tactical skill compensating for inferior numbers. It offered a closer link between the two tiers of the defense, the semi-mobile infantry divisions and the mechanized formations. Rommel's plan made it less likely that the former would regard themselves as pawns for sacrifice, and correspondingly less likely that they would break or capitulate. One of the reasons for the German infantry's Homeric combat record on the Eastern Front was the widespread knowledge that surrendering to Ivan involved high levels of immediate risk and complete certainty of subsequent discomfort. By contrast, conditions of British or American captivity were so favorably mythologized that not a few prisoners taken during the D-Day campaign seemed surprised when their first meal did not include steak.

Rommel was never a blind admirer of Hitler; and his direct contact with the Führer was more recent and more extensive than that of anyone else in High Command West. His faith in "final victory" had been correspondingly weakened. In that, at least, Rommel had much in common with almost every senior officer west of the Rhine River. But while his counterparts were content to play the cards in their hands with a cynical shrug, Rommel thought in wider terms. Repulsing the landings at the shoreline would buy military time that might be exploited politically. A decisive victory presented to the Führer by his favorite marshal might well prove an entering wedge for a negotiated peace. If not, there was always the German Resistance, whose plans and hopes for direct action against "history's greatest warlord" were increasingly open secrets among those in the know at High Command West. Best evidence indicates Rommel was not directly involved in any conspiracies. He was, however, tactician enough to profit from any opportunities created by Hitler's removal.

Rommel's principal critic was not von Rundstedt, but Leo Geyr von Schweppenburg. An experienced staff officer and long-time commander of armored forces, with extensive experience on the Russian Front, Geyr had been appointed commander of Panzer Troops West in July 1943, and immediately began developing his own plans for using armor against an Allied invasion. Like Rommel, Geyr recognized the potential impact of Allied sea and air power – in particular, the probable use of airborne forces to disrupt rear areas and communications. His proposed response was to keep available mobile forces well clear of the coast, in camouflaged positions out of range of naval guns. Geyr was no admirer of the battle group tactics that had emerged in Russia as a response to a chronic shortage of tanks. These small formations, he argued, would be particularly vulnerable to Allied firepower. What was needed were large-scale counterattacks against the invasion beaches, counterattacks in divisional strength or more. Air power did not stop movement, it only delayed it. To reach the operational zones, the mechanized forces would have to move by night, but properly trained troops under competent officers could expect to arrive in time.

Rommel, unlike Geyr, had spent a fair amount of his time in North Africa personally dodging Allied aircraft. He expected the invasion to have higher levels of air support than anything previously seen in history. The terrain, moreover, was ideally suited for tactical air power. In contrast to the wide open desert, northern France was so heavily built up that only relatively few roads could be used for major troop movements. These led across rivers and through cities. Bridges and buildings alike offered inviting targets for Allied medium and heavy bombers. Rommel did not expect any feelings for the French people to restrict such uses of air power. The French Resistance was also likely to be a factor, both directly in partisan operations and by providing up-to-date intelligence to the Allied airmen. It was unreasonable, Rommel argued, to expect divisions positioned according to Geyr's proposals to reach the battle zone, reorganize, and refit, in less than ten days or two weeks. That was all the time and more the invaders would need to establish a bridgehead impregnable to anything High Command West was likely to bring against it.

Perhaps as important as the debates over deployment and force structures was the growing conflict in High Command West between mind-sets. Rommel did not embody a specific National Socialist way of war so much as reflect the actual military situation facing Germany in 1944. Will power, striking power, and tactical virtuosity were keeping the Reich alive. They were not, however, bringing victory – only prolonging an end game. To Geyr's supporters, that general's approach offered a last chance to wage a mobile campaign the way one ought to be waged, against an enemy that from Africa to Anzio had shown significant vulnerability to German operational skills. And if it failed, the panzer arm would at least expire in a final blaze of glory rather than being destroyed one tank at a time.

The decision was von Rundstedt's, and the field marshal remained torn between his commitment to defeating the invasion at the water line and the lure of Geyr's arguments for attempting something more decisive. Rommel, Geyr, von Rundstedt, all by now agreed that events on the French coast would determine the fate of the German people. Rommel sought Hitler's intervention. The Führer was reluctant to decide, particularly since a decision in Rommel's favor meant the corresponding necessity of relieving von Rundstedt. Geyr did not have Rommel's access to the supreme commander, but his patron, Heinz Guderian, was still in good favor at the *Führerhauptquartier*. As the jockeying intensified, von Rundstedt found himself in the position of a poker player who antes in every hand but fails to bet: his stack of military/political chips was steadily diminishing.

SPLIT COMMAND

The initial result was something the German army had rejected in principle since the days of Frederick the Great: division of authority. In February 1944, as more and more armored divisions began arriving in France, Rommel's Army Group B was given the right to command any formations of Panzer Group West in its operational area as part of its preparation for the invasion. Rommel also received the right to recommend sector assignments and command appointments for the mobile formations directly to von Rundstedt, thus bypassing Geyr. The result was an increase in friction among the senior officers that led Hitler to intervene directly. He began in April by stating he reserved the decision to determine when mobile formations should be assigned to Army Group B. Until that point, High Command West retained full control of those divisions. A month later, the Führer became even more

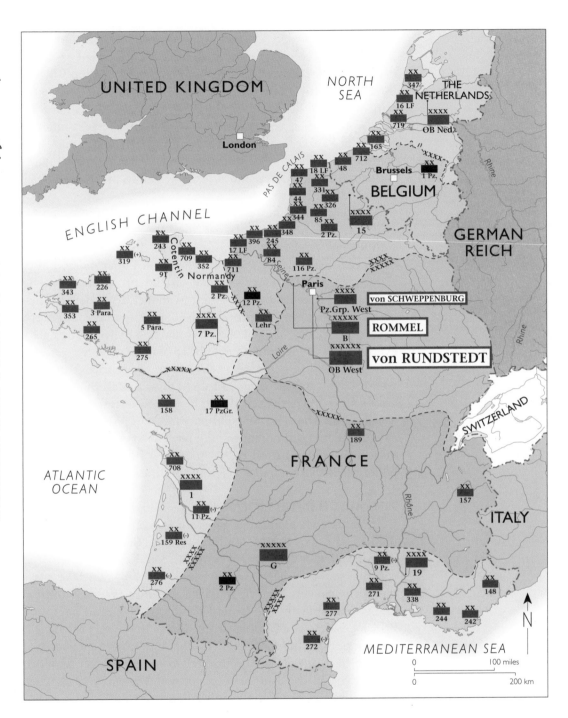

GERMAN DISPOSITIONS IN THE WEST, JUNE 6, 1944

specific. He created a new army group headquarters under von Rundstedt to control southern France, and assigned it three panzer divisions: 9th, 11th, and 2nd SS. Rommel's Army Group B also received three panzer divisions: the 2nd, 21st, and 116th. The mobile units that remained were the cream of the crop: 1st and 12th SS Panzer, 17th SS Panzer Grenadier, and the army's Panzer Lehr. They remained under control of Panzer Group West – but not exactly under von Rundstedt's command. Instead, the Panzer Group was designated part of the Wehrmacht High Command reserve, which in practice placed it under Hitler's direct control.

This reorganization invites dismissal as no more than another example of Hitler's high-test meddling in matters outside his competence. Assigning three mechanized divisions to southern France left seven available for the decisive sector. Either massed as a central reserve or posted close together on the prospective beaches, they represented a force strong enough to shape, if not decide, the coming battle – not a queen but, properly used, perhaps a pair of knights. Their division not only created the obvious possibility of being too weak everywhere. It generated a subtler risk of making everyone just strong enough to generate a false sense of security. Von Rundstedt's well-known sarcastic comment that Hitler's decision left him only the authority to move the sentries in his headquarters is, however, at best a half-truth. The field marshal had forgotten a fundamental military axiom: the first duty of a commander was to command, specifically, to decide the organization of his theater. War abhors vacuums. Adolf Hitler filled that created by Gerd von Rundstedt.

TOO MUCH INTELLIGENCE?

German defense planning's general focus on Normandy, Brittany, and the Pas de Calais hardly required General Staff training. A schoolboy with a Mercator map and a compass could expect to reach a similar conclusion. But where exactly would the invasion take place? Here the Germans were tapping in darkness. Since 1940, the entire network of German spies in the United Kingdom had been operating under British control. The Double-Cross system involved providing accurate information to the German Abwehr, but information of no importance or just out of date. Systematic counterintelligence efforts might have revealed the true state of affairs. The Abwehr, however, was increasingly involved in the anti-Hitler resistance – involved, perhaps, to a point where its senior officers may have chosen not to ask awkward questions about the nature of the material they received from the British Isles.

To the Double-Cross system was added in late 1943 an even more elaborate deception plan. Operation FORTITIUDE created entire armies out of whole cloth and radio call signs. It suggested possible invasion sites from Norway to Marseilles, and was spectacularly successful in encouraging Hitler to retain 13 divisions in Norway to secure the bases of a U-boat arm that had been ineffective for almost a year. By the end of May, FORTITUDE persuaded High Command West's intelligence that the Allies had no fewer than 89 divisions, with enough landing craft to bring 20 of them ashore in the first wave. The actual figures were 47 and six, respectively. FORTITUDE'S heart, however, was its effort to convince the Germans that the major invasion would take place in the Pas de Calais. A non-existent First US Army Group (FUSAG) was placed under the command of the very real George S. Patton – a man the Germans regarded as the Allies' best and most daring commander. With a mixture of real and imaginary divisions under its command, FUSAG seemed not a pistol, but a cannon aimed at the area which years before von Rundstedt had described as posing the greatest long-term risk to Germany's "Fortress Europe."

The course of the operation is a classic illustration of the risks of becoming over-involved in intelligence operations. Had part of the energy devoted to monitoring and analyzing FORTITUDE'S communications been directed instead to common-sense evaluation of possibilities, it seems likely that some bright colonel or major might have questioned whether an exhausted Britain and a US fighting a two-ocean war could, in fact, provide such huge forces even for a decisive operation. German intelligence, however, like the Wehrmacht of which it was a part, tended to focus on tactical and operational problems rather than production statistics and manpower pools. FORTITUDE was a German failure as well as an Allied success.

The effect of Operation FORTITUDE on German planning must not be exaggerated. Rommel might have been an unconventional soldier, but he unconditionally accepted the traditional maxim that to be strong everywhere meant being strong nowhere. The Pas de Calais was the most likely invasion sector, and the most threatening. It was, moreover, small enough that its fixed defenses could be concentrated to a degree that would pose a genuine threat to a landing force. Normandy–Brittany, in contrast, offered such a broad front that it absorbed concrete as a sponge absorbs water. It was not gambler's intuition but common strategic sense that led Rommel, as the spring of 1944 waned, to concentrate his available resources around the port city of Calais and its environs – even in the face of Hitler's intuitive belief the landings just might come farther west, in Brittany and the Cotentin Peninsula.

D-DAY APPROACHES

Statistics help tell the final story. The Fifteenth Army in the Pas de Calais sector eventually grew to a strength of 18 infantry and two panzer divisions, responsible for about 340 miles of coastline. The Seventh Army, responsible for Normandy and Brittany, had 14 infantry divisions and a single panzer division. It was responsible for 995 miles of coast. One of its divisions had a defensive sector of 62 miles; another was expected to secure no fewer than 167 miles.

The figures must not be taken literally. Large sections of the Seventh Army's zone of operations were completely unsuitable for major landing operations. In crucial areas, including the actual D-Day beaches, German force-to-space ratios were a good deal more favorable. Nevertheless, by June 6 the discrepancy was clear. The Pas de Calais was something approximating a true fortified zone, along lines High Command West had hoped to achieve since 1942. Its combination of mutually supporting fixed defenses, relatively large infantry forces, and two mobile divisions in sector reserve represented the best the Germans were likely to achieve in the foreseeable future. Normandy, in contrast, was still a network of isolated, thinly garrisoned, strong points. Its armored reserve, the 21st Panzer Division, was still partly equipped with French tanks captured in 1940.

Even in that context D-Day was no walkover. German soldiers, from division commanders to rear-rank *Landser*, stressed Allied material superiority. Not only were the Allies' fighter-bombers everywhere, it sometimes seemed that every infantryman had his own radio to call for air support. And if British and American tanks were individually inferior to the Mark IVs, Tigers, and Panthers, there nevertheless seemed to be an endless supply of them.

D-Day, however, was a German defeat as well as an Allied victory, and the roots of that defeat ran deeper than a single day's fighting. Hitler's control of operational details remains a target of criticism, with the Führer's alleged late sleeping on that morning of June 6 sometimes even described as among the war's turning points. What was important was not the exact time Hitler arose, but his long-entertained wariness of Allied diversionary moves – a concern shared by High Command West. Once awake, he remained skeptical until the daily lunch conference. Only then did he agree to send two more panzer divisions to Normandy. The delay, in other words, was not a direct function of terrified adjutants unwilling to awaken their Führer with bad news. Committing the armored reserves meant the die was indisputably cast, and for all their alleged battlefield virtuosity the generals were just a bit reluctant to throw that final switch.

That uncertainty makes moot the question of whether Rommel or Geyr was right about the panzers. German preparations for D-Day did not begin with Rommel's arrival in Normandy. Nor did they develop in a vacuum. They reflected four years of war experience. They reflected the internal dynamics of the German army and the National Socialist system. And they reflected a series of individual decisions dating back to 1940. Hitler himself, Rommel, von Rundstedt, Geyr, the officers and men under their commands, approached the Longest Day with the intention of being victors at its end. That instead they tasted defeat to the dregs was in part a consideration of German failures and shortcomings. But it was ultimately the result of men, British and Americans, Canadians, Poles, Czechs, and Free French, who put their lives on the line to storm the Atlantic Wall, to fight their way through the hedgerows to the green fields beyond, and to final victory in the Liberation Campaign.

Chapter 6

"In the air, on the ground and in the factories"

(General Henry H "Hap" Arnold,
Commander of US Army Air Forces,
Christmas 1943 address)
*"Destroy the enemy air force wherever you find them,
in the air, on the ground and in the factories."*

Air power

Professor Williamson Murray

On June 6, 1944, the great Anglo-American invasion of Europe began. Overhead, a cloud of Allied aircraft flew against targets across the length and breadth of France, while fighter-bombers and medium bombers hammered German positions throughout the Norman countryside. The previous evening, transport aircraft had dropped the main elements of three airborne divisions – the American 82nd and 101st on the western side of the amphibious landings, and the British 6th on the eastern side. Overall, Allied air forces flew over 14,000 sorties on D-Day in support of the invasion; the Luftwaffe barely 100. That air superiority, which bordered on air supremacy, was the result of a sustained aerial campaign against Germany's population and its economic strength that had begun in 1940. In the end it was to make a number of contributions, direct as well as indirect, to the landings. Before World War II, air power theorists had claimed that air power would win the next war. It did not. However, OVERLORD's success and the eventual victory of the Western Powers in World War II was inconceivable without the great effort in the air. That is our story.

By summer 1943, the Royal Air Force had been bombing Germany for over three years. Its efforts had begun in 1940 with attempts to attack German industrial targets using night precision bombing. That had been a non-starter. Analysis of bombing photos in August 1941 indicated that only one in three RAF bombers were dropping their loads within five miles of their target – a bull's eye over 75 square miles in area. The technology to allow true precision bombing was, at this stage, not sufficiently developed. To all intents and purposes, the RAF was bombing trees and killing cows. As a result, from 1941 through to the war's end, the RAF's Bomber Command turned to attacking the German population directly by blasting the Reich's cities in an effort to break German morale. The attacks reflected earlier RAF assumptions about war, and did succeed to a considerable extent in affecting German morale. Reports of the SS secret service, the infamous SD (*Sicherheitsdienst*) indicate that bombing had a serious and negative impact on the morale of the German population, especially during the last two years of the war, but in view of the ruthless control that Hitler's regime exercised over the Reich there was little the Germans could do.

By summer 1943, the British bombing was achieving considerable success. Under the ruthless leadership of Air Marshal Sir Arthur Harris, Bomber Command was finally receiving the aircraft and technological support that allowed it to mete out terrible punishment to its German targets. In late July, Operation GOMORRAH devastated the city of Hamburg with a firestorm that killed nearly 40,000 civilians

OPPOSITE A Typhoon fighter-bomber of the 2nd Tactical Air Force (RAF) taxiing from the dispersal point preparatory to take-off. Note the large quantity of jerricans, containing 100 octane fuel, in the forefront of the photograph. (Laurier Centre for Miltary, Strategic and Disarmament Studies, Wilfrid Laurier University, Canada)

and destroyed the city's heart. After the war, the tsar of the German war economy, Albert Speer, claimed that, if the RAF had managed several other successes on the scale of Hamburg over the last half of 1943, the war would have ended that year. Luckily for the Germans, the RAF required perfect conditions to achieve such successes. It was not able to achieve an equivalent level of effect for the remainder of 1943 and for all of 1944. In addition, beginning in November 1943, Bomber Command's losses went through the roof. In the Battle of Berlin (November 1943 to March 1944), the command lost 1,128 bombers. On its worst night, a raid against Nuremberg in March 1944, it lost over 100 bombers. Yet, the damage that the command dealt out to German cities was terrifying. From early 1943, British bombers were paying the Germans back for the terrible damage inflicted on Europe over the past three years.

Meanwhile, the Americans had entered what was now to be called the Combined Bomber Offensive. By summer 1943, they were able to send great formations of B-17s to attack targets deep in Germany. The theory behind the American bomber campaign was that B-17s, with their heavy defensive armament and by flying at high altitude, could defend themselves without fighter escort in daylight against the Luftwaffe's fighters. The theory also posited that such formations could hit key targets in the Reich's economy, the destruction of which would lead to its collapse. But the theory proved wrong on a number of counts. Targets proved harder to hit; Luftwaffe fighters were much deadlier than presumed; German air defenses more effective; and the Reich's war economy more resilient. Eighth Air Force, responsible for the American strategic bombing effort from bases in England, had an horrendous summer and fall. On August 17, 1943, 60 bombers were lost whilst attacking the ball-bearing factories at Schweinfurt. In a

A B-17 goes down over Germany. (Official US Air Force photo)

return attack against Schweinfurt on October 14, Eighth lost another 60 bombers with virtually every bomber that survived returning in damaged condition. From April 1943 through October 1943, Eighth was losing 30 percent of its crews *each month*.

Yet for all the difficulties that the Combined Bomber Offensive was experiencing in the last half of 1943, the Germans were in an even worse position. The Luftwaffe was losing nearly 15 percent of its fighter pilots every month – a loss rate it was far less able to sustain than its American enemies. The simplest way to understand the extent of the losses suffered by the opposing side is the fact that a young American had a better chance of surviving the war in 1942 by joining the marines and fighting on the island campaigns in the Pacific than by joining the Army Air Forces and flying in bombers over Germany in 1943. Similarly in 1942 a young German had a better chance of surviving by joining the Waffen SS and fighting on the Eastern Front than by joining the Luftwaffe and becoming a fighter pilot.

The fact that the Allies were gaining an edge on the Germans, despite the heavy losses of US bombers, underlines the extent of Hitler's miscalculation in declaring war on the United States in December 1941. Despite its appalling loss rates, Eighth Air Force's front line strength continued to grow throughout the long summer and fall months of 1943 – a mark of the mobilization of the massive US economy and the ability of that economy to mass-produce even complex weapons systems such as bombers. For example, the great Ford plant in Willow Run, Michigan, stretched out for two miles, over what had once been farmland; at one end the production line started with a tail assembly and out the other end came a finished B-24 bomber. In effect, the Americans were mass-producing bombers just as they had refrigerators.

Meanwhile, not only was German production of new fighter aircraft falling off in the last half of 1943, but the quality of the weapons being produced was also declining. Perhaps even more important was the fact that the quality of newly trained Luftwaffe fighter pilots was also declining, as the Germans cut back on the training hours devoted to prepare their pilots for combat. On the other side of the hill, the US Army Air Forces and the RAF were increasing the training hours in the syllabi required for a pilot to master before his commitment to combat.

Moreover, the bombing onslaught was forcing the Germans to disperse their production, which only exacerbated the inefficiencies created by the Nazi system and ideology. It was also having other second order effects. Hitler and Göring determined to respond to the bombing offensive and the impact that it was having on German morale with an extraordinarily expensive, and in the long run ineffective, rocket program, which would eventually result in the world's first ballistic missile, the V-2. After the war, the *Strategic Bombing Survey* determined that the V-2 had used up sufficient resources to build the equivalent of 25,000 fighter aircraft.

However, the direct impact on German military resources was one of the most important contributions the Combined Bomber Offensive would make. In the last half of 1943, the Germans transferred virtually all of their fighters back to Germany to defend the skies over the Reich against the increasing American bomber offensive. Moreover, by 1943 the Germans had well over 10,000 high-velocity 88mm and 105mm anti-aircraft guns, firing huge amounts of ammunition against the American and British bombers that were attacking targets throughout Germany. By spring 1944, that number would climb to well over 15,000 pieces of modern artillery, manned by over half a million soldiers – all of whom could have had an enormous impact on the war, had they been fighting on the Eastern Front or in Normandy. Ironically, the only reason they were there was because of the impact that the Combined Bomber Offensive was having on the morale of the German population, a factor about which Hitler and his advisers had considerable worries. In fact, German flak, as the Luftwaffe knew as early as 1942, was largely cost-ineffective against high-flying bombers.

THE BATTLE FOR AIR SUPERIORITY IN EUROPE

Nevertheless, so heavy were the losses suffered by Eighth Air Force in fall 1943 that its commanders had to pull back from unescorted raids deep into German territory. From October 15, 1943, American raids no longer reached beyond the range of fighter escorts, which was barely over the Rhine. Not surprisingly, but rather late in the game, Eighth's commander, Lieutenant General Ira Eaker, was desperately cabling the commander of US Army Air Forces, General "Hap" Arnold, that his command needed a long-range-fighter escort to protect the bombers – a capability that had remained among the lowest of his priorities until losses in October 1943 served to underline how dangerously askew his priorities had been.

At the end of 1943, the prayers of Eighth's crews were answered, although largely by accident, with the appearance of the P-51 "Mustang". The initial plans for this aircraft came as the result of negotiations in 1940 between the RAF's purchasing mission in the United States and a struggling new firm, North American, which had no product, but a bank loan and a number of bright engineers who thought they could cash in on ballooning defense budgets. The British asked whether the firm could build the Curtis-Wright P-40 under license. The engineers replied that they had a design for a better aircraft. The British accepted their claims, and the result was the P-51 "Mustang" – an aircraft which was considerably underpowered with its Allison engine, but which could perform satisfactorily enough at low altitudes. In 1942, the engineers at Farnborough, the RAF's main research and development base, discovered that the Mustang possessed extraordinary aerodynamic qualities despite its unimpressive flight profile. By October 1942, the Farnborough engineers had replaced the Allison engine with a Rolls Royce engine. What they got was the hottest piston-engine fighter of World War II. Further tests in 1943 discovered that the aircraft could carry an internal fuel tank in its fuselage without making it unflyable. With that fuel tank and a drop tank the Mustang could reach out to ranges over 400 miles. Further refinements in 1944 would give it a range of over 600 miles – sufficient to take it beyond Berlin and accompany B-17 formations at their farthest range.

In January 1944, Eighth Air Force received a new commander, Lieutenant General "Jimmie" Doolittle, who had led the famous Tokyo raid in April 1942, where B-26 bombers had flown off US carriers to attack targets throughout Japan's Home Islands. Eighth's bomber strength had now reached well over 1,000, and it was beginning to receive a significant number of P-51s. Its raids deep into Germany would now be covered by Spitfires over the Channel and into the Low Countries. There P-47 Thunderbolts and P-38 Lightnings would pick up the bomber formations, and on the far side of the Rhine the Mustangs would assume responsibility for keeping the Luftwaffe fighters off the back of the B-17s. For the Germans, the appearance of the P-51s so deep into Germany would prove to be their worst nightmare, particularly since the American fighter was superior to anything currently in the German inventory.

For all of January and much of February 1944, northern Europe suffered its normal appalling weather. For much of that period, American crews watched, waited, and prepared for the fight to come. Raids, when they occurred, were against targets where radar bombing could be used. Yet the task ahead was clear. For his Christmas 1943 message, the commander of US Army Air Forces, General Arnold, sent out a clear and unambiguous message of what he expected of Eighth Air Force's crews over the course of the coming months: "Destroy the enemy air force wherever you find them, in the air, on the ground, and in the factories."

On February 20, the extended period of bad weather finally broke. Eighth was ready with 539 P-38s, 416 P-47s, and 329 P-51s and well over 1,000 bombers, while Fifteenth Air Force, operating out of Italy, now contributed to attacks on the German aircraft industry with its B-24s. For the next week, the weather remained largely clear and the greatest air battle in history began; it would last into May before the

Spring 1944: an FW-190 erupts in
flames under fire from US fighters.
(Official US Air Force photo)

Luftwaffe's fighter force was finally broken as an effective instrument of military power. The intensive week of aerial combat that now ensued was called "Big Week," with considerable accuracy, by the Army Air Force public affairs officials. Four great raids, each with over 1,000 bombers, struck the Luftwaffe's production base. Aircraft production facilities, factories that produced engines, and electronics production facilities all received massive blows. The aim to destroy the German economy's ability to produce aircraft was clear from the first.

To protect that production base, the Luftwaffe's fighters rose like angry hornets. During Big Week the Americans lost over 200 bombers. While German losses for the week are no longer available, Luftwaffe returns for the month indicate that it lost 33 percent of its single-engine fighters and 17.9 percent of its fighter pilots in February. Things got worse in March; Luftwaffe losses in aircraft totaled 56.4 percent of its single-engine fighters, while 22 percent of its fighter pilots were dead, wounded, or missing.

In March, having completed their mission to protect the bombers, Doolittle released his fighter pilots to attack targets of opportunity throughout the Reich, particularly the Luftwaffe's airfields. This intercepted ULTRA message indicates how widespread the threat to German air crews had become:

"During flights into the home war zone, enemy fighters have repeatedly carried out attacks on aircraft which were landing or on the airfields themselves. In doing so, they imitate the landing procedure of German fighters or effect surprise by approaching the airfield in fast and level flight. The difficulty in distinguishing friend from foe often makes it impossible for the flak artillery to fire on them."

The massive American attacks on the German aircraft industry failed to stop the Germans from transferring production resources from other aircraft. Thus, German fighter production rose over the course of the first half of 1944, but only at the expense of total aircraft production. The real contribution of these attacks was that the enormous battle of attrition that was taking place was killing off German fighter pilots – good, bad, and indifferent – at a rate that the Luftwaffe could not sustain. On January 1, 1944, the Luftwaffe had had 2,395 single-engine fighter pilots on active duty. Of that number, 1,491 were fully combat-ready, 291 were partially combat-ready, and the rest were not considered combat-ready. Over the course of the next five months, the Luftwaffe lost no fewer than 2,262 single-engine fighter pilots – equivalent to 99 percent of the number present for duty at the beginning of the year. In May, the Luftwaffe's resistance began to crumble, even in the air battles over the Reich. From this point onwards, daylight bomber losses dropped precipitously, and most of the bomber losses after May were the result of anti-aircraft fire.

A Luftwaffe bomber burns: the result of a US low-altitude attack on a German airfield. (Official US Air Force photo)

The largest contribution that the Combined Bomber Offensive made to OVERLORD's success did not lie in the destruction it wrought on Germany's cities or industry, but rather in the fact that it forced the Luftwaffe to fight a massive battle of attrition. That long, sustained battle resulted in its defeat, ironically not because it ran out of aircraft, but because it ran out of trained pilots. When the Allied invasion of Europe came, the Germans were no longer capable of putting significant numbers of aircraft over the beaches to contest either the landings or the vessels that fed the swelling flow of men, machines, and supplies into the countryside of northern France.

THE TRANSPORTATION PLAN

In March 1944, a furious row occurred among the senior leaders of the Allied High Command in Europe. It pitted the overall commander of the upcoming invasion of Europe, General Dwight David Eisenhower, against the "bomber barons." Eisenhower demanded that control of the strategic bombing forces be turned over to him on April 1 to begin a campaign against the French transportation network, the destruction of which would make it difficult, if not impossible, for the Germans to reinforce and supply their forces defending the Norman coast. The overall commander of the US strategic bombing effort, which included Fifteenth Air Force in Italy as well as Eighth Air Force, General "Tooey" Spaatz, strongly objected. Not surprisingly, his British counterpart, Air Marshal Harris, also objected. Harris disingenuously argued to Churchill that attacks by Bomber Command aircraft would kill large numbers of French civilians. (After the war he admitted that he didn't give a damn how many French were killed, since they had run away in 1940.) On the other hand, Spaatz argued that his B-17s could make a far larger contribution to Allied victory by beginning a campaign to destroy Germany's petroleum industry. Spaatz also argued that he wanted to keep the pressure on the Germans, and that if attacks on railroads forced the Luftwaffe to come up and fight, they would help him accomplish his task of destroying them. In this respect he was right, and Eisenhower did allow him to keep the pressure on the Germans throughout April and on into May by continuing raids into Germany.

The supreme allied commander was forced to take the argument all the way to Roosevelt and Churchill to gain control of the strategic bombers. He won the argument, because nearly everyone except the airmen understood that OVERLORD represented the most important strategic and political military operation that the Western Allies would mount during the course of World War II. Eisenhower was able to dispense with Spaatz's argument, because whatever contribution attacks on the petroleum industry would have (and they would be considerable), they would be longer-term and less immediately helpful than attacks on the French transportation network. With respect to Harris' arguments, there was a longer period of disagreement, because Churchill was desperately worried that the collateral damage of attacks on French marshaling yards, for example, would kill large numbers of civilians and permanently harm post-war Anglo-French relations. In fact, over the past several years Bomber Command had developed bombing capabilities that allowed its Lancasters and Halifaxes to hit targets more accurately than the American daylight formations could. This was particularly the case with targets in France, because blind-bombing navigational devices would be closer to their signaling stations in the United Kingdom and were thus more accurate. Equally important was the fact that each bomber would drop its load individually. Several raids soon indicated that Harris had completely underestimated the accuracy with which his crews could hit targets. Churchill then ruled that Eisenhower would control the bombers.

On April 1, 1944, Eisenhower received de facto command over all Allied air forces and the transportation plan began. Obviously, the attacks could not be limited to isolating the Normandy beaches. Instead, to keep the Allied landing objective secret, Allied air forces had to attack railroad marshaling yards, repair depots, bridges, trucks and other vehicular traffic, and transportation targets from Belgium across the length and breadth of northern and western France. Not surprisingly, because of the battering that it was taking in the skies over Europe, the Luftwaffe was able to offer no support to defend the transportation network. Eighth Air Force received the tasking to attack 23 of the major transportation targets in Belgium and France, while Allied tactical air forces attacked 18. Bomber Command carried the major load by attacking 39 of the targets on the Allied list.

In the latter half of May, Allied fighter bombers began the task of striking bridges throughout France with notable success, although at considerable cost, since Luftwaffe anti-aircraft batteries were particularly accurate in hitting aircraft attacking at low level. From May 21, Allied fighter bombers – over 800 Spitfires, Typhoons, and Thunderbolts – began a locomotive-busting campaign. Over the last week of May, Allied air attacks managed to destroy 500 locomotives. By late May, just before attacks on the Seine bridges, overall rail traffic was down to 55 percent of January's. Destruction of the bridges lowered the level to 30 percent. Attacks on the system in western France were particularly effective; by mid-June that portion of the French railroad system had entirely ceased to operate. The effect on the transportation of troops and supplies in western France was disastrous. In June, the Germans could run only 7 percent of what they had run in March. Even in the north along the Belgian frontier the drop was significant; the figure for June was only 27 percent of what the railroads had carried in March.

Nevertheless, the transportation campaign came at considerable cost. Between the beginning of April and June 5, 1944, the Allies were to lose over 2,000 aircraft and 12,000 aircrew, dead, wounded, or prisoner. Was it worth the cost? A German report of June 3 concluded:

"In Zone 1 [France and Belgium], the systematic destruction that has been carried out since March of all important junctions of the entire network – not only of the main lines – has most seriously crippled the whole transportation system (railway installations, including rolling stock). Similarly Paris has been systematically cut off from long-distance traffic, and the most important bridges over the lower Seine have been destroyed one after another. As a result … it is only by exerting the greatest efforts that purely military traffic and goods essential to the war effort … can be kept moving … The railway network is to be completely wrecked. Local and through traffic is to be made impossible, and all efforts to restore the service are to be prevented. The aim has so successfully been achieved – locally at any rate – that the *Reichsbahn* authorities are seriously considering whether it is not useless to attempt further repair work."

Perhaps the greatest testimony to the transportation campaign's success comes from the difficulties the Wehrmacht confronted in moving its formations across France to reinforce its desperately hard-pressed troops in Normandy. It took no less than five days for the 17th Panzer Grenadier Division to cover 200 miles; movement by railroad was out of the question. The SS Division *Das Reich* probably set the record for transportation frustration. Tracked elements of the division left Limoges on June 11, but failed to arrive in Normandy until the end of the month. The movement of divisions immediately adjacent to the beachhead was hardly easier. The Wehrmacht's Panzer Lehr Division had to move towards the Allied landings on five separate roads, and even then its commander described one of those routes as a "fighter bomber race course." On June 6 alone, it lost 80 half-tracks, self-propelled guns, and prime movers.

AIR POWER AND THE GERMAN DEFEAT IN NORMANDY
The contribution made by Allied air to Normandy's success hardly ended with the landings on June 6. Allied air power slaughtered the Luftwaffe's formations as they moved forward to reply to the landings. It continued the terrible pressure on the roads and railroads, so that reinforcements

An ME-109 plunges earthward, after being hit by gunfire from a US fighter. (Official US Air Force photo)

and supplies could move forward only with the greatest difficulty. The situation for the Germans was clearly hopeless, and reinforcing the battlefront, in the eyes at least of one German, represented "a race in which conditions inevitably favor the enemy." Allied air superiority was troublesome enough for the Germans, but when combined with ULTRA intelligence its results could prove devastating. British intercepts of high level German radio transmissions on June 9 indicated the exact location of the headquarters of Panzer Group West. An attack the next day destroyed the Panzer Group's communications gear entirely, and killed 17 staff officers, including the chief of staff. The headquarters never became operational. ULTRA intelligence also kept Allied commanders fully informed of the difficulties their aerial attacks were causing the Germans. One decrypt on June 14 indicated: "C-in-C West report morning ninth included: In large-scale operations by thousands of bombers and fighter bombers, Allied air forces stifled German tank attacks and had harassing effect on movements."

CONCLUSION

Before and during the early years of World War II, airmen and air power theorists had proclaimed that the airplane alone would be the decisive weapon of the war. They were wrong. But their extravagant claims should not mislead us into missing how critical air power proved as a contributor to the overall battle. Without the Combined Bomber Offensive, the Anglo-American air forces could not have won air superiority over the European continent. Without that superiority, OVERLORD would have taken place under a massive Luftwaffe aerial assault, which would have placed everything in jeopardy. Moreover, the Combined Bomber Offensive significantly retarded the growth of the German war economy in 1943, and even more so in 1944. Equally important was the distortion it caused in the production and distribution of German military resources. In the case of the former, the resources lavished on the V-2 ballistic missile – with an accuracy delineated by a target area the size of southern England – set the stage for the post-World War II missile era, but did the German war effort no good at all. In the latter case, the 15,000 high-velocity 88mm flak guns and half a million soldiers defending the Reich's cities would have made a significant difference in the fighting on either the Eastern or Western Fronts. Finally, the transportation plan of spring 1944 ensured that the Germans had lost the battle of the build-up in Normandy even before it began. Thus, we might say that while the contribution of air power was not by itself decisive in the winning of the war, it played a decisive role in the eventual victory of the Western Powers and OVERLORD's success.

Chapter 7

"The greatest military armada ever launched"

(Kenneth C Garrett, LSR2, ret'd)
"During the next few months, our ship faced extensive training to prepare us for the D-Day invasion, the greatest military armada ever launched against an enemy."

Operation *NEPTUNE*

Dr Andrew Gordon

No European belligerent in World War II began hostilities expecting to mount a major opposed, seaborne invasion, and it was only because the early course of the war went wrong for both sides that amphibious landings became so crucial to subsequent strategy. For the British, such an eventuality would be necessary only if they were ejected from the European mainland – a hypothesis which could not possibly be entertained in pre-war planning (allied, as they expected to be, to the French). For the Germans, such an alien prospect would rear its head only if the British were obtuse enough to refuse terms after being soundly defeated by Blitzkrieg in France and Belgium. Both these unlikely prospects, of course, came about.

ELEPHANT AGAINST WHALE

Napoleon characterised Continental powers as elephants, and Great Britain as a whale. The metaphor is applicable to Britain and Germany after the fall of France in 1940: the 'whale' having disengaged and escaped back to the sea, the 'elephant' could only stand on the shoreline and puzzle out what to do next. In global terms the four years after Dunkirk were among the most dramatic in history, but the basic strategic face-off in north-west Europe remained. Neither side was equipped by nature, doctrine or capability to do decisive harm to the other, and the trans-Channel stalemate would endure until one of them learned how to enter, and dominate, the other's habitat. For some considerable time, the Germans, with their U-boat campaign in the Atlantic, looked the more likely to achieve that goal, while the Anglo-Saxon 'whale' struggled in fits and starts to develop the amphibious skills of crawling up defended beaches to give battle ashore.

Under two Chiefs of Combined Operations, firstly Admiral of the Fleet Sir Roger Keyes, and latterly Acting Vice Admiral Lord Louis Mountbatten, myriad issues of method, doctrine, equipment and training were progressively tested in a series of increasingly ambitious – and sometimes costly – amphibious landings, from Commando raids such as Vaagso (December 1941), through St Nazaire (March 1942) and Madagascar (May 1942), to Dieppe (August 1942), before the first big, permanent lodgement was attempted. The Dieppe disaster demonstrated how much preparation remained to be done, and seemed to prove that a frontal assault on a heavily defended port would fail unless the place had first been pounded to rubble by air and sea bombardment – which would defeat the point of its capture. This presented a major stumbling-block to the would-be invaders. It also helped to reconcile the Americans to the idea that the first major 'stay-ashore' landing in the 'European' theatre should be in North-West

OPPOSITE MULBERRY B at Arromanches. (IWM BU695)

129

Dieppe, 1942. Three quarters of the 5,000 troops landed during this disastrous raid were lost. Important lessons were learned from this tragedy. (National Archives of Canada, C-14160)

Africa, against – as in Madagascar – the uncomfortably neutral Vichy French. Hence Operation TORCH.

These opposing campaigns by elephant and whale to master the other's environment were inter-linked, insofar as an Allied victory in the Battle of the Atlantic was preconditional to a full-scale cross-Channel invasion of the Continent. At the time, this issue of strategic sequencing was unappreciated by those (mainly Americans and Russians) who wanted the invasion mounted in 1943, and were impatient and suspicious at what they considered to be British prevarication. But Operation TORCH, in November 1942, as the Battle of the Atlantic reached its peak, was attended by major miscalculations as to the shipping-intensive (and shipping-retentive) nature of offensive operations. Although the invasion convoys themselves escaped serious attack, in terms of global maritime resources, TORCH was launched too soon. The diversion of shipping capacity from the trans-Atlantic trade depressed food stocks in Britain to their lowest wartime level, and Anglo-American 'shipping politics' to their most acrimonious.

In the late spring of 1943, when planning for OVERLORD was still at a tentative stage, and the Allies were progressing towards TORCH's logical follow-up – HUSKY (the occupation of Sicily) – Admiral Karl Dönitz's U-boats were at last defeated in a series of decisive convoy battles, and never recovered. Within a few months, as a result of HUSKY and the subsequent surrender of Italy, the Mediterranean through-route was re-opened, bringing the windfall-equivalent of a million tons of shipping-capacity. Meanwhile, American shipbuilders reached their full stride and Allied output now decisively outgrew declining war-losses. It remains impossible to see how the three million tons of shipping needed to support the invasion of France could have been presumed with realism by the planners for much earlier than 1944. In the long view, however, Hitler really lost his leasehold on Western Europe at sea in 1943 rather than ashore the following year, for once Dönitz's U-boats had been hounded out of the Atlantic, it was only a matter of time before the decisive industrial might of the Allies would be thrown ashore at a place of their choosing, exploiting the freedom of relatively safe, maritime, exterior lines.

As an aside, one can speculate as to what the Allies might have done if victory over the U-boat had not been achieved in good time for OVERLORD – if the U-boats had continued to appear undefeatable at sea (as with Hitler's V weapons in the air, in the summer of 1944). Perhaps a desperate assault would have been launched across a hostile sea, with the object of capturing the Biscay ports from which the U-boats sailed. Happily, as it was, by the spring of 1944 the Atlantic war was over, Brittany was strategically benign, and the Allies were free to wheel left out of Normandy, towards Paris and Germany.

BACKGROUND TO NEPTUNE

By the summer of 1942, the Americans, having agreed the previous December – in the face of the national fury towards Japan which naturally followed Pearl Harbor – that the defeat of Germany should take priority over the war in the Pacific, were urging a prompt lodgement on the Continent (SLEDGEHAMMER) to be followed in 1943 by a major push towards Germany (ROUNDUP). The British considered such an agenda to be premature with the resources then available, but were anxious to keep the Americans committed to the war in Europe. There was therefore established in July a planning staff under Admiral Sir Bertram Ramsay, who took the somewhat premature title of Naval Commander Expeditionary Force (NCXF), and set up shop in Norfolk House in St James's Square in central London. There, in consultation with the Chief of Combined Operations, Ramsay's staff laid the groundwork of analysis and doctrine on which the largest invasions of World War II were founded.

Before long, Ramsay was diverted to work on TORCH: the invasion of French territories in North-West Africa to which Churchill had, at

Admiral Sir Bertram Ramsay.
(IWM A9232)

length, managed to convert Roosevelt. TORCH was to be a predominantly American affair. The Vichy French had a substantial list of grievances against the British by this time in the war; and a relatively unknown US lieutenant general, Dwight D. Eisenhower, was named Allied C-in-C. Admiral of the Fleet Sir Andrew Cunningham, Britain's most celebrated wartime admiral, was in Washington at the time, and he accepted the post of naval commander, and thereafter worked hard to give Eisenhower (his junior by two ranks) the best possible maritime support – ably assisted by Ramsay, who took his notional demotion in good heart. It was a team that worked well, and remained largely in place for HUSKY, the following summer.

While Ramsay was away from Norfolk House, his work was progressed by Lieutenant General Frederick Morgan, who took the title of chief of staff to the supreme allied commander (COSSAC) – although for many months the post of supreme commander was to remain vacant. Morgan was one of the unsung 'fixers' behind the invasion of Normandy, and he proceeded with his planning on the presumption that his work would be accepted, more or less in its entirety, by the eventually appointed supremo.

Initially, he was told to prepare for a three-division landing, but he made the bold (and correct) assumption that the figure would be

increased to at least four, and planned accordingly. It was in his watch
that the stretch of coastline in Normandy between the rivers Vire and
Orne was identified as the optimum landing area (notwithstanding its
lack of a substantial port); and it was in his watch that the ideas behind
the MULBERRY harbours and the pipeline-under-the-ocean (PLUTO)
were first accepted.

THE AIM OF MULBERRY

As with most good ideas, the origins of MULBERRY are disputed.
Disregarding Churchill's claim to have thought of it first, the most
usually accepted story is that, at the end of a long COSSAC meeting
at which the difficulties of capturing a port on the 'far shore' were
discussed, Commodore John Hughes-Hallet (from the staff of Combined
Operations) simply stated that if we can't capture a port "we must take
one with us". The throw-away remark was taken seriously by, among
others, the commodore's boss, Mountbatten, who in turn persuaded
Churchill. If the problem was huge in scale, it was simple in nature: to
provide a sheltered deep-water anchorage within which large merchant
ships could speedily unload onto jetties which responded to the rise and
fall of the tide. The engineering solutions, by contrast, were complex
and ground-breaking. (Like the idea itself, the origins of the codename
'MULBERRY' are disputed. One theory is that Churchill was amused by
the way his Scottish housekeeper pronounced the name of his ancestor,
Marlborough.)

The eventual material commitment to MULBERRY, combined with
the mass-construction of landing craft and other engineering
commitments connected with NEPTUNE, pushed British industrial
capacity to its very limits. The basic components of the harbours (of
which there were to be two) were the 146 concrete caissons, known as
PHOENIXES, which were to be sunk along an outer perimeter to act as
breakwaters and ensure calm water inside. These items were up to
6,000 tons and 200 feet in length. Their construction – by some of the
big-name engineering firms which, 40 years later, started work on the
Channel Tunnel – required 330,000 cubic yards of concrete and 31,000
tons of steel. When every possible building slip accessible from the sea
was already occupied, huge trenches had to be dug out of riverside
meadows for some of these giant blocks. Many of the other modular
items – floating pontoons, roadways and pierheads – were novel and
complex. Some of them contained pumping equipment, generating
plants, crew accommodation and anti-aircraft guns. MULBERRY also
consumed the UK's entire stock of ground tackle, which is why the
PHOENIXES, having been delivered to sheltered anchorages, had to be

A PHOENIX under construction in London docks. (IWM H37606)

sunk, rather than moored, and subsequently raised before being towed across to France.

The importance of MULBERRY harbours goes far beyond the operational issue of how efficacious they were. Until their invention, it was axiomatic that invading armies would need to capture a major, functioning port soon after landing, to replenish those forces already ashore and to sustain the build-up. The Germans' own abortive plan for SEALION in 1940 had been built around this necessity, and it made the task of the would-be defenders relatively clear: deny the invader a major port (or, failing that, wreck it beyond short-term repair) and any successful landing will probably wither on the vine through lack of life-support.

In 1943–44, the Germans assumed that such a constraint would apply to the expected Allied landing in France, and so planned their defences accordingly. The invaders would need rapidly to grab a port with the capacity of, say, Cherbourg, Le Havre, Dieppe, Boulogne or Calais, and so the landings must take place in the near vicinity of at least one such place. The potential pairings of Le Havre and Dieppe, or Boulogne and Calais, were self-suggestive – the more so as they coincided with easy range from airfields in southern England. Meanwhile, having persuaded themselves (wisely or not) that their logistical needs could be met, for an extended time after the landings, by transportable harbours, the Allied planners freed themselves to think in a rather different geographical box from those German staff-officers whose job it was to second-guess their plans. MULBERRY was not conceived directly for the purpose of deception, but by nullifying received wisdom it permitted the Allies to avoid confronting those segments of the 'Atlantic Wall' to which the Germans would, quite rationally, give top priority. Its implicit purpose, indeed, was to enable an exercise in manoeuvrism of a scale unsurpassed since Hannibal.

THE ROLE OF ADMIRAL SIR BERTRAM RAMSAY

The COSSAC plan for what was now known as OVERLORD was approved in principle by the Allied leaders at Quebec in August 1943. In September, the Admiralty announced that naval activities within OVERLORD would be called Operation NEPTUNE. In October, Ramsay returned from the Mediterranean and resumed his work, now as Allied Naval C-in-C Expeditionary Force (ANCXF): the first of the three component commanders to be appointed to OVERLORD.

Admiral Sir Bertram Ramsay was best known to the public as the mastermind of the desperate but spectacularly successful evacuation of Dunkirk in the early summer of 1940. However, as we have seen, he had by now also gained an unrivalled track-record as the organiser of the opposite process: of joint and combined amphibious landings on the largest scale, having served as second-in-command to Cunningham in TORCH, and then as the British naval supremo in HUSKY. He had proved himself gifted at both extemporisation and organisation, as circumstances demanded, and no-one got on better with the Americans in general, and Eisenhower in particular, than he. His appointment as ANCXF brought him back to waters he knew well both from his time as C-in-C Dover in the early years of World War II, and, indeed, from his naval apprenticeship as a young CO in the previous war.

Ramsay's two World War I command-appointments had a future significance which would not become apparent for a quarter of a century. The first, in 1915, was to a small gun-boat monitor operating along the Belgian coast in support of the army. The second, in 1917, was to a destroyer in Sir Roger Keyes's famous Dover Patrol. The navigational log of HMS *Broke* shows how his time was spent: about equal measures in Dover and Dunkirk, sometimes anchored outside if the harbours were full, punctuated with occasional brisk pursuit actions with enemy torpedo-boats. So habitual was this routine that the log sometimes fails to make clear which port the ship was at, and only by unravelling the scant navigational references can one hope to work it out. So young Ramsay gained intimate, first-hand knowledge of how to work small ships in the shallow, hazardous, rip-tidal, 'littoral' waters, which would bring him fame in the next war.

In interpersonal terms, at least where his seniors were concerned, Ramsay never quite curbed a headstrong directness of manner. As a lieutenant in 1914 his diary reflects a bursting frustration at the errors of admirals; as a commander in 1919 his annual report alluded to a regrettable want of tact. His wilfulness actually terminated his career (or so it seemed at the time) in late 1935, when, as a rear admiral and chief of staff to Sir Roger Backhouse (C-in-C Home Fleet), he felt driven to distraction – and to resignation – by his boss's refusal to delegate. It was most unfortunate, not least of all because Sir Roger was an old friend, and many in the Service thought Ramsay had been high-handed. Compulsory retirement followed in 1938, and he had to watch from the sidelines as European affairs slid towards war, unaware that Backhouse, in his brief stint as First Sea Lord (before dying from over-work), had arranged for him to be given the Dover command in the event of hostilities.

The wisdom of that appointment was amply demonstrated over a ten-day period in May–June 1940, when the defeated British Expeditionary Force (BEF) lay trapped against the coast at Dunkirk and along the ten miles of beaches to the north-east of the town, with no obvious prospect except surrender. The rescue of a third of a million men needs no elaboration here. It brought Bertram Ramsay, as Vice Admiral Dover, a well-earned knighthood, although technically he remained on the retired list.

The only wartime failure with which Ramsay can be associated was the transit through the Straits of Dover of *Scharnhorst* and *Gneisenau* in February 1942. The two battlecruisers were abandoning the doctrine of Atlantic operations, and making a dash from the Biscay coast of France to German home waters, but their success was an affront to the Royal Navy and the Royal Air Force. The enemy ships were Ramsay's responsibility only while in his local command area; he had at his disposal only a few old destroyers and Swordfish torpedo-bombers, and he lost most of them. A less iconic 'Vice Admiral Dover' might have been made a scapegoat for the embarrassment, but Ramsay easily rode out the storm, and a few months later he was in Norfolk House,

beginning the planning processes which would lead, via circuitous diversions mentioned above, to Normandy.

Evacuation of Dunkirk, 26 May– 4 June 1940. 338,000 Allied troops were evacuated. (Ann Ronan Picture Library)

The command-team which eventually came together to invade France had such a shared track-record of successes that it is hard now to understand how there could have been so much apparent dithering over selecting the supremo. The Deputy Supreme Commander, Air Chief Marshal Sir Arthur Tedder, had been a great proponent of inter-service 'jointery' in the desert, and had served as British air component commander in HUSKY – where Montgomery and Ramsay had played the equivalent roles for the Army and Navy. The only 'newcomer' was OVERLORD's air component commander, Air Chief Marshal Sir Trafford Leigh-Mallory, who had made his name in the Battle of Britain. Eisenhower, and his chief of staff General Bedell Smith, had worked and won with these officers from as far back as TORCH – indeed, they belonged to a very select, and mostly British, web of professional collegiality which a lesser American than Eisenhower might have found daunting, and of which few others could claim membership. Ramsay was at its centre.

For a start, Churchill readily came to trust the Admiral's counsel and company in the months after Dunkirk, not just because he had saved his prime-ministership from catastrophe before it was a month old, and provided the miracle-myth on which to build Britain's 'finest hour' defiance, but because his father, Colonel William Ramsay, had commanded Winston's first regiment, the 4th Hussars, and the Prime Minister could remember Bertram as a boy in Aldershot in the mid-1890s.

Additionally, Admiral of the Fleet Sir Andrew Cunningham, with whom Ramsay had worked closely and harmoniously during TORCH in the tunnels of Gibraltar, was now First Sea Lord and was effectively fire-proof even from Churchill (who had offered the First Sea Lordship to someone else for that very reason).

Then there was the Army high command, in the forms of Field Marshal Lord Alanbrooke and General Sir Bernard Montgomery. These

Admiral of the Fleet, Sir Andrew Browne Cunningham. (IWM MH 31338)

two went back a long way, the latter having been in the former's syndicate at Staff College in 1921. Both men were in the BEF in 1939–40, Brooke (as he then was) a three-star corps commander, Monty, a two-star divisional commander. Braced for captivity, they watched their khaki masses being spirited away from the Dunkirk beaches by Ramsay's armada of little ships before wading into the surf themselves; and got back to Blighty holding their saviour's abilities in understandably high esteem. In the ensuing months, while awaiting German invasion, both (promoted) soldiers would lunch or dine with Sir Bertram at Dover Castle, and Monty would invite him to lecture to his staff in 5 (and later, 12) Corps on the naval dimensions of combined operations.

Ramsay never relinquished the high ground he had gained in relation to the vain and often bombastic Montgomery. Two and a half years later, while he was doing the groundwork-planning for HUSKY, and Montgomery was busy with Rommel in Tunisia, Ramsay found it necessary to send the hero of El Alamein a letter which, while friendly in tone, clearly warned him to stop claiming presidential rights over plans for which he was not responsible. Monty professed to be delighted, wrote back to say he was having the letter framed, and Ramsay must come and stay. Later, the general lamented Ramsay's departure from the Mediterranean theatre, and acknowledged that "you understand us soldiers and you know more about the land battle than any other sailor". The quiet but self-assured admiral was able to ensure that NEPTUNE's three component commanders (in today's jargon) would comprise a triumvirate of equals, and not merely a Montgomery fiefdom.

Alanbrooke, meanwhile, had long been Chief of Imperial General Staff (the head of the British Army) and Churchill's closest military adviser. Having swallowed his disappointment at not getting the top job himself, he took a benign overview of preparations for OVERLORD and kept in personal contact with Ramsay.

With some of Ramsay's immediate naval collaborators and subordinates, too, the wartime bonds were strong. His 'Senior Naval Officer Afloat' at Dunkirk, Rear Admiral Frederick Wake-Walker, was now Third Sea Lord and Controller of the Navy – the Admiralty high official responsible for the production and delivery of the hundreds of landing craft which the NEPTUNE plan required. Likewise, his 'Senior Naval Officer Ashore' at Dunkirk, Captain William Tennant, was now 'Rear Admiral MULBERRY and PLUTO' (RAMP) – the officer responsible for giving effect to those remarkable solutions to the Army's future logistical demands ashore.

The Americans, it should be noted, had their own rarefied network in England: Admiral Harold Stark, their senior naval officer in the

European theatre – "a shrewd old man" in Ramsay's opinion – had served in the Grand Fleet with King George V (Prince Albert, at the time) in 1918, and successfully used this link to bring to Churchill's attention concerns to which the British military authorities appeared impervious.

PLANNING, LOADING UP AND MOVING OUT
Eisenhower was not appointed supreme commander until January 1944, when most of the planning had been done. One of his first actions was to support Morgan and Montgomery in demanding that the scale of the initial landings be enhanced from three to five divisions. This very necessary step had important ramifications for the maritime resources needed in support. Extra landing-craft of all types, bombardment vessels, escorts, minesweepers and so on would have to be found, and even with the postponement of an intended landing in the South of France, and delays to the build-up of British naval forces in the Far East, it was apparent that the Royal Navy could not do it all. The American Chief of Naval Operations, Admiral Ernest King, was petitioned for support, and after the expected churlishness, responded generously. (King had, rightly or wrongly, gained a reputation for being both anti-British and hostile to Roosevelt's commitment to putting the war in Europe first.)

Only in the early spring of 1944 could the final size and shape of NEPTUNE be settled. Landings would take place in divisional strength on five separate beaches: two – UTAH and OMAHA – in the Western Area, which stretched from the base of the Cotentin Peninsula to the tiny harbour of Port en Bessin, and three – GOLD, JUNO and SWORD – in the Eastern Area which stretched on to Ouistreham at the mouth of the Orne. To each beach was allocated a flag-officer, who would monitor the progress of events and intervene where necessary, answerable to one or other of two task force commanders. The two major task forces (TFs), Western (mainly American) and Eastern (mainly British), comprised naval units from eight nations, with each TF commanded by a rear admiral (afloat) directly answerable to Ramsay. The Western TF fell under Rear Admiral Alan Kirk USN, and the Eastern under Rear Admiral Philip Vian RN. Ramsay came to have misgivings about both these officers, and what he saw as their diffidence at shouldering responsibility – which perhaps says as much about Ramsay's driven, exacting standards, as about the rear admirals. Vian was a tough destroyer-flotilla commander by habit, and had acted with force and decision in the 'Altmark affair' in 1940, the *Bismarck* pursuit in 1941, and at the Second Battle of Sirte in 1942. He was taciturn to the point of disagreeability, and unaccustomed to close supervision, and one might question whether his known talents necessarily matched the patient, complex, low-speed team-work of a task force commander in such crowded, regulated waters as those off Normandy in June 1944.

Three months before D-Day, Ramsay (who had, to his delight, been restored to the Active List of the Royal Navy) moved his staff down to HMS *Dryad*, in Southwick House, in the hinterland of Portsmouth, and there combed over the plans, adding here, tweaking there. The full scale of Operation NEPTUNE, of the painstaking training, the coordination and the administration, were all stupendous. The total number of landing craft, barges, trawlers and ancillary vessels in the assault areas, each one with its specialised tasks and operational orders, was slightly over 4,000. Of them, the landing craft themselves numbered 2,468 (of which 346 were American), and fell into 46 distinct categories, from the Landing Craft Tank (Rocket) to the Landing Craft (Emergency Repair) or the Landing Craft Personnel (Large) Smokelayer. Other miscellaneous minor craft moving about the assault areas numbered 1,656. Each vessel had to be loaded at the designated point of departure (the Americans, west of Portland Bill, the British, east), with the correct men and equipment, in the correct 'tactical' order, and then take up its designated position in the right shipping stream at exactly the right time. Turnaround times for landing craft and merchant ships were calculated and simplified. Command ships, canteen barges and hospital ships were all provided for.

Backing them up, clearing mines, patrolling perimeters and providing gunfire support were 1,213 warships of all types, including a few units held in reserve. The majority of them were British; some 17 per cent were US; others were Canadian, or from the free forces of Holland, Poland, Norway, France and Greece. Among them were six battleships (three US); two monitors; 23 cruisers (three US, two French, one Polish); 81 destroyers (30 US, two Polish, one French, one Norwegian); 247 minesweepers and danlayers (25 US).

The big-gunned ships had fixed bombardment positions, with allocated targets ashore. The battleships were matched against the heaviest-known German gun-batteries. (The cruiser HMS *Black Prince*, in the Western Task Group, was allocated targets above the beach at Morsalines on the Cotentin Peninsula, where the Black Prince was knighted by Edward III in 1346.) The destroyers were allowed to range close inshore – in pre-swept channels – in opportunistic support of the troops.

To get the whole show going, Beach Reconnaissance Parties were covertly put ashore on dark nights to ascertain the nature and gradients of the sand, and Combined Operations Pilotage Parties were sent to survey the beach approaches, under the noses of the Germans. The

Warship lending shelling support,
HMS *Ramillies* bombards a coastal
position. (IWM A 23918XC)

flotillas of minesweepers would have to adhere minutely to the schedule laid out for them – and would be in sight of the French coast before dark on D-1 (in the event, the Germans, having withdrawn their patrols because of bad weather, either failed to spot them or failed to identify them).

An enormous responsibility for accurate navigation rested on the shoulders of very junior officers (almost entirely reservists), and extreme measures were taken to try to ensure accurate landfalls. Off SWORD, where the coastline was low-lying and featureless (especially if the church spires were knocked down), two midget submarines, X20 and X23, were carefully pre-positioned to come to the surface and act as beacons for the first wave of landing craft. At OMAHA, the steep headlands promised good radar echoes, and artists' impressions were drawn of what the 'paint' on the screen should look like if the ship was in the right position. Still, some of the problems at that bitterly fought beach began with an under-estimation of the easterly current, and a failure by inexperienced personnel to allow sufficient offset. Naval beach-masters had to be rigorously practised, their authority enforced by military police who would ensure compliance and channel traffic off the beaches.

The master 'OpOrd' (operation order) for NEPTUNE was several telephone-books thick, and each vessel had to be issued with the correct few pages, incorporating the appropriate last-minute amendments. Ramsay presided over the whole massive, sprawling operation, pulled it together and made it work, with very little margin for error.

THE DECISION TO GO

It was at Ramsay's HQ at Southwick House that Eisenhower and the other senior commanders came together in the final countdown. And it was in the library, in the early hours of 4 June, that the crucial decision was made, on the advice of the meteorological experts, to postpone for 24 hours – which involved turning around hundreds of ships, and thousands of seasick soldiers, already at sea. It was there also, in the small hours of 5 June, that a brief break in the bad weather was forecast, and the decision had to be made either to postpone the whole enterprise for at least a fortnight, or to go ahead and take a chance. Montgomery was all for cracking on. Leigh-Mallory wanted to postpone, fearing that low cloud would compromise the accuracy of the air forces' bombing. Ramsay merely said that the Navy would do whatever was asked of it. The buck stopped with Eisenhower. After a few seconds' silence he decided to go.

The harsh test of battle brought to light some locally expensive failures of intelligence, errors of coordination and omissions in training; but in such a vast and complex enterprise, in which so many disparate organisations and military cultures were interwoven, it would have been miraculous had there been none of these. In war, the perfect is the enemy of the good. By the end of 6 June 1944, some 125,000 US, British and Canadian troops had been put ashore, and total casualties had been lighter than feared. After a week, 430,000 men, 62,000 vehicles and 105,000 tons of stores had been landed. After a month – in spite of a storm which partially demolished the American MULBERRY – those figures had grown to a million, 200,000 and 700,000 respectively. The British MULBERRY at Arromanches remained operating at full capacity until well after France had been liberated. Its remains may still be seen. Bertram Ramsay had provided Dwight D. Eisenhower with a 'bridge to France'.

Chapter 8

"A visitor to hell"

(Pvt. Charles Neighbor, 29th Division)

"As our boat touched sand and the ramp went down I became a visitor to hell."

On the beaches

Professor Williamson Murray

In the early morning hours of June 6, the military forces of the Western Powers came ashore on the coast of France. There were five main amphibious landings. On the far west would be the American landing at a place codenamed UTAH Beach at the base of the Cotentin Peninsula. Ten miles to the east, US forces would land to the west of the Norman capital of Bayeux at OMAHA Beach. To the east of Bayeux, lay GOLD, JUNO, and SWORD beaches, which the British and Canadians would assault. The span of these landings covered nearly 55 miles – a distance that reflected the Allied need to seize a beachhead sufficiently wide to funnel in the necessary forces and supplies to win the build-up phase, defeat German reinforcements as they arrived, and eventually break out into central France.

Whilst each of the amphibious assaults had a specific task, it was their combined success which was crucial. This chapter will examine the planning, conception, the course of events, and the degree of success that the Allies achieved against the dogged, effective German defenders. On the success of these landings would rest the ability of the Western Powers to project military strength onto Europe's northwestern plains, effect the defeat of Nazi Germany, and lay the seeds for eventual victory in the Cold War – the latter in the then far distant future of the late twentieth century.

AMPHIBIOUS OPERATIONS

Of all military operations, the most difficult and complex is that of projecting combat power from the sea, across the beaches, to the land beyond. This aspect of warfare, termed amphibious warfare, was the centerpiece of Britain's success in conquering a great world-wide empire in the eighteenth and nineteenth centuries. In the twentieth century, however, the problems confronting the conduct of amphibious warfare had grown more difficult. Advances in technology provided the defender with weapons that allowed small numbers of soldiers to wreak havoc on troops struggling ashore through the surf. Even more important was the fact that modern communications and transportation allowed defenders to reinforce threatened sectors faster than the amphibious forces could bring their troops ashore. Thus, those planning amphibious operations had to consider not only the effectiveness of the enemy's beach defenses and obstacles, but the likely weather conditions and sea state when a landing would take place. So complex were such operations that a sine qua non was air superiority, the lack of which caused Hitler to postpone and then cancel Operation SEALION – the proposed German amphibious assault on the British Isles – in September 1940.

Amphibious forces confronted a number of intractable problems. First, they had to suppress enemy forces defending the beaches – in some cases

OPPOSITE This photo was taken from a US P-38 Lightning reconnaissance plane a month before D-Day, and shows German soldiers laying beach obstacles. (IWM EA 64465)

147

THE BEACHES OF NORMANDY

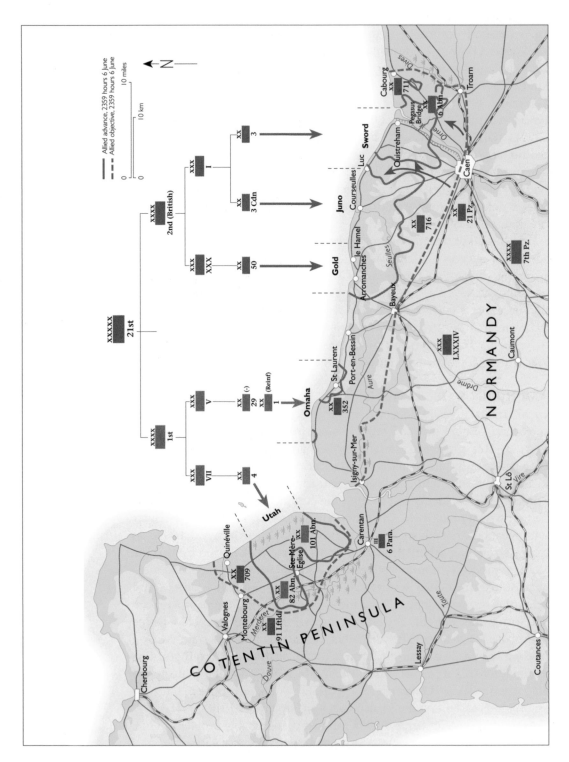

in fortified positions. Then, the landing force had to seize a beachhead sufficiently deep and broad to allow follow-on forces to defeat enemy reinforcements, arriving by train or automotive transport. And finally, it had to funnel supplies, ammunition, and troops across beaches in sufficient numbers and strength to sustain the battle. Exacerbating these difficulties was the fact that troops and supplies had to be trans-shipped to some type of landing craft, which then required unloading, often under enemy fire, on the beaches, all of this occurring under the conditions of uncertainty and ambiguity that have characterized war throughout history.

The British and Anzac landings on the Gallipoli Peninsula in April 1915, and the subsequent landings at Suvla Bay later that August underlined the difficulties involved in modern amphibious operations. On some landing sites, British troops were slaughtered before they could even reach solid ground. On others, troops achieved surprise, but the task of getting ashore, or the lassitude induced by surviving what had appeared to be a deadly mission, led troops as well as commanders to miss opportunities that beckoned. Invariably, as the British hesitated, often for understandable reasons, the Turks reacted with vigor to hold the assault to narrow and operationally ineffective beachheads. The failure at Gallipoli sealed the fate of the one strategic alternative to the Western Front. There would be no further major attempts at amphibious warfare in World War I by Allied forces.

In the ensuing post-war period, European militaries concluded from Gallipoli's failure that amphibious operations were no longer possible. Only the United States Marines, with help from their naval comrades, believed that amphibious operations might still be achievable. However, the collapse of France in May 1940 forced the British to change their attitudes towards an amphibious assault. Other alternatives were considered. There were, of course, strategic bombing advocates in the RAF, who believed that bombing alone, if sufficiently massive, could bring about the collapse of German morale and accomplish the defeat of the Nazi regime. While he was a strong supporter of Bomber Command's efforts, Churchill never subscribed to such a view. He was, however, an enthusiastic believer in special operations, and his brief to the new heads of the Special Operations Executive was to "set Europe ablaze." Nevertheless, whatever the success of British special operations in stirring up trouble, it was clear by 1942 that the defeat of Germany was going to require a landing on the Continent.

THE PLANNING FOR THE NORMANDY LANDINGS
The entrance of the United States into the war in December 1941

reinforced the position of those who argued for a great amphibious assault on the Continent. The American attitude was that the Reich's defeat would require a landing on the shores of northwest Europe – and the sooner the better. In 1942 and 1943, the British deflected American efforts into the Mediterranean. There, by May 1943, Anglo-American forces had cleared North Africa of the Germans, by July they had conquered Sicily – a victory which led to Mussolini's fall – and by September they had invaded Italy itself. By then the massive productive power of the United States and its swelling military forces gave it predominance in the making of Anglo-American strategy. There *would be* an invasion of northwest Europe in spring 1944.

To accomplish that task, the combined chiefs of staff brought the first team back from the Mediterranean to command the upcoming invasion. Planning was already underway in the United Kingdom by a staff called COSSAC under the leadership of a British general, Lieutenant General Sir Frederick Morgan. The initial plans reflected the fact that Morgan was never in a position to demand a certain-sized force. Rather, he was given certain resources for planning purposes, and ordered to plan the invasion on that basis. The target area Morgan's team chose was Normandy, and their reasons for selecting that location proved persuasive to OVERLORD's eventual commanders. But the original planners foresaw only a three-division amphibious assault, running from Vierville-sur-Mer in the west to Lion-sur-Mer in the east, with a one-division airborne drop. As the foremost historian of the Normandy campaign has noted: "In retrospect, the ... outline plan seems terribly flawed. The three-divisional invasion was far too small, spread too thinly, and much too vulnerable to defeat by counterattack before adequate units, ammunition, and equipment could be brought ashore."[1]

Shortly before Montgomery returned to Great Britain in early January 1944, he had an opportunity to discuss the plan, its conception, and the initial strength of the landing force with Dwight Eisenhower, soon to assume the mantle of supreme allied commander, and Eisenhower's chief of staff, the always acerbic Walter Bedell Smith. All three were in agreement that a three-division landing was completely inadequate to achieve a lodgement that could sustain the battle that would ensue. Both Eisenhower and Montgomery had the political clout, gained from the prestige of their victories in the Mediterranean, to make their demands for a larger landing stick heard.

By May 1944, the plans for the landing had increased the amphibious force to five divisions, supported by three armored brigades (the equivalent to over a full division). In addition, instead of one airborne division, the Allies would launch three in support of the landings. Such increases required major changes in the force structure as well as massive changes in the logistical planning and the requirements for landing craft – relatively small vessels such as Landing Craft Vehicle and Personnel (LCVPs or Higgins Boats) and Landing Craft Mediums (LCMs) were carried on assault transports on davits. A landing across beaches would require far larger beaching ships such as Landing Ship Tanks (LSTs), Landing Ship Infantry (LSIs), and Landing Craft Utility (LCUs), which could carry heavier loads and survive in the strong swells of the ocean. The variety of amphibious shipping proved a particularly contentious issue, because there was a seemingly insatiable appetite for such craft in the Pacific, where the Americans were mounting two massive amphibious drives in their war against Imperial Japan.

Despite opposition from Admiral Ernest King, the US Navy's chief of naval operations, the Allies found sufficient landing craft to support the increase in the invading force's size. Five divisions would now land on five separate beaches, stretching from the Orne River to the base of the Cotentin Peninsula. By landing on the southeastern corner of the peninsula, the Allies gained a direct shot at seizing the major port of Cherbourg early in the battle, to ease the logistical strain of supplying their forces over the Normandy beaches. The US 4th Infantry Division would land here on what was codenamed UTAH Beach. Inland were the drop zones of the 82nd and 101st Airborne Divisions – their mission, to ensure that the Germans could not interfere with the establishment of a beachhead on the Cotentin Peninsula. A second American landing to the west of Arromanches near Vierville-sur-Mer, codenamed OMAHA, aimed at securing the connection between US forces in the west and British landings to the east. In overall command of the OMAHA landing was the 1st Infantry Division, but half of the landing force came from the 29th Infantry Division.

The British beaches were closer together, but the thinking was that the British forces would face more sustained German counterattacks. On the right, the British 50th Division, supported by the 8th Armored Brigade, was to land between Arromanches and La Rivière on GOLD Beach. Immediately to its left was the Canadian 3rd Division, supported by the Canadian 2nd Armored Brigade, on JUNO Beach, while on the far left the British 3rd Infantry Division, supported by the 27th Armored Brigade, would land on SWORD. The task of this last division was the most difficult of any of the landing forces. First, it was to secure the bridges over the Orne and Dire rivers to support the seizure of the high ground east of the Orne by the British 6th Airborne Division. Once that high ground was secure, the Germans could not counterattack the Allied lodgement from that direction because of the Seine River's swamps. But

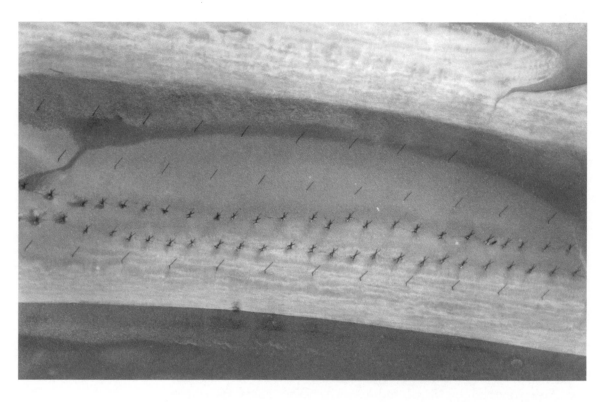

Taken by a Ninth Air Force reconnaissance unit, this photograph shows some of the beach defenses set up by the Germans on the coast of Normandy. (NARA)

the troops landing on SWORD also had the mission of seizing the crucial transportation and road junctions that lay in the city of Caen. With Caen in Allied hands, Montgomery, the overall ground forces commander, could then fight a mobile battle on the flatter, more open fields lying to the south and east of the *bocage* country.

Overall, the Allied plan aimed at achieving a massive lodgement, into which they could pour forces and supplies sufficiently fast to win the battle of the build-up. Here they were depending on the success of the air campaign that had begun in early April to disrupt German transportation in northwest France, rail as well as road. But the success of the landings would depend on a number of factors beyond the control of Allied planners. The first, and most difficult to predict, at least until the immediate hours before the invasion, was the weather. Intelligence on how the Germans were preparing to meet the invasion was easier to come by, but a number of items remained ambiguous and uncertain. On one hand it was obvious that the Wehrmacht, under Field Marshal Erwin Rommel's driving leadership, was making every effort to build obstacles on the beaches, construct field fortifications immediately behind the beaches, and lay minefields in areas where the Allies might attack. On the other hand, Rommel's superior, Field Marshal Gerd von Rundstedt argued that German reserves be held back from the beaches with the intent of fighting a mobile battle across northern France. In retrospect, Rommel's approach was entirely correct, because the overwhelming superiority of Allied air forces made a mobile defense virtually impossible. Some German dispositions remained opaque right up to the actual invasion. Intelligence officers were unsure as to the general nature of Rommel's reserves; in some cases they overestimated German ability to respond. The 21st Panzer Division, for example, was spread out in a number of different locations, which made it difficult for the Germans to launch a powerful combined-arms counterattack, but it also made it difficult for Allied intelligence to work out German movements. Luckily for the Allies, Rommel was overruled by his superiors in his desire to bring the 12th SS Panzer Division up to Isigny, close to what would eventually prove to be the UTAH and OMAHA beaches. Along the OMAHA Beach sector, the 352nd Infantry Division received the responsibility for the defense of that area. Rommel urged the division commander, Lieutenant General Dietrick Kraiss, to move his regiments up close to the coast, but for reasons that remain unclear, Kraiss refused. In the aftermath of the near disaster at OMAHA, army historians were to claim that the "unexpected" positioning of the 352nd had caused the difficulties at OMAHA. In fact, the Germans had only two regiments up on the beaches. Had the whole division been up on the coast, the landings at OMAHA would undoubtedly have failed.

In making their landing the Allies would confront intractable problems. The first was the fact that, since early winter, the German engineers had embarked on a massive construction program to build

One of Hobart's "funnies" – the Sherman Crab, lies knocked out on GOLD Beach. The metal chains on the revolving drum at the front of the tank were designed to smash into the ground in front of the tank, exploding any mines before the tank hit them, and clearing a path for following vehicles.

obstacles between the low and high tide marks. Large girders, welded together, many of them armed with mines (known as "hedgehogs"), rested in the tidal areas off the beaches. They threatened to blow up or rip the bottom out of any landing craft attempting to land at high tide. To land at low tide, however, would expose Allied troops to a longer killing zone, in the case of OMAHA nearly 300 yards. Behind the beaches the Germans had constructed bunkers and fortified strong points to cover the beaches with machine-gun fire. On British beaches, many of these positions were built into the houses along the seawall. Along OMAHA, they were sited in the draws that led up the long, laborious climb to the cliffs overlooking the beaches below. Behind the beach defenses a number of artillery positions and naval batteries in massive turrets would support the defenders.

The British had been looking at the coast of occupied France for nearly four years. They had selected one of their most imaginative generals from the inter-war period, Major General Percy Hobart, to develop a series of armored vehicles to help troops cross the killing zones. Hobart's "funnies" – which included flame-throwing tanks, flail tanks to clear minefields, and bridging equipment – were to make a major contribution to the success of the British landings. Omar Bradley, the senior American ground commander, was not interested in such contraptions. American troops would cross the killing zone without the help of specially designed tanks.

The knottier problem was how to destroy German defenders lying behind the beaches. The deep artillery positions could be taken out by air or naval bombardment. Heavier German batteries closer to the coast could be taken out by direct assault, as with the batteries at Pointe-du-Hoc. Air and naval bombardment would also prove essential to taking out German bunkers and fortified positions that threatened Allied forces as they disembarked. Here arose a considerable difference between the Americans and British. The latter delayed their landings for almost an hour and a half after the American landing, to provide additional time to bombard the German beach defenses. However, Omar Bradley and his planners, counting on a massive attack by Army Air Force aircraft, laid on only a 20-minute naval bombardment. Unfortunately for the troops landing on OMAHA, the cloud ceilings on June 6 were too low, and the bombers entirely missed the German defensive positions.

By this point in the war, naval gunfire support in the Pacific for marine and army amphibious operations had reached epic proportions. The landing of the 4th Marine Division and the army's 7th Division at Kwajalein in March 1944 had received the support of no fewer than seven battleships – the two US divisions at Normandy would be supported by

Aerial photograph of UTAH Beach. (Courtesy of the Wilfrid Laurier Centre for Military Strategic and Disarmament Studies, Wilfrid Laurier University, Canada)

only three of the oldest battleships in the US inventory. George Marshall was so impressed by the Kwajalein operation that he ordered the 7th Division's Commander, Major General Pete Corlett, to England, to pass along his experiences in the Pacific to American commanders in Europe. The attitude of Bradley and other senior commanders was anything but open minded – best characterized by a belief that "anything that happened in the Pacific was strictly bush-league stuff."[2] The fact that a Brooklyn-class cruiser could fire 1,500 five-inch shells in ten minutes underlines the kind of support that the navy could have provided the OMAHA landing. When directed by spotter aircraft, or line-of-sight, naval gunfire was deadly, as the Germans discovered at Sicily, Salerno, and Anzio. Yet Bradley, with his deep prejudices against the US Navy, had no interest. In the end, the air attacks entirely missed their targets and killed more Norman cows and chickens than Germans; the naval bombardment was so short that it hardly had time to damage the German defenses. Nevertheless, when it became clear that the landings at OMAHA were in trouble, a number of the destroyer skippers would take their vessels so close to the beaches that they nearly grounded, in order to support the hard-pressed troops. That support would prove enormously useful in helping soldiers suppress the German defenses in the draws that led inland.

UTAH BEACH

The American landing at UTAH Beach was the easiest of the landings undertaken by Allied forces on June 6. The airborne drops of the 82nd and 101st Airborne Divisions behind the 4th Division's beaches contributed considerably to the lack of German resistance. Moreover, the airborne units were able to destroy a substantial portion of the German artillery. In one case, one of the finest soldiers in the US Army, Lieutenant Richard Winters, almost single-handedly took out a German battery.

This aerial view of OMAHA, taken in 1945, shows how the German strongpoints, built into the rock and especially up the draws, could cover the beach with enfilading fire. (Military History Institute)

Uncertain as to what was happening and bedeviled by reports of American paratroopers landing across the Cotentin Peninsula, the Germans never managed to launch a coherent counterattack on either the landing or the paratroopers beating up the rear areas.

Despite a strong tidal current that swept the amphibious forces 2,000 yards farther south than plans had called for, the landing at UTAH ran into minimal opposition. The 4th Division was a well-led, well-trained outfit ready to go about its business of killing Germans. Its commander, Major General "Tubby" Bartan was one of the most respected infantry division commanders in the US Army. He was ably assisted by superior subordinates. The assistant division commander, Brigadier Theodore Roosevelt, Jr, the son of the president, would receive the Medal of Honor for his actions on that day. He would die of a heart attack later in the campaign on the night before he was scheduled to take over command of a division. He lies next to his brother, Quentin – killed in a flying accident in 1918 while flying for the US Army – in the great American cemetery overlooking OMAHA Beach.

From the first, things went right for the Americans at UTAH. Twenty-eight of the 32 amphibious tanks made it to the shore, where they helped the landing infantry destroy German defensive positions. The greatest problem the 4th Division's infantry confronted was the difficulty of moving through the dunes and the flooded fields lying behind the beach to link up with the paratroopers inland. By late morning, some of the link-ups had been made, and the Americans were expanding their lodgement against light German resistance. The fact that the 4th Infantry Division suffered only 197 casualties out of the 23,000 men landed on June 6 underlines UTAH's success.

OMAHA BEACH

If the landing at UTAH was relatively easy, that at OMAHA was a near disaster. The official histories – followed by most historians who have written about the campaign – argued that the difficulties encountered at OMAHA were largely the result of the fact that the 352nd Panzer Division had recently moved into the area, replacing the 716th – a move not picked up by Allied intelligence. In fact, the 352nd had not moved into the area; rather it had been given control of the area. Despite Rommel's advice to move the 352nd up to the coast, the division commander had kept the bulk of his division well back from the beaches. Thus, when the landings occurred, there was only one battalion from the 352nd Division and one from the 716th defending OMAHA out of the ten battalions available. Those two battalions were more than enough to give the US Army one of the worst days in its history – but things would have been much worse had the division commander followed his orders.

There are some military operations dogged by bad luck. OMAHA was one of them. The air bombardment entirely missed the German beach defenses. The naval bombardment of 20 minutes hardly damaged German defenses. The naval officer in charge of releasing the amphibious tanks lost his nerve and sent them into the deep swells of the Channel well before he reached the release point. Out of 34 amphibious tanks released, 29 would founder and sink, taking most of their crews with them. And then the attacking Americans confronted the terrible reality of OMAHA Beach's terrain. Landing at low tide, they confronted a distance of nearly 300 yards across the tidal zone, then 100 yards of beach, then the dunes, and beyond them swamps, barbed-wire, and tangled undergrowth, before a survivor could begin working up the draws or cliffs that led to the high ground.

View of OMAHA from inside a landing craft. The troops on the craft ahead have already disembarked and are wading towards shore. (NARA)

The result was a slaughter. Many in the first wave were hit and died in a rising tide. As the tide began to flood in, reinforcing landing craft ran into the beach obstacles planted under Rommel's direction. A few dodged their way through the obstacles to the dunes, where German machine-gun and rifle fire pinned them down. Those huddling in the dunes, many badly wounded, were not even in the position to return fire. Only the fact that some destroyer commanders moved their ships almost to grounding depth and brought the fire of their 5″ guns to bear on the German defensive positions provided some relief. Casualty rates were so bad that the official histories do not give the total losses for OMAHA on the first day. Reconstructed from the records of the 1st Infantry Division, the 29th Infantry Division, the supporting engineer units, the two tank battalions, the two artillery battalions and the rangers, US forces lost over 2,500 soldiers killed on OMAHA before the sun had set – one of the most costly operations US military forces have ever mounted.

Conditions over the course of the morning were so bad that Bradley considered sending the reinforcing waves over to UTAH, instead of adding them to the slaughter. Luckily, General Kraiss, commander of the 352nd division, believed reports coming from his forward battalions that things were going well and failed to reinforce the defenders. Instead, he took the reserve battalions and moved off towards the eastern beaches, where the British had broken through. By midday, German defenses began to break down. Naval gunfire significantly attrited the defenders. The American survivors began to recover their nerves after their shattering experiences in crossing the killing zone, and began working their way up the cliffs and clearing the draws. Good leadership from the general officer level down to sergeants pushed the survivors forward. Brigadier General Norman Cota's heroism would win him a Distinguished Service Cross for his actions in getting the troops moving off the beach. As Lieutenant Leo Van de Voort simply stated: "Let's go,

Royal Marine Commandos land on GOLD Beach. On the left is a bulldozer towing a trailer filled with wooden fascines, used for filling ditches. (IWM B5246)

goddamn, there ain't no use in staying here, we're all going to get killed!"[3] By late afternoon, the Americans had captured solid footholds on the heights and had cleared most of the draws from the rear. With no German reinforcements, the Americans moved inland, while the flow of battalions from the 1st and 29th Divisions could begin. But, as the Duke of Wellington had commented about Waterloo, it had been the nearest-run thing you ever saw in your life.

GOLD BEACH

The British landing on GOLD Beach aimed to establish the basis for a link-up with the Americans further west at OMAHA. After a sustained naval bombardment, the landing troops overwhelmed the German defenders in most places. One of the main centers of German resistance was at Le Hamel, which fell only after a sustained assault by the 1st Hampshires, who took heavy losses. Meanwhile, succeeding waves continued to take losses as they piled up on the beach nearby. For many in the landing force, the experience was not that of a smooth, unopposed ride:

"We hit two mines going in – bottle mines on stakes. They didn't stop us, although the ramp was damaged and an officer standing on it was killed. We ground on a sandbank. The first man off was a commando sergeant in full kit. He disappeared like a stone into six feet of water … The beach was strewn with wreckage, a blazing tank, bundles of blankets and kit, bodies, and bits of bodies. One bloke near me was blown in half and his lower half collapsed in a bloody heap on the sand."[4]

Once the thin crust of German defenses was broken, troops of the 50th Infantry Division advanced almost to the suburbs of Bayeux; the town would fall the next day, one of the few major Norman cities to fall without a serious fight – and one of the main reasons it still retains much of its medieval splendor. The success at GOLD was crucial to creating the means to link up the American and British landings. The relatively quick British success was also essential in pulling most of the regiments of the 352nd division away from the OMAHA Beach landings, where their presence might have made a terribly real difference.

JUNO BEACH

The assault by the Canadian 3rd Division in the center of the British landings succeeded equally well, but at higher cost. In particular, the Canadians had the bad luck to hit their beaches late. Consequently, the tide was already rising, and Rommel's obstacles took a serious toll, particularly as the landing craft attempted to back off the beaches after unloading. No fewer than 20 out of 24 of the lead boats were damaged or lost; nearly one third of those engaged on JUNO would be lost or damaged by the end of the day. Again, the German defenses put up some sustained resistance. It took the Canadians over three hours to take the town of St-Aubin-sur-Mer. But once the crust of the German defenses broke, the Canadians found it relatively easy to push inland. The German defenders would receive no reinforcements until the next day, when the murderous juvenile delinquents of the Waffen SS Hitlerjügend arrived, and launched a savage counterattack. By then the Canadians had the depth and the forces to absorb what the Germans threw at them. While they would suffer heavy losses in killed, wounded, and captured – many of the captured murdered by the Germans in the most brutal fashion – they would inflict heavy casualties on the Germans. By late afternoon, one of the lead battalions of the Canadian 9th Brigade reported that the road to Caen lay open before it and requested permission to move into the city. The brigade commander denied permission, since such a move was not in the plans. In retrospect, the senior officer may have been correct. An advance into Caen's outskirts might only have served to make the Canadians more vulnerable to the counterattacks that would come the next day.

SWORD BEACH

The landing on SWORD went considerably easier than the landing at JUNO. For the most part, the heavy naval bombardment suppressed German strongpoints. Nevertheless, the German stronghold at La Brèche held out for three hours. Troops coming ashore in that area had to move through heavy small-arms fire. In one place, British soldiers caught sight of a French girl struggling to pull their wounded out of the pounding surf. Two problems confronted the attackers: the first was clearing the beaches as succeeding waves piled in. Here, the specialized armor did its job neatly in clearing lanes through minefields and burning the defenders out of fortified positions. The second problem was that of indirect artillery fire from inland, which caused considerable losses both in landing craft and among those on the beaches.

The double mission, requiring the 3rd Division to link up with the airborne by securing Pegasus Bridge across the Orne, as well as to move south and capture Caen, represented an impossible challenge. The link-up with the British airborne was accomplished with relative ease. The 185th Brigade had the mission of capturing Caen, and by 11:00a.m. its three battalions were assembled near Hermanville for the push south. From that point on things went wrong. The supporting tanks failed to get off the beach because of the congestion. Exacerbating British difficulties was the German defense of strongpoint "Hillman" – a virtual fortress that

Canadian troops come ashore with their bicycles at JUNO. A span has already been created to bridge the sea wall and allow the vehicles to get off the beach. (IWM A23 938)

stood directly in the 185th Brigade's path. Naval gunfire had been tasked to bombard the position, but German fire had killed the bombardment liaison officer, and there was no one else available to control naval gunfire. The result was a nasty fire-fight that took most of the afternoon. Finally, as the lead elements approached Caen from the northeast, they ran into elements of the 21st Panzer Division. Caen would not fall until the middle of July.

Yet, perhaps it was all to the best, because a move into Caen on the late afternoon of June 6 would have led the British straight into the jaws of the Hitlerjügend, who were spoiling for a fight and who would give the Canadians a very bloody nose the next day. Considering the campaign as a whole, the failure to take Caen may have been a blessing in disguise, forcing, as it did, the Germans to fight a static battle of attrition, in which superior British firepower eventually ground down the Wehrmacht's panzer and panzer grenadier formations and set the stage for the great American breakout.

CONCLUSION

By the time that June 6 had become a defining day in history, the Allies had managed to insert onto the continent of Europe over 155,000 men – 75,215 across the British and Canadian beaches, 57,500 across the American sector, and 23,000 by parachute and glider. Altogether, Montgomery had eight divisions and three armored brigades ashore despite tenacious German resistance. Moreover, Allied deception plans had been so successful that the Germans had barely begun to react to the invasion by the day's end. Only one German division, the Hitlerjügend, would arrive the next day. The Allies were well on the way to winning the battle of the build-up before it had begun. In the end, OVERLORD's success rested entirely on the success of Allied amphibious forces in securing the five bridgeheads, through which Allied armies and supplies could pour over the coming months.

Chapter 9

"Blood upon
the risers"

(The paratroopers' song)
"There was blood upon the risers, there were brains upon the 'chute."

Airborne

Professor Allan R Millett

The Allied airborne assault on D-Day rivaled the amphibious landings in complexity, risk, drama, heroism, losses, and effort. It can be debated whether the physical and psychological damage the two American and one British airborne divisions inflicted on the Wehrmacht truly justified the airborne operation. What is certain is that the airborne operations did not go as planned. In some zones of operations, particularly those of the British 6th Airborne Division, the missions, although altered in battle, added a useful degree of confusion to the German Seventh Army's response to the invasion. In no case could operational flaws be attributed to the skill and ardor of the airborne troops themselves or to most of the transport and glider pilots who carried them into a day of death and near disaster.

THE DEVELOPMENT OF AIRBORNE OPERATIONS

The airborne phase of Operation OVERLORD had its origins in the German invasion of Crete (May, 1941) and less ambitious Allied operations in North Africa, Sicily, and Italy in 1942–43. The concept of airborne assaults, however, predated World War II and grew from the awareness that the new air forces might provide a unique operational capability to ground forces, an ability to conduct a "vertical envelopment" of an enemy force too strong for a surface offensive to dislodge. As developed principally by the German, British, Russian, and United States armies by 1941, the concept took on more precise form. An airborne operation should be part of a larger ground offensive, probably an amphibious landing. The mission of an airborne assault would be to seize and defend critical terrain and military objectives that would impede enemy counterattacks on the landing forces. The airborne forces might also occupy key defensive terrain in a pre-emptive assault, thus disrupting the enemy's defensive plans. Even if casualties in the airborne troops were high on a percentage basis, airborne operations might reduce overall field army losses if the enemy lost its ability to conduct a cohesive, coordinated defense that required rapid counterattacks, a staple in German operational thinking.

An airborne operation that would be an important element in a larger offensive required three phases and three different kinds of air-landing forces. The first phase required the dropping of parachute infantry on or near critical objectives. A mission might require no other force but parachute infantry, but if a commander required sustained operations, the next phase brought glider-borne air-landing forces and critical amounts of ammunition, rations, and medical supplies.

OPPOSITE Two ready to load. (Airborne and Special Operations Museum)

Loading a .57mm anti-tank gun on a glider. (Airborne and Special Operations Museum)

The air-landing forces would be a mix of more infantry with mortars and heavy machine guns, field artillery batteries, and anti-mechanized artillery companies. Glider-borne units could also bring light vehicles and mounted, powerful radios to the assault force. If a glider-borne force was an operational necessity, then the initial parachute infantry objectives had to include clear glider-landing fields that would be safe from enemy direct-fire weapons like anti-aircraft machine guns and automatic cannon. If the first two phases of the airborne assault were successful, a third phase might occur, the landing of transport aircraft on a captured airfield or "heavy" air-landing operations that would bring medium artillery, heavier vehicles (including Bren gun carriers, perhaps light mechanized forces), sustaining logistics, and fresh infantry. If the planning included the heavy air-landing phase, then the first and second phase forces had to capture an enemy airfield capable of handling large, loaded transports and becoming an instant full-service airport. Such sites were obviously few in number, heavily defended, vulnerable to air and ground attack, and seldom located for the convenience of the attacking forces, the same limitation amphibious forces faced in capturing a major port like Cherbourg. In the Normandy operation the only feasible location for a complete three-phase, corps-sized airborne operation was a four-airfield complex around the French city of Évreux, some 80 kilometers from the Normandy beaches and right in the middle of the German mechanized reserve forces south of the Seine River.

DIVIDED OPINION ON THE USE OF AIRBORNE TROOPS

The Allied and German airborne experiences in the Mediterranean theater provided a very mixed body of operational expertise that guaranteed continuous, heated arguments over the employment of airborne forces. The Wehrmacht simply opted out of division-sized operations after the capture of Crete, because senior army and Luftwaffe officers thought the losses of elite paratroopers (Luftwaffe forces) and aircraft were excessive; the Germans, however, received plenty of relevant experience in how to defend against an airborne assault. The Allied experience – principally by US Army airborne regimental combat teams (about 2,000 officers and men) – did not offer convincing proof that even a phase-one operation (parachute infantry only) was worth the risk.

For its impact on Allied airborne operational planning for D-Day, the US 82nd Airborne Division provided the bulk of the sadder and wiser experiences in Sicily, July, 1943. Transport aircraft could not find the drop zones; "friendly" anti-aircraft units ravaged the transport formations; paratroopers landed miles from their objectives; parachute infantry too light to stop mechanized enemy forces fought without adequate artillery and air support. The 505th Parachute Infantry Regiment (Col. James M. Gavin) had less than one-fifth of its 2,000 assault paratroopers land on or near the proper drop zones in Sicily; the scattered combat groups found themselves locked in mortal combat with a German panzer division. In a week of fighting in Sicily, the 82nd Airborne Division took 27 percent casualties, but stopped the German counterattack on Gela with close combat, artillery, and naval gunfire. Two smaller operations by the British 1st Airborne Division also endured friendly-fire losses on the transports and gliders; half the paras came down around the actual drop zone and actually closed the bridge assigned as their objective. Of 16 gliders, three landed near the bridge, and 12 were lost to enemy action. The British took 23 percent casualties in a 3,856-man force. Subsequent airborne operations in Italy did not convince most senior commanders that divisional airborne operations had much future.

Despite the Mediterranean experience, Allied planning made airborne operations a centerpiece of the cross-Channel offensive. The late 1943 initial plans for NEPTUNE, the amphibious phase of OVERLORD, included an airborne assault deep behind the narrow three-division beach. A British division would land east of the Orne River to guard the landing forces' left flank. Two American divisions would take Bayeux. Airborne operations had political–military support at the highest levels. On the British side, Winston Churchill, although skeptical about OVERLORD, remained transfixed by high-risk special operations, the coup de main that used British pluck and ingenuity to offset Axis numbers and material excellence. He also admired Britain's unconventional airborne generals, Richard N. Gale and Frederick A. M. "Boy" Browning, both heroic Western Front lieutenants in World War I.

Browning was pure Victorian in background: an Eton and Sandhurst athlete, wealthy, a matinée idol in manner and appearance, a Grenadier Guards officer, and the husband of a literary lioness, the novelist Daphne du Maurier. Richard Gale, known to his peers as "Windy," shared Browning's enthusiasm for adventurous warfare. Of common means and family background, Gale, a machine gun officer in World War I, spent almost all of the inter-war years on regimental duty. An obscure major in 1939, he proved a great trainer as an infantry battalion commander, 1940–41, and took command of the 1st Parachute Brigade (September, 1941). When Browning took the British 1st Airborne Division to the Mediterranean, Gale succeeded him as War Office director of army air operations, which included the Parachute Regiment and the Glider Pilot Regiment.

The American champions of airborne operations included Army Chief of Staff George C. Marshall and General Henry H. "Hap" Arnold, commanding general, US Army Air Forces. With Marshall and Arnold committed to the wide use of American air power, airborne operations needed no other advocates. Almost all other major Allied army and air force generals saw no special magic in battalion and brigade parachute special operations (the British model) or the Marshall–Arnold concept of corps-sized strategic air landing assaults on the Crete model. Even if the Allies could form airborne divisions (and there were four in Europe early in 1944), the transport and glider requirements looked insurmountable. The American army, however, did not have to deal with the equivalent of the Royal Air Force in buying transports since the USAAF had no separate service status. Marshall and Arnold could build an airborne army if they so desired, and they did. Based on their notions of strategic air landing operations, the two American generals created enough parachute and glider infantry regiments and C-47 transport groups for as many as seven airborne divisions. With this investment beyond recall in 1944, someone needed to find a use for this elite force.

Brig. Gen. James Gavin briefs pathfinder teams, 82nd Airborne Division, June 5, 1944. (Airborne and Special Operations Museum)

THE PLANNED ROLE OF AIRBORNE OPERATIONS

When Generals Eisenhower, Montgomery, and Bradley came to England in the winter of 1943–44, they found a great deal to dislike about the preliminary planning for OVERLORD. They agreed that five major beaches were needed, over which six divisions could land on D-Day. One new western landing would open the Cotentin Peninsula and the road to Cherbourg. Bradley's first plan (December, 1943) was to cut the Cotentin Peninsula in one assault with the 82nd Division establishing an airhead (an area that would assure the continued arrival of troops and materiel by air) west of the Douve River at the city of St-Sauveur-le-Vicomte. Gavin, now a brigadier general and the chief airborne planner, was disturbed by the risks. As elements of the German 91st Airlanding Division began to appear along the Douve, Air Chief Marshal Sir Trafford Leigh-Mallory, RAF, and commander, Allied Expeditionary Air Forces, demanded that the plan be changed. The RAF's Cassandra predicted an aerial slaughter and a ground combat disaster that would endanger the whole Cotentin campaign. The next alternative Bradley saw was the Marshall–Arnold Évreux concept, even more frightening, and fueling Leigh-Mallory's opposition. Bradley and Gavin crafted another Cotentin plan,

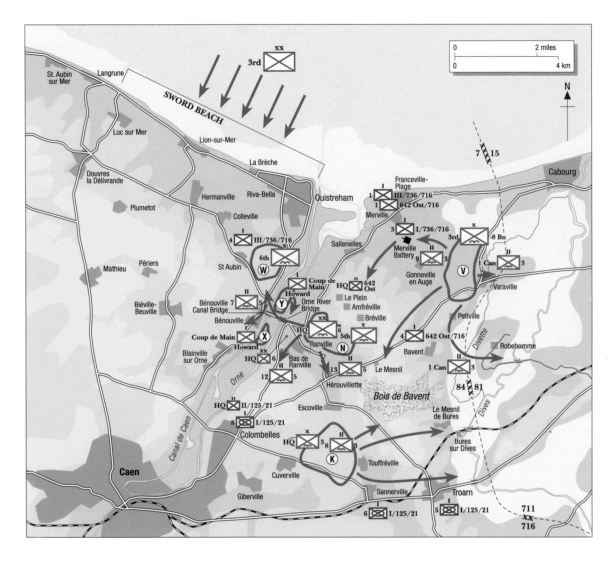

British 6th Airborne Division,
D-Day, June 6, 1944

completed May 26, that moved the 82nd Airborne Division eastward to
the Merderet River valley and closer to the 101st Airborne Division.
Still worried that Leigh-Mallory would persuade Eisenhower to
cancel the American air assault, Bradley insisted that there would be
no UTAH Beach assault without the airborne operation. As Gavin
recalled: "We received the new plan without a single regret."

The final plan committed the 82nd Division to drop its three
parachute infantry regiments on either side of the Merderet River. West
of the river the paratroopers would control a plateau and two major
roads north of the Douve River before it joined the Merderet and
flowed to the sea. The division's eastern sector included the town of

Ste-Mère-Eglise, five roads, a railroad, and two small towns – La Fière and Chef-du-Pont – that commanded two causeway-bridges that spanned the broad Merderet. The critical road east of the Merderet ran along a low ridge of small fields and thick woods that led to the city of Carentan, about ten miles to the south. The 101st Division's sector, about 40 square miles, lay east of the Ste-Mère-Eglise–Carentan road. Bradley assigned the division the mission of driving east to open the four causeway-roads that would bring the US 4th Infantry Division off UTAH Beach, isolated from the farmlands by marshes and flooded tidal plains. The paratroopers would attack the Germans, especially field artillery batteries, between them and the beach. The 4th Division would bring medium artillery and a tank battalion to give weight to the paratroopers' fight, especially against German mechanized counterattacks. Tactical air support might be available as well as naval gunfire. The 101st Division would try to capture Carentan even before help arrived, and defend the southern perimeter while the US VII Corps wheeled north toward Cherbourg.

The British 6th Airborne Division assumed a similar set of interdiction missions. The 5th Parachute Brigade would land just east of the Orne River/Caen Canal and prevent German use of the twin bridge complex at Bénouville ("Pegasus Bridge"), the only such crossing between Caen and the sea. The 3rd Parachute Brigade would drop to more dispersed drop zones farther to the east and seize four bridges, three of them over the Dives River. The paras would also capture a German battery at Merville and set up roadblocks to confuse German troop movements east of Caen. The 6th Airlanding Brigade (less one battalion) would come in by glider to provide light vehicles, heavy machine guns, pack artillery, and towed anti-tank guns. The 1st Special Service Brigade (Commando) would spearhead the amphibious force that would link up with airborne forces at Pegasus Bridge, to be captured by the glider-borne Company D, 2nd Battalion, Oxfordshire and Buckinghamshire Light Infantry (Major John Howard).

OVERLORD planners at all levels became aware of the known risks and unpredictable perils that faced the three airborne divisions. It was no comfort that Air Chief Marshal Leigh-Mallory did not favor the airborne assault, since he had the direct responsibility for the operation's success. With extrapolations from Mediterranean losses and assuming no improvement in airborne tactics and techniques, Leigh-Mallory first predicted catastrophe in March and hectored Eisenhower with memos of doom up until May 30. Leigh-Mallory's estimates ran from one-third to half the transports and gliders in flight, "colossal losses" of aircraft, gliders, and embarked soldiers. Eisenhower finally told Leigh-Mallory to stop spreading his gloom, which must have affected the transport and glider pilots who had little or no combat experience and knew a C-47 as transport or glider tug made a slow, fat target.

THE OPPOSING FORCES

By the spring of 1944, the German commanders on the Cotentin Peninsula and the Norman coastline believed they might face a simultaneous amphibious and airborne assault. Their planning for counter-airborne operations differed with their perception of Allied plans, the terrain, and the forces at hand, but plan they did. In the

Enemy forces in Cotentin Peninsula
(Courtesy, U.S. Army Center of
Military History)

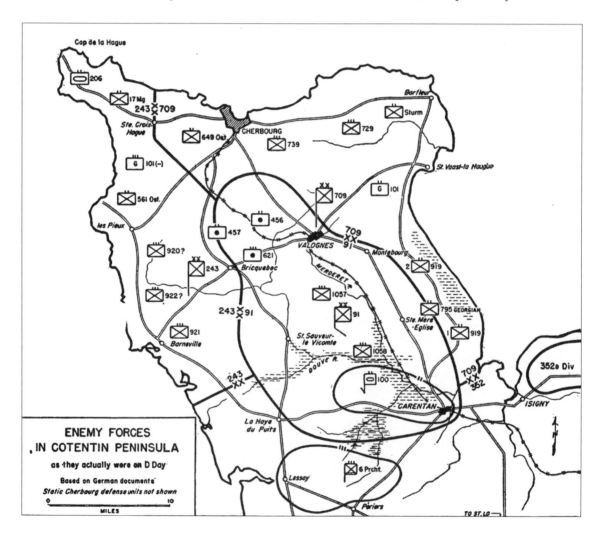

172

future drop-landing zones of the British 6th Airborne Division, the LXXXIV Corps (General der Artillerie Erich Marcks) controlled two third-rate infantry divisions (716th and 711th), committed to beach and air defense with an armored force, the war-weary 21st Panzer Division, in reserve. At the other flank of the planned amphibious objective area (UTAH Beach), the German 709th Infantry Division manned the fortifications that began at the mouth of the Vire River and extended to Cherbourg. Positioned west of the Merderet–Douve Rivers and south of Carentan, the 91st Airlanding Division and 6th Parachute Regiment had the mission of eliminating any Allied airhead. The British paras faced the greatest challenge, outnumbered and exposed to their worst nightmare, an armored attack on their landing zones. The American divisions faced about equal numbers (20,000 more or less), but German forces with no substantial mechanized forces. The biggest German deficiency was the Luftwaffe's departure for the air defenses of the Third Reich.

The German forces in the Caen-Orne River valley depended primarily on light, automatic, multi-barreled 20mm cannon for air defense, deadly against low-flying transports. They also erected anti-glider poles ("Rommel's asparagus") and other obstacles and mines in fields likely to be landing sites. The UTAH Beach area provided an additional option – flooding. The low tidal marshlands behind the beaches required no engineering magic. Inland, however, German pioneer troops dammed the Merderet and Douve rivers and their tributaries, thus turning the river valleys into temporary lakes and swamps. Most of the water obstacles were not over six feet deep, but the paratroopers (total landing weight as much as 400 pounds of man and equipment) were not prepared for survival-swimming under fire. Bundles of weapons, ammunition, and supplies easily disappeared in the murky waters. General Marcks also received some additional units to improve his anti-airborne capability: a special infantry assault battalion, a rocket battalion, a machine gun battalion, and a tank battalion. Marcks' immediate superiors – Generaloberst Friedrich Dollman (Seventh Army), Generalfeldmarschall Erwin Rommel (Army Group B) and Generalfeldmarschall Gerd von Rundstedt (Army Group West) – did not believe that an airborne assault in the LXXXIV Corps area would open the expected Allied amphibious invasion.

The not-so-watchful waiting by the German generals, encouraged by the storms of June, influenced their army. Although the lower ranks labored away at building obstacles, storing ammunition, and checking their weapons' fields of fire, the tactical commanders showed little urgency in organizing counterattack plans that could be mounted at night when Allied confusion would be greatest and air and naval fire support almost useless. The soldiers of the German infantry divisions in 1944 were a mix of veterans, foreign conscripts, and overage and teenage Germans, held together by cadres of officers and NCOs whose authority to punish (including field executions) was backed by the feldpolitzei. Panzertruppen and fallschirmjäger remained more formidable enemies. Although German infantry battalions had fewer troops, they had more light mortars, AT weapons, and MG-42 machine guns, the most effective single infantry weapon the Allies faced in Normandy.

The Allied airborne divisions presented a sharp contrast to their German foes. Except for a handful of recent veterans in the British 6th and the US 82nd Airborne Divisions, the Allied paratroopers and

American glider infantry on the way to Normandy. (82nd Airborne Division War Memorial Museum)

glider infantry had endured almost two years of rigorous training, but no combat. They had become physically fit to their armies' highest standards and skilled in a wide range of infantry weapons. Continuous field exercises weeded out many ineffective leaders. Field training stressed tactical initiative at every level, since few paratroop leaders believed that any night drop would work as planned in terms of unit concentration and cohesion. Contrary to post-war mythology, often nourished by German veterans, the Allied airborne combat units were not armed with weapons that outclassed the Germans. The Allied airborne troops had to depend on surprise, speed, tactical ingenuity, physical stamina, sheer courage, and leadership at all ranks, not material superiority.

THE TRANSPORTS

Getting the elite paratroops and the glider infantry, with their supporting light artillery, to the battlefield in intact battalions proved more than their transports could manage. The glider pilots, another elite in the British service, had little choice but to find the best place to land when their tug-transports broke the two-rope connections. Transport pilots, USAAF or RAF, were not the pick of their service's aviators, and their aircraft matched their own low status. The British created transport groups of bombers and bomber air crews, a solution that provided excellent groups, but too few in numbers for even a British division. British heavy bombers could serve as glider tugs, but their flight characteristics made them poor troop-carriers. The success of the D-Day airborne assault depended, therefore, on the three C-47 wings of the US IX Troop Carrier Command (Brig. Gen. Paul R. Williams, USAAF), a force of 1,176 aircraft and 1,004 air crews assigned to the US Ninth Air Force and then attached to the Allied tactical air command. The flying officers of the IX Troop Carrier Command were the least effective pilots in the USAAF, rejected for offensive air operations and plagued by air and ground problems in attitude and behavior. One enlisted crew chief who became a command historian noted that transport pilots seldom developed primary groups or worked well with their commanders (often experienced airline pilots) or ground crews. Glider pilots, on the other hand, developed strong common bonds based on their lowly ranks, ground combat experiences, and shared danger and contempt for gun-shy transport pilots.

The C-47 had positive qualities that endeared it to its air crews and passengers. It was easy to fly and maintain. It remained a stable aircraft at slow drop-speeds (100–120 knots), and its reduced prop-wash (the surge created by the propeller) reduced the dangers of 'chute-fouling for the jumpers. Beneath its military color scheme, however, the C-47 was still the Douglas DC-3 commercial airliner. It was not a high-priority USAAF acquisition and had not been altered much for airborne operations. Its gas tanks lacked armor and self-sealing features, increasing the chances of fires and fatal explosions. The pilot, co-pilot, and enlisted navigator had little protection. The crew chief had to stand in the narrow hatch to kick out the bundled arms, ammunition, and supplies before the paratroopers shuffled to the door, jumped right out, and counted to four. The greatest challenge was night navigation and formation flying. Flight leaders had SCR 717 radar, but it was too complex for time-urgent flight corrections. The ground terminal radio beacons ("Eureka") did not always reach their airborne partners ("Rebecca"). The ultimate source of direction was the group leaders' navigator and crew chief, which meant that humans under stress had to make the "red" signal (four minutes out) and "green" signal (jump) by hand-held lights to around 25–30 aircraft. The flight profile for a tight, safe drop demanded a high order of skill and courage. The concealment of darkness provided some element of surprise, assisted by low-level (600–800 feet) flying.

The optimum altitude for a drop was 600 feet at an airspeed of 100–120 knots. A higher-faster flight profile scattered a "stick" of 13–17

American airborne dead, Cotentin Peninsula, June 1944. (82nd Airborne Division War Memorial Museum)

parachutists and exposed them to dangerous prop-wash, other aircraft, and enemy flak for more than 30 seconds. A high-speed drop meant that gravity forces would rip away a jumper's weapons and equipment when his 'chute blossomed. A reduction of altitude meant that a paratrooper's 'chute might not fully open. A partial or complete "Roman candle" (when a parachute failed to open) meant that a jumper landed at a speed of 35 to 150 miles an hour.

The gliders themselves were barely adequate in design and numbers. The American contribution, the CG4A "Waco," was too heavy and large in packaged form to ship in scarce cargo space and too small in payload capacity (15 troops or one jeep); only 3,750 Wacos reached the global war. British gliders flew or landed in a controlled crash with better aerodynamic characteristics. The Horsa (6,900-pound payload or almost twice a Waco's) and the Hamilcar (16,000-pound payload) provided space for towed anti-tank guns, heavy radio jeeps, and Bren gun carriers. The Hamilcar's weight meant that a four-engined bomber had to fly as tug while a C-47 could tow a Horsa. The British glider pilots (enlisted volunteers) had high morale and felt privileged to be members of The Glider Regiment. They received additional combat training and expected to join para or air-landing battalions in combat, a policy that created pilot shortages but enhanced esprit de corps and bonded air crew to their passengers.

THE BRITISH AIRBORNE ASSAULT

The 6th Airborne Division's missions on D-Day had few complexities and many difficulties. The division knew its objectives in February, 1944, and they remained unchanged. The purpose was to buy time and space for the Allied forces landing over SWORD Beach by commanding the high ground between the Caen Canal–Orne River and the Dives River. The bridges over the canal and western river were to be seized and held intact; those over the Dives would be destroyed, thus slowing a German panzer counterattack. An added (but crucial) mission was to destroy the German heavy coastal battery at Merville that endangered the SWORD landing. The transports and tugs for the 6th Division came from the RAF's 38th and 46th Groups (470 aircraft, 1,120 gliders), on the whole better-trained than their USAAF counterparts.

The 6th Division plan provided for four waves of assault before D-Day's dawning. Shortly after midnight, the reinforced company of the 2nd Ox and Bucks in six gliders would land near the Caen Canal–Orne River bridges and seize them intact. Within the same hour, pathfinder teams parachuted into three drop zones east of the Orne

and set up terminal guidance systems for the main force, six parachute
battalions of roughly 4,200 officers and other ranks, who landed
between 12:30a.m. and 1:00a.m.. At 3:20a.m. 68 Horsa gliders would
deliver critical supplies, ammunition, anti-tank guns, engineers with
mines and demolitions, communications jeeps, and light howitzers as
well as the division's forward headquarters. During dusk of D-Day
another glider force would bring in the 6th Airlanding Brigade (less
one battalion) and the rest of the division's "heavy" units.

The plans did not produce complete success, but on the whole the
6th Division accomplished all its missions within acceptable time
limits and casualties. The transport force experienced fewer losses
than anticipated; all but five of 129 transports dropped their "sticks"
somewhere between the Orne and Dives. Of the 264 transports that
flew D-Day missions for the Sixth Division, only seven were lost. The
glider force lost 22 of 98 gliders, a more serious statistic that included
71 glider pilot casualties. The actual placement of the troops was
another matter through flak avoidance and poor navigation. The
3rd Brigade, which had five missions for three battalions, had two
zones, V for Varaville and K for Touffréville, separated by six miles.
Some of its pathfinders landed in Zone N (the 5th Brigade's area) and
guided planes to the wrong place. Only about half of Zone V's two
battalions (9th Para and 1st Canadian) found their rendezvous, and

The perils of glider landings,
Normandy June 6, 1944.
(82nd Airborne Division War
Memorial Museum)

only one of 11 gliders found the zone. The brigade lost most of its
mortars and demolitions engineers. It also lost its naval gunfire party.
The 9th Paras took the Merville battery by unsupported direct assault
with only 170 men, led by the battalion commander. Two gliders of
assault troops arrived for a coup de main, but missed the battery. The
storming party lost half its men, but captured the complex from the
716th Division's defenders, only to find no heavy guns inside the
battery.

The 1st Canadians destroyed two Dives River bridges with two
composite companies of its own and errant paras from two other
battalions. One Canadian company almost became a complete casualty
in a flooded area, but its remnants and some late-arriving engineers
destroyed one bridge. To the south, the 8th Para battalion mustered only
141 officers and men in Zone K, since only four of 37 C-47s found the zone
while the rest of the battalion landed miles away in Zone N. Nevertheless,
the 8th Paratroopers fought their way into Bures and Troarn and battled
the Germans while the gallant sappers of 3rd Parachute Squadron Royal
Engineers rushed the bridges under fire and blew away one span. All
of the 3rd Brigade's battalions returned to pre-planned defensive
positions west of the Dives, brought in some stragglers, and beat back the
half-hearted local counterattacks of the 716th Division and one battalion
of panzergrenadiers, 21st Panzer Division.

The 5th Parachute Brigade faced a sterner challenge, serious counterattacks by the 21st Panzer Division to recapture the Caen–Orne bridges. The first two parachute battalions (7th and 12th Para) arrived in disarray. Without most of its crew-served weapons and with about half its troops, 7th Para rushed to reinforce the Ox and Bucks company at Bénouville and Le Port west of the Caen Canal. The 12th Para had half of its "sticks" hit Zone N, but its own stragglers and those of 7th Para allowed it to establish a good position east of the Orne, facing south. The reserve 13th Para had the best drop and held Zone N while helping the other battalions beat back two panzergrenadier battalions that began probing attacks around 3:30a.m. The critical reinforcement was the 3:20a.m. glider wave; 50 of 68 scheduled Horsas arrived with 11 anti-tank guns, mines, and machine guns as well as General Gale and his staff. With good ground and sufficient men and munitions, the 6th Division had arrived to stay. The commandos of the 1st Special Service Brigade reached Pegasus Bridge at 1:00p.m., followed five hours later by infantry and tanks from the British 3rd Infantry Division. The 6th Airlanding Brigade made its glider entry as scheduled at dusk, with 248 of 258 gliders landing west of the Caen Canal. By dark, the airhead contained 14 infantry battalions, medium artillery, armor, and a full complement of engineers, air control parties, naval gunfire spotters, and service troops. The German 716th Division presented no threat, and the bloodied 21st Panzer Division broke off its attacks along the Caen Canal–Orne axis to await the arrival of I SS Panzer Corps. With ingenuity, initiative, and determination, the 6th Airborne Division had secured the Allied left flank at a cost of 821 dead, 2,709 wounded, and 927 missing, about evenly divided between the dead and prisoners.

THE AMERICAN AIRBORNE ASSAULT

The American airborne operation behind UTAH Beach by the 82nd Airborne and 101st Airborne divisions remains second only to the OMAHA Beach landing in near disaster. The excessive losses and general confusion are usually blamed on Air Chief Marshal Leigh-Mallory and the C-47 transport pilots, convenient scapegoats for Generals Bradley, Ridgway, and Taylor, a trio of senior officers consumed by ambition, peer rivalry, and an indecent desire to please the media and their superiors. The only airborne skeptic in the Normandy operation was Brigadier General Gavin, assistant division commander of the 82nd Airborne, who served as COSSAC airborne planner after commanding the 505th Airborne Infantry Regiment, the only combat-tested regiment in all the American airborne forces in

England. Gavin watched one poor decision after another eventually ruin three American airborne regiments, two in his own division. He helped make the plans, too. Never have so many dropped in so small an area with so little purpose and so much loss. Only the fighting heart of younger officers and sturdy troops saved the operation.

The difficulty began with General Bradley's decision, approved by General J. Lawton Collins of VII Corps, to use both American divisions at the base of the Cotenin Peninsula. Leigh-Mallory didn't like the plan: too many gliders (almost 700 by the eve of D-Day), too much risk in isolation for the 82nd Division, out of range for naval guns and any 4th Division artillery. Leigh-Mallory might have committed USAAF tactical aircraft to inland targets in the drop zone, but he resisted any use of fighter-bombers in close air support, and the Americans, scared of "friendly fire" but unwilling to train to eliminate it, did not protest. Leigh-Mallory insisted that predawn glider operations be cut from 260 to 100 tugs and gliders and the evening waves from 400 to 200. Bradley made the change, and neither Taylor nor Ridgway objected. The final change the Americans accepted was to create three new drop zones for Ridgway's division closer to those of the 101st Airborne, which made sense since both divisions would be short on anti-tank guns and howitzers, victims of the glider reductions. The battle would be borne by some 13,000 paratroopers of six airborne regiments wedged between the beach marshes and flooded Merderet River valley. There was a better option, but it required the cooperation of Maxwell D. Taylor, no friend of either Ridgway or Gavin, who regarded Taylor as a dilettante artilleryman of too much quick intelligence, great charm, sycophantic brilliance, questionable courage, and convenient ethics. Ridgway's former chief of staff and division artillery commander, Taylor had escaped Ridgway's wrath for inattentive work by promotion to brigadier general and a transfer, championed by Bradley, to the 101st Division. Taylor replaced Maj. Gen. William C. Lee in March, 1944 when Lee, the true airborne pioneer, collapsed from a heart attack. Taylor regarded Ridgway as a relentless egotist of limited intelligence, boundless energy, more physical courage than judgment, and a sanctimonious hypocrite who surrounded himself with dim-witted staff officers and commanders he manipulated through intimidation. Taylor may have excluded Gavin (who loathed him) from this characterization because he regarded Gavin – a poor orphan from coal-mining Pennsylvania who completed West Point without a high school education – as a social inferior. Taylor would accommodate Ridgway only as much as Bradley demanded. Fearing that internal battle would fuel Leigh-Mallory's demands to scratch the whole operation, the

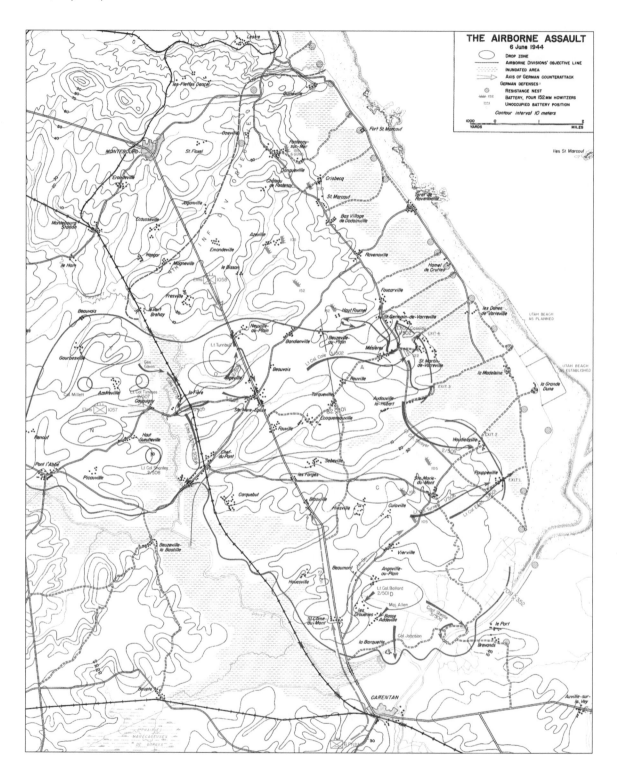

THE AIRBORNE ASSAULT
6 June 1944

airborne generals and Bradley stopped the operational adjustment with one change too few.

The adjustment untaken was the assignment of the 101st Airborne's 502nd Parachute Infantry Regiment (PIR) to take causeway Exits Four and Three right behind UTAH Beach. Absorbed with training and buried in trivial matters his obsessive personality could not ignore, Ridgway did not propose one more logical change: shift the 502nd PIR to Exits Two and One to the south and use the proven 505th PIR to take Exits Four and Three, the 507th or 508th PIR to take Ste-Mère-Eglise and the Merderet bridges from the east bank, and the remaining regiment to hold the river's western bank or concentrate at Chef-du-Pont, another east bank crossroads. As Ridgway doted on the 505th PIR, so Taylor regarded the 502nd PIR as "Max's Own." Its commander, Colonel George Van Horn Moseley, Jr., a general's son, was mediocre and obliged everyone by breaking a leg just before he emotionally collapsed. His executive officer and replacement, Lt. Col. John H. "Mike" Michaelis, was a true warrior as were the three battalion commanders, Patrick Cassidy, Steven Chappius, and Robert G. Cole. Three, deservedly, became generals, but Cole died in Holland before learning he had been awarded a Medal of Honor. Taylor would not deny the 502nd PIR the best mission on D-Day.

In the face of Ridgway's and Taylor's demands to stage realistic parachute exercises, Bradley and Maj. Gen. Lewis H. Brereton, the Ninth Air Force commander, had no stomach for revising the airborne plan. Like a vulture at Agincourt, Leigh-Mallory hovered around the IX Troop Carrier Command, looking for fatal flaws. Taylor held to his high risk, high glory scheme unchallenged. Two of his regiments would open UTAH Beach while the third (the 501st PIR) drove south to take and hold a canal lock, bridge system, and road around the city of Carentan, key to the Douve-Taute and Vire River valleys and the roads to OMAHA Beach. This zone was the responsibility of the German 6th Parachute Regiment and the reinforcements it was likely to receive from LXXXIV Corps. The 501st PIR had the most demanding mission, but Taylor put one of its battalions in division reserve while the 506th PIR opened Exits One and Two, well south of the planned UTAH Beach. Basically, the division would put two regiments behind the beach and only one in the most menacing entrant to the battlefield. Moreover, the 4th Division's scheme of maneuver would send it north, not to reinforce the 501st PIR.

82ND AIRBORNE DIVISION

By midnight June 6 in a clear, moonlit night, the American aerial armada (917 transports with 96 towing gliders) formed up over the Channel, then turned south away from the invasion fleet below it. In a

OPPOSITE The Airborne Assault. (Courtesy, U.S. Army Military History Institute)

V-of-Vs, the transport groups droned on at 1,500 feet above the water, crossed over the occupied Channel Islands, and began their west–east run across the 23-mile-wide base of the Cotentin Peninsula. Pathfinders would drop from the first wave on six drop zones: T, N, and O for the 82nd Division and (north to south) A, C, and D for the 101st Division. The transports dropped to 600 feet and slowed down – and ran into a dense cloud bank. Alerted by their radars, the German flak batteries fired in blind abandon at the passing aerial host. The leading waves escaped almost unscathed, the 21 transports actually shot down coming from the rear serials. The clouds and flak, however, broke up the neat Vs as some transports climbed as high as 2,000 feet, others dropped below 500 feet, and many increased their airspeeds well above 120 knots. Many of the transports, overloaded at take-off, had to increase their airspeeds to avoid stalling. Controlled navigation disappeared. Individual air crews had less than ten minutes to plot adjusted courses. Dropping bundles added to the miscalculations. Confused and terrified air crews missed or misread terminal guidance beacons and lights. In four zones, the pathfinders fought more and guided less. One pilot made three passes to find the right drop zone for his stick; few had equal faith and determination. Weapons and equipment came down willy-nilly, torn by gravity from the parachutists. The transports carrying the 505th PIR found Ste-Mère-Eglise, in part because a large house on its square had caught fire. The better half of three battalions and Ridgway and his staff (60 of 118 sticks) landed in Zone O or at least within two miles of it. Eight sticks landed as much as 14 miles from the zone. Confused by the rain of paratroopers, the Germans fought only briefly for the town and then fled; a flak company riddled the troopers who came down within the town, but moved off for Cherbourg. The 505th PIR set up an extemporized defense with about half its jump strength, the only one of Ridgway's regiments to fight with any degree of cohesion.

The rest of the 82nd Division met a cruel fate west of the Merderet. The 507th PIR missed Zone T almost completely. About 20 sticks landed around Ste-Mère-Eglise and joined the 505th PIR. Most of the regiment landed in the flooded Merderet; those not drowned, or shot or captured by the 1057th Infantry Regiment, 91st Division, were too exhausted and weaponless to fight. There were some exceptions. Expecting trouble west of the Merderet, Jim Gavin, M-1 tied to his body, jumped with the 508th PIR west of the Merderet marshes. Most of the 508th PIR landed on high ground, but badly scattered. Thirty sticks landed east of the river, nine almost on UTAH Beach. Gavin and the regimental commander rallied about 50 men and then joined

150 more survivors of the 507th PIR and 508th PIR. This demi-battalion, all that could join the 505th PIR, entered the fight to hold the Merderet bridges. By nightfall, Ridgway commanded about one-third of his original division. Most of the 507th and 508th PIRs died or were captured in three isolated pockets west of the Merderet; of 12 parachute and glider battalion commanders, only four survived the battle in command, three of them wounded. Half of their replacements became casualties. About half of the three Ridgway PIRs became casualties on D-Day alone, establishing a division loss rate that held for 33 more days of fighting for control of the Merderet valley and Ste-Mère-Eglise. Of the division's 5,436 casualties, only an estimated

82d Airborne Division Drop Pattern.(Courtesy, U.S. Army Military History Institute)

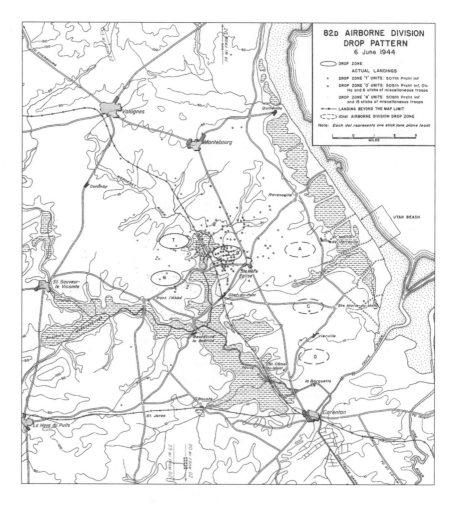

272 were lost in the drop itself, but the scattered drop doomed hundreds more.

The 82nd Division glider serial (52 gliders) completed the debacle at about 4:30a.m. on June 6 by crashing in the woods, hedgerows, orchards, cattle herds, German obstacles, and stone walls around Ste-Mère-Eglise. Thirty-one gliders landed within two miles of their goal, Zone O of the 505th PIR. Twenty-two gliders (wherever they landed) crashed and ruined their cargo: 26 soldiers, eight precious anti-tank guns, 11 jeeps, medical supplies, the division's best radio equipment, and much of Ridgway's staff became casualties. Six big 57mm anti-tank guns, however, went into the 505th PIR's position, Ridgway's greatest fire power until late on D-Day when his sea echelon (mostly artillery) arrived and D+1 when the 325th Glider Infantry arrived in a glider lift.

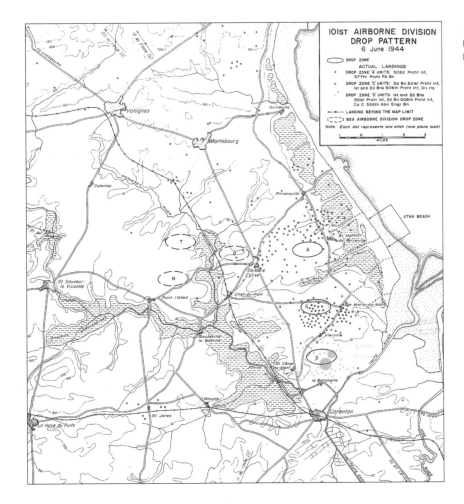

101ST AIRBORNE DIVISION

The experiences of the three parachute regiments of the 101st Division mirrored those of the 82nd Division, but with variations on the confusion theme. In the broad sense, the division accomplished one of its two missions, eliminating the German positions at the western ends of the Exits Four-One Causeways. It did not take Carentan or stop the German 6th Parachute Regiment from counter-attacking deep into the division's position. The paratroopers did, however, capture or isolate six artillery batteries of the German 709th Division, as well as engage that division's infantry to such a degree that it posed no threat to the landing. The initiative and tactical skill of individual leaders and the fragments of companies and battalions carried the day, since General Taylor and his regimental commanders never controlled their organizations.

The reinforced 502nd PIR (it had an attached artillery battalion) landed in disarray behind Exits Four and Three. Fifty-two sticks came down outside the division's northern boundary; another 25 sticks landed around Zone C to the south among the 506th PIR. The transports evened the maldistribution by dropping over 30 sticks of the 506th PIR among the 60 or so 502nd sticks that came down around Zone A. Probably around 30 sticks hit the tidal marches behind the beach. Private David Webster of the 506th PIR found himself on a swamp hillock with six castaways from four different regiments. Blessed with superior leadership once Colonel Moseley departed, the three 502nd PIR battalions, really mixed groups of 200 paratroopers each, attacked the German batteries and garrisons between them and the causeways. The drop itself wrecked the 377th Parachute Artillery Battalion, which lost all 12 of its howitzers in a drop that varied from three to 12 miles from Zone A. Of 2,500 Zone A paratroopers about 600–800 fought the Germans on D-Day. It was enough – barely. Cassidy and Cole took their teams against the Germans between them and the beach while Chappius's scattered battalion defended the zone to the north and south. Cole's 3rd Battalion, 502nd PIR controlled Exit Three by 7:30a.m. where it met the advance guard of the US 8th Infantry Regiment early that afternoon after the battalion had ambushed a fleeing German company. Cassidy's battalion had to fight its way through four fortified villages to open Exit Four. Colonel Michaelis with 200 troopers arrived to hold Exit Four while Cassidy pushed north to block the roads on the regiment's flank. A handful of paratroopers actually outfought the Germans. The best example was the feat of Staff Sergeant Harrison Summers, who almost single-handedly killed or captured the 150-man garrison of La Mézières in five hours of house-to-house fighting. Summers then admitted: "I'm sure I'd never do anything like that again."

The drop of the 506th PIR (Col. Robert F. Sink) and the 3rd Battalion, 501st PIR (Lt. Col. Julian Ewell, a future general) on Zone C behind Exits Two and One did nothing to reassure General Taylor, who made his second jump into Normandy. (He wore jump wings for one "qualifying" jump that Ridgway approved for his division staff in 1943.) Sink's 2nd Battalion landed in Zone A, far from its objectives, Exits Two and One. The scattered battalion fought its way back to its zone, but arrived at Exit Two that afternoon to find it in the hands of other paratroopers and the 8th Infantry. Colonel Sink sent his 1st Battalion (fewer than 100 effectives) to clear the exits, but it made little headway against German resistance. General Taylor, initially part of a group of 15 led by two generals and two colonels, sent

Ewell's battalion (again perhaps 100 men) to take the defended towns of Houdienville (Exit Two) and Pouppeville (Exit One). Ewell's force drove the Germans out of Pouppeville and held the exit until the 8th Infantry arrived at mid-morning. In the meantime, Colonel Sink gathered some of his 1st and 2nd Battalions around Ste-Marie-du-Mont where he waged an all-day battle in the hedgerows with a battalion of the 191st Artillery Regiment and a force of German paratroopers. This sharp local fight was shaped by Sink's responsibility for holding a new Zone E for the late afternoon glider operation that would bring in 32 Horsas. Twenty-four landed more or less on location under German fire; the enemy fire and crashes eliminated 54 of the 157 embarked soldiers, including Brig. Gen. Don F. Pratt, Taylor's assistant, dead of a broken neck. The operation improved Taylor's supply situation, but he already had heavy weapons support from the 4th Infantry Division. Sink ended the day with 650 men in two battalions.

The destruction of a four-gun battery of 105mm howitzers positioned near a French farm-fortress, Brécourt Manor, typified the sort of independent action that kept the Germans off-balance. With the 506th PIR still scattered in the early morning of June 6, Colonel Sink sent an extemporized platoon of 20 officers and men from three different companies to silence the guns, defended by perhaps 50 enemy infantry. The risks were acceptable since the guns had begun to shell the "new" UTAH Beach. Lieutenant Richard D. Winters (Company E, 506th PIR) got the assignment since he, another lieutenant, and nine enlisted men would be the initial assault force. With a classic example of supporting fires (two machine guns) and close assault with grenades, rifles, and submachine guns, Winters' group killed or routed the crews, spiked the guns, and held the Germans at bay before ending the raid with four dead and two wounded. Winters returned later in the afternoon with a 4th Division tank-infantry team to kill or capture the remaining Germans in the strongpoint.

The 101st Division's non-beach oriented mission went to the 501st PIR (Colonel Howard R. "Skeets" Johnson) and the attached 3rd Battalion, 506th PIR. Johnson's regiment (less Ewell's battalion) and the 506th PIR battalion were supposed to capture Carentan and its canal-river locks and bridges. The Germans prevented this success. Despite heavy flak, the transports dropped Johnson's force almost all on or near Zone D, just west of the Vierville–St–Côme-du-Mont road. Only ten sticks went wildly out-of-area. The German defenders, however, had Zone D under heavy machine gun and artillery fire. The 1st Battalion, 501st PIR lost its battalion commander, his staff, and all

its company commanders and half its troops, thus leaving the battle without making any impact. The 3rd Battalion, 506th PIR fared little better. Its senior surviving officer, a staff captain, gathered 50 men and reached the Taute River, but could go no farther. Johnson's headquarters and his 2nd Battalion, also disorganized by its landing, split into two groups of about 150 each. Johnson and his operations officer took one group to a canal lock, one objective, but again met stubborn German defenders. The second group found too many Germans at St-Côme-du-Mont to advance. Naval gunfire from a US Navy cruiser, directed by a team of naval gunfire controllers, kept the Germans immobile, but the stand-off ended when two battalions of the 6th Parachute Regiment slipped north of Carentan and attacked both the 501st and 506th PIR, supported by troops from the German 91st and 709th Divisions. Johnson concentrated his faux regiment (perhaps 500 effectives) for a defense well short of his D-Day objectives and awaited help. The help could not come from the 101st Division, which mustered about 2,500 men of the 6,500 troopers who had made the night drop.

THE UTAH BEACH LANDING

The UTAH Beach landing by the 4th Infantry Division rescued the airborne divisions. For once, fortune smiled on the Americans. For one thing, the presence of the airborne divisions forced the navy to use pinpoint naval gunfire against the beach defenses, its doctrinal preference, rather than area fire inland. The Ninth Air Force's pre-landing attacks came down the beach's long axis (north to south), not at a right angle, the bombing pattern at OMAHA Beach. A wave of B-26s missed their primary targets, but their "overs" smashed the strongpoint La Madeline and damaged La Grande Dune strongpoint. The initial waves of landing craft drifted south 2,000 yards, which brought them into the accidental gap in the beach defenses and gave them direct access to Exits Two and One, not to Exits Four and Three, still defended by stubborn German troops. The American infantry with tanks pushed forward through Exits Three–One, which stiffened the 101st Division's positions. Since Taylor's 327th Glider Infantry Regiment and two missing artillery battalions did not come ashore with any urgency, the reinforced 8th Infantry made a welcome appearance. It took another whole day for the 4th Infantry Division to shore up Ridgway's fragile line along the Merderet and his division's northern perimeter. Like the 82nd Division, the "Screaming Eagles" left Normandy in July reduced by 4,670 casualties, but it was impossible to be precise about how many paratroopers fell on D-Day. The estimate is that 40 percent of the division's parachute force of June 6 became casualties, about 2,600 officers and men.

SUMMARY

No one quibbles about the fortitude and tactical skill of the three Allied airborne divisions that participated in Operation NEPTUNE. It is easy to forget how few of them from colonel to private had been in combat before June 6, although they had certainly trained hard and long. There was no appreciable difference between the combat performance of the British and Canadian paras and their American comrades. All three divisions fought a mix of first rate and second rate German troops; the 6th Parachute Regiment, 91st Airlanding Division, and 21st Panzer Division were as good as any unit in the regular German army, and the 701st and 709th Divisions had infantry that would defend fixed positions under the command of veteran NCOs, and both divisions had good artillery, field and fixed. Why did the British 6th Airborne Division accomplish all its missions and the American divisions did not? The answer is not the quality of the transport air drops. Although the British C-47 squadrons flew slightly steadier and tighter formations, they also faced somewhat lighter flak and thinner clouds. The British did use more and bigger gliders, flown by skilled pilots, and they timed the glider force arrival more expertly. Therefore, the British parachute brigades had more light artillery and anti-tank guns to face German counter attacks. The amphibious forces brought up tanks and heavier artillery slightly more rapidly from SWORD Beach. None of the divisions received much naval gunfire or any close air support, common in the Pacific in mid-1944.

The essential American problem revolved around two airborne division commanders (both eventually chiefs of staff, US Army) and their willingness to pressure Bradley and, to a lesser degree, Collins into approving an overly ambitious plan based on heroic assumptions about IX Troop Carrier Command and their own parachute regiments. The plan wasted the 507th and 508th Parachute Infantry Regiments (82nd Division) and allocated at least one regiment too few to the capture of Carentan. Clearing the four beach exits received too much emphasis; naval gunfire, close air support, and the US 8th Regimental Combat Team and its attached tank battalion could and did force three of four beach exits, only one with a serious fight shared with the paratroopers. Future planning, for example Operation MARKET in Holland, September 1944, reflected the lessons of Normandy: flak suppression by tactical aircraft, the earlier introduction of big gliders with artillery and anti-tank guns, and a drop in broad daylight with more effective terminal guidance in more hospitable landing zones. This time the planning errors would be British – Montgomery's and "Boy" Browning's to be precise – and the cost at Arnhem worse than D-Day. Learning remained an early casualty in war.

Chapter 10

"Their road will be long and hard"

(President Franklin D Roosevelt's prayer to the nation, June 6, 1944)
"Their road will be long and hard. For the enemy is strong. He may hurl back our forces. Success may not come with rushing speed. But we shall return again and again."

The push inland

Ronald J Drez

On the morning of June 7, the Allied High Command assessed the results of the previous day's invasion. Nowhere had any of the units achieved all their ambitious D-Day objectives. The British Second Army was ashore at GOLD, JUNO, and SWORD beaches, but the key city of Caen was still very much in German hands, as was Carpiquet Airport to the west, both important D-Day objectives. Only the British 50th Northumbrian Division and the Canadian 3rd Division had linked their flanks. Elsewhere the invasion forces remained confined in isolated enclaves.

The dispersion of the forces of the First US Army to the west was the most severe. The attack at OMAHA Beach had been a very close call, and the dead still littered the beaches, testament to the ferocious fight of the preceding day. The American lodgement was narrow indeed. The forces of V Corps at OMAHA were isolated from the British 50th Division to the east and from the American VII Corps to the west on the Cotentin Peninsula.

The forces of VII Corps now faced a two-fold task. First, to link up with V Corps, and second, to attack to the north, away from the main German forces, to seize the critical port of Cherbourg. To do this they would have to cut the neck of the peninsula all the way to the Atlantic in the west. The OVERLORD invasion could succeed only if the Allied Army built up rapidly and poured in supplies. Each infantry division required 400 tons a day to remain effective, and each armored division 1,200. Providing such supplies required a deep-water port, and Cherbourg was the only one in the invasion area. The lack of port facilities had originally worked to the Allies' advantage in deceiving the Germans that Normandy was not the invasion site, but now that the invasion was ashore, the advantage had shifted to the Germans. An Allied Army in short supply, unable to attack and maneuver, was an army the defenders could bottle up and stall. The end result would be stalemate and possibly the beginning of trench warfare, as had happened in World War I.

TAKING CARENTAN

The attack to link up VII Corps from UTAH Beach with V Corps at OMAHA Beach would have to come through the town of Carentan, which stood like a wedge between the American flanks. So important was this strategic town that General Omar Bradley, First Army commander, was ready to smash it into oblivion:

"Put 500 or even 1,000 tons of air on Carentan and take the town apart," he said to Major General Lawton Collins, commanding VII Corps. "Then rush in and you'll get it."[1]

OPPOSITE After a hard battle for Carentan, soldiers sleep in a doorway. (IWM 480705)

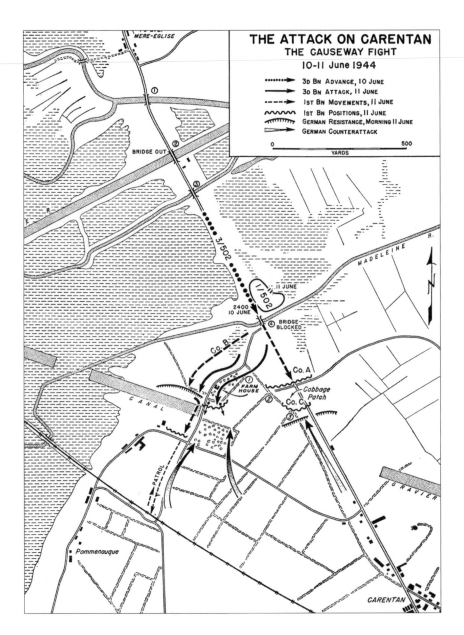

THE ATTACK ON CARENTAN
THE CAUSEWAY FIGHT
10–11 June 1944

Rushing in and getting it was more easily said than done. An attack on Carentan would have to be delivered by the 101st Airborne forces holding St-Côme-du-Mont to the north. The attack would be a commander's nightmare, down the macadam road that was Route National 13, and restricted to the narrow highway itself, rising just above the flooded land on either side. The flooding was part of the successful German plan to restrict Allied infantry maneuvers.

"The causeway was a raised roadway with marshland on either side," said trooper Ken Cordry. "In the marshes were small raised areas that concealed German machine-gun nests."[2]

Adding to the difficulties of the restricted assault were four bridges along the highway approaching Carentan. The retreating Germans had blown the second bridge, but airborne engineers had moved material up to repair the 12-foot gap. To the north of Carentan, the youthful 6th German Parachute Regiment was well positioned to defend the town. Under the command of Lt. Col. August von der Heydte, the 6th Regiment was well-trained and devoted to the Führer, although its soldiers were not quite 18 years old. They were also undetected in their position. American intelligence reported that Carentan had been evacuated.

The 101st Airborne's attack of Carentan began at 12:15a.m., June 11; the 3rd Battalion of Lt. Col. Robert G. Cole led the way. Down the moonlit causeway went the Screaming Eagles, as if marching down a bowling lane. To each man, the sound of his footsteps seemed magnified on the hard-surfaced road. The paratroopers crossed the first bridge without incident.

By 1:30a.m. the squad at the point of the column reached the second bridge, and by the light of the moon discovered that, although the repair material was stacked nearby, the bridge had not been repaired. Instead, the soldiers found a small boat and crossed the stream, three at a time, bathed in uncomfortable moonlight. The squad made its way past the third bridge without incident and approached the fourth, where the German defenders had positioned an iron Belgian Gate across the road. It could only be prized open 18 inches, forcing the men to squeeze through one by one. Fifty yards past the gate, the well-positioned German paratroopers opened fire, pinning the small American patrol down and finally forcing it to withdraw at 5:30a.m.

Back at Bridge #2, Lt. Col. Cole used the repair material to improvise a shaky footbridge over the missing span. He began his attack in the early afternoon. His men were strung out over the length of the highway and moved low, mostly along the small slopes of the road embankment, to avoid enemy fire. By the time the head of the column began slipping through the Belgian Gate at Bridge #4, the end of the battalion was 700 yards to the rear, still at Bridge #2. American artillery poured fire into German positions for six hours to cover the dangerous man-by-man passage through the Belgian Gate, but despite that support, German mortars and machine guns blasted the Americans. Then the Germans unleashed another weapon.

To the soldiers of the 101st, accustomed to seeing Allied aircraft flying unopposed in the Normandy skies, the sudden appearance of two German planes was a shock. The attacking aircraft pounded the men on the confining road. Company I alone lost 25 percent of its men.

"Two German dive bombers came down and bombed us," said Ken Cordry. "One strafed the river bank and the other attacked the troops on the road. I was sent out on a litter-bearing detail. Most of the men had been hit in the back and buttocks."[3]

By 4:00a.m., however, three of Cole's companies had managed to successfully negotiate the Belgian Gate and deploy on the south side of the bridge on both sides of the highway. To the right side was a large farmhouse rising above the flooded fields and surrounded by hedgerows. Inside, the young German paratroopers of von der Heydte's force waited for the Americans.

Company H attacked toward the farmhouse and into the hornets' nest. Machine guns, rifle fire, and mortar fire greeted the attackers, and even Lt. Col. Cole's supporting artillery fire seemed to have little effect on the German gunners smothering his men with deadly fire. Company H's attack withered. Cole moved with the hard-hit company watching the German forces shred his line and considered withdrawing, but a withdrawal would be more dangerous than his approach. To withdraw, each man would have to renegotiate the Belgian Gate with German guns zeroed on the constricting spot. It would become a massacre. Cole decided that retreat was not the answer. Locating Major John Stopka, his executive officer, he issued his order to attack:

"We're going to get some artillery smoke on that goddamn farmhouse," said Cole. "Then we're going to make a bayonet charge!"[4]

His exec blinked with disbelief, but passed the word to the scattered men of Company H, and soon the two officers heard the distinctive clicks of bayonets snapping onto rifle muzzles. But the order for the bayonet charge remained unheard by many of the soldiers who were out of earshot or deafened by the din of battle.

At 6:15a.m. the smoke rounds began impacting in an arc around the farmhouse. Gripping his whistle and pistol, Colonel Cole waited to signal his 250-man charge. At the proper moment, the whistle shrieked in the air and Cole was off at a run. As he turned to encourage his men on, he was shocked to see that only 70 men followed Major Stopka and him, but the charge did not stop. The charge surprised the other paratroopers who had not heard the order, but upon seeing their comrades rise up with fixed bayonets, many clamored after the charging colonel. The momentum of the charge swept across the field towards the farmhouse and broke the German defense. Despite fierce German resistance and counterattack after the charge, the enemy was not able to dislodge the Americans, and follow-up forces strengthened

Cole's attack and smashed into Carentan. On June 12 the city was liberated. UTAH Beach had linked with OMAHA Beach.

For his conduct in leading the bayonet charge that cracked the German defense, Colonel Robert G. Cole was awarded the Medal of Honor. It was presented to him posthumously since he was killed in action in Holland on September 19. Major John Stopka received the Distinguished Service Cross but, like Cole, did not survive the war.

BRIDGING THE MERDERET RIVER

The task of securing a bridgehead across the Merderet River fell to the 82nd Airborne Division. If that bridgehead could be secured then it would be possible to launch a further attack to cut the neck of the Cotentin Peninsula. The Merderet River was five miles west of Ste-Mère-Eglise, which had been liberated on D-Day. The Merderet River, normally a small flowing body of water, was in full flood as a result of the German control of the locks that regulated the twice-daily high tides from the Channel. By leaving the locks open, the rush of water filled the rivers and drains to overflowing. The flooding stretched 500 to 1,000 yards past the normal banks, turning the entire area into a marshland.

On June 9, after a failed attempt to secure the La Fiére bridgehead by crossing the flooded area north of the bridge, General Gavin, the Assistant Division Commander of the 82nd Airborne, decided to force the crossing of the Merderet at the bridge itself. The attack would cross the bridge from the east but would then face difficult progress down a 500-yard causeway between the flooded fields. Like the attack on the Carentan causeway, the 82nd soldiers would be exposed to German fire while in a virtual single-file attack formation.

Defending the west bank of the Merderet, at the end of the causeway, was the German 1057th Grenadier Regiment occupying positions on relatively high ground and in the buildings of nearby villages. Supporting the American attack would be 12 Sherman tanks and the artillery of the 90th Infantry Division. The spearhead of the bridge attack would be the 82nd Airborne Division's glidermen of the 2nd Battalion, 325th Regiment. General Gavin recognized that the attack would be daunting, because unlike the similar approach to Carentan, there would be no welcomed concealment under cover of darkness. The glidermen would cross La Fière Bridge and the ensuing 500-yard causeway in daylight, on the dead run, in full view of the German defenders.

Gavin scheduled the attack for 10:45a.m., to be preceded by a 15-minute artillery preparation. Taking positions a few hundred yards east of the

La Fière bridgehead.
(Courtesy, U.S. Army
Military History Institute)

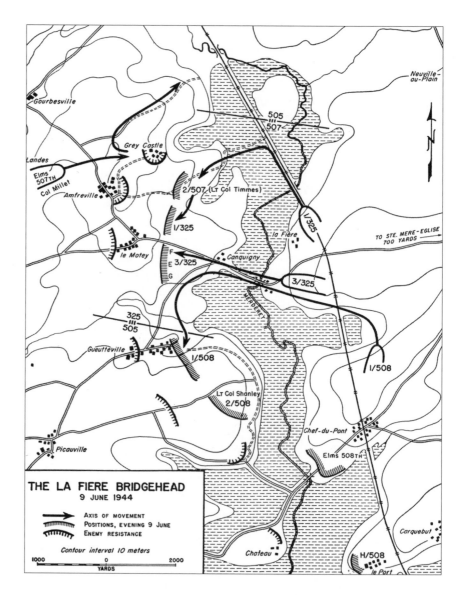

bridge, with their barrels just clearing a hedgerow, the 12 Sherman tanks
lined up abreast almost track to track, and when the first artillery rounds
impacted on the German defensive positions, the Shermans fired point
blank into the enemy lines like a ship delivering a broadside. Mortars,
rifles, and machine guns in the area of the bridge also lent the weight of
their fire to the bombardment. At 10:30a.m. the west bank of the Merderet
disappeared under a shroud of smoke and fire. For 15 minutes the fearful
barrage enveloped the German defenses. The last rounds to fall were
phosphorus rounds, meant to provide billowing smoke to conceal the

glidermen's charge across La Fière. But the smoke was slightly off-target, and not concentrated, and the veil was thin. The charging glidermen were not concealed from German eyes.

The demanding 500-yard run under mortar and machine-gun fire left Company G with only a few men unscathed as they reached the west end. The heavy casualties and sprawled bodies became obstacles on the causeway, and created hesitation among the soldiers who were following. That hesitation slowed the charge, causing a traffic jam, and making the German fire more effective. A tank, attempting to cross, struck a mine and further blocked the narrow causeway.

Company E, following Company G, arrived at the far end of the bridge, with its ranks terribly thinned, and swept to the right. Company F charged behind E and jammed into the pocket that had become the western bridgehead. On the east bank, General Gavin, confused by the smoke, congestion, and retreating wounded, assumed the attack had faltered. He ordered a reserve paratrooper company across, further jamming the tiny bridgehead.

Despite all setbacks, the Americans managed to push into a small town at the far end of the causeway and commanded some high ground. But luck was still not with the Americans, as friendly artillery pounded the town, still thinking it was in enemy hands, and forced the soldiers to give up their hard-won ground. By late afternoon, however, the three companies of glidermen had formed a hasty defensive line and repulsed a German counterattack. By sheer tenacity, the glidermen and paratroopers had carved out a bridgehead on the west end of La Fière causeway.

This bridgehead over the Merderet River became the springboard for the continued drive to the Atlantic, and the 90th Division passed through 82nd Airborne lines to press the attack against the enemy. Four days later, however, the 90th Division gains were scant, measured in yards, especially as the fighting shifted into the hedgerows. The slow progress and high casualties led to the relieving of the division commander and several of his subordinates.

NORMANDY'S HEDGEROWS

The tentativeness of the 90th Division had, in part, been due to the difficulties of fighting in hedgerows or *bocage*. These man-made barriers, dating back to Roman times, had been constructed to divide fields and served as fencing for grazing livestock. But their construction was perfectly suited to aid defending forces. A solid earthen embankment, almost trapezoidal in shape with steep faces, formed the base of the hedgerow. That base rose from three to six feet and was topped with

This photo clearly shows how claustrophobic the *bocage* could be, and the natural defensive positions it provided.

impenetrable branches and tangled growth. In many areas the hedges grew to a height of 20 feet and often arched over the road to meet the opposite hedge, forming a canopy that blocked out the sun. A soldier trapped on a road flanked by hedgerows could move only forward or backward. Small openings in the hedgerow, permitting entry into the enclosed field, were always covered by enemy fire. The road became a sunken passage and a very dangerous place to be.

"Normandy had no fences," said PFC Adolf Rogosch with the German 352nd Division. "They [the hedges] blocked the view in all directions, and we received specialized training for combat there. It all looked the same. Everywhere you looked, four lines of hedges criss-crossed one another. It played tricks on your eyes. We trained to fight there as individual soldiers. We caused the Americans heavy losses there because they had to come toward us and could not deploy their tanks because of the hedges."[5]

Despite such obstacles, the 82nd Airborne and the fresh 9th Division passed through 90th Division and continued the attack. In the face of fierce resistance, they hacked and fought their way through the dug-in German forces in the drive to the west. Five days later, the Americans finally reached the west coast overlooking the Atlantic. On June 18, they had cut the 18-mile wide Contentin Peninsula and turned to the north, toward Cherbourg and its vital port.

SEIZING CHERBOURG

The German forces north of the American line were trapped between that line and the sea that surrounded them on three sides. Major General J. Lawton "Lightning Joe" Collins proved worthy of his nickname by launching his VII Corps attack toward Cherbourg within 24 hours of cutting the Peninsula. His attack occurred, however, at the same time as a massive attack launched against Allied supplies and shipping. It was not a German attack, but an attack of nature. A tremendous storm formed in the English Channel and pounded and battered Allied vessels, shipping, and unloading facilities. The newly installed MULBERRY

Lt. Gen. Karl Wilhelm von Schlieben, Commander Cherbourg Military Garrison, is shown surrendering to General J. "Lightning Joe" Collins of the 7th US Army Corps at General Collins' HQ. The capture of Cherbourg on June 27, 1944, by US forces turned the Normandy bridgehead into a solid front. (IWM OWIL 27884)

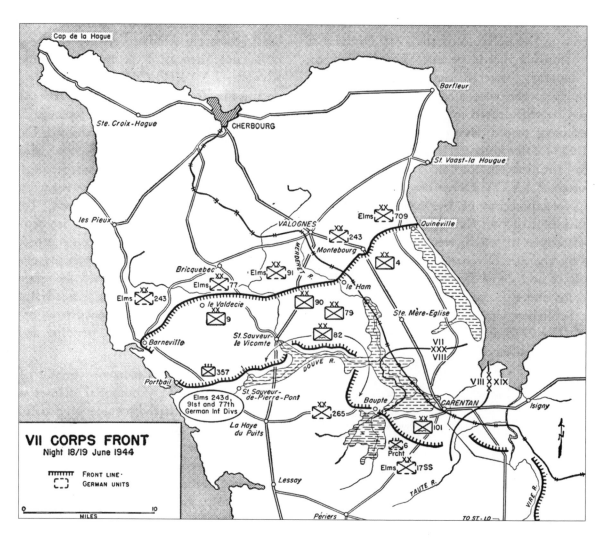

VII Corps Front on the night of June 18/19, 1944. (Courtesy, U.S. Army Military History Institute)

harbors at OMAHA and Arromanches received the full force of the most severe storm in 40 years.

When it was over, the MULBERRY at OMAHA was completely destroyed and the one at Arromanches was gravely damaged. Over 800 craft of various types had been sunk or hurled and smashed onto the coastline. Even in their wildest expectations the German Navy could not have delivered such a crippling blow against the Allies. All unloading was stopped. The attacking forces ashore were limited to the supplies and ammunition on hand. The air forces were grounded.

The damage resulting from the great storm added an extra urgency to VII Corps' attack to seize the port of Cherbourg, and General Collins drove his three-division attack forward. Sweeping aside

German resistance at Montebourg and several critical crossroads, VII Corps pressed inexorably ahead. Allied air pounded the German forces in defensive positions and along the roads retreating toward Cherbourg. Sherman tanks accompanied VII Corps infantry and delivered machine-gun and cannon fire into sparse hedgerows and pockets of resistance.

The German defenders fell back into Cherbourg. They were doomed. VII Corps encircled the city. On June 24, Lieutenant General Karl Wilhelm von Schlieben radioed higher headquarters from his command post in the besieged city. His situation was desperate:

"Communications to several battalions no longer available," he signaled. "Phosphorous shell has put eight batteries out of action. Tomorrow heavier enemy attack expected…"

Then as if to express the total hopelessness of the situation, he concluded: "Completely crushed by artillery fire."[6]

Fortress Cherbourg surrendered on June 27. VII Corp casualties numbered 22,000. German killed and wounded were not known but 39,000 prisoners surrendered. The port had been shattered by German demolitions. Although the Americans had expected damage, the destruction was beyond belief. American engineers called it: "beyond a doubt the most complete, intensive, and best-planned demolition job in history."[7]

FAILURE AT VILLERS-BOCAGE

The British attack on the left flank of the OVERLORD invasion area had successfully gained lodgement on GOLD, JUNO, and SWORD beaches, but moving inland against the German defenders had proved difficult. Stiff resistance held the British 3rd Division away from the city of Caen.

By June 9, Field Marshal Montgomery had conceded that to launch a frontal assault to take Caen was to invite a military disaster in men and materiel. "I have decided not to have a lot of casualties by butting up against the place," he said.[8]

Instead, Montgomery planned a double envelopment of the ancient city. He would attempt to squeeze the German defenders in a pincer movement thus bringing about a decisive victory, but just as he began his June 10 attack, the Germans also attacked and engaged the British paratrooper forces holding the bridgehead to the east. Although the British airborne defeated the attack on June 12, Rommel's attack had blunted and upset Montgomery's plan.

On June 10 the left pincer was defeated by elements of the German 21st Panzer Division. With the center of the German line anchored by

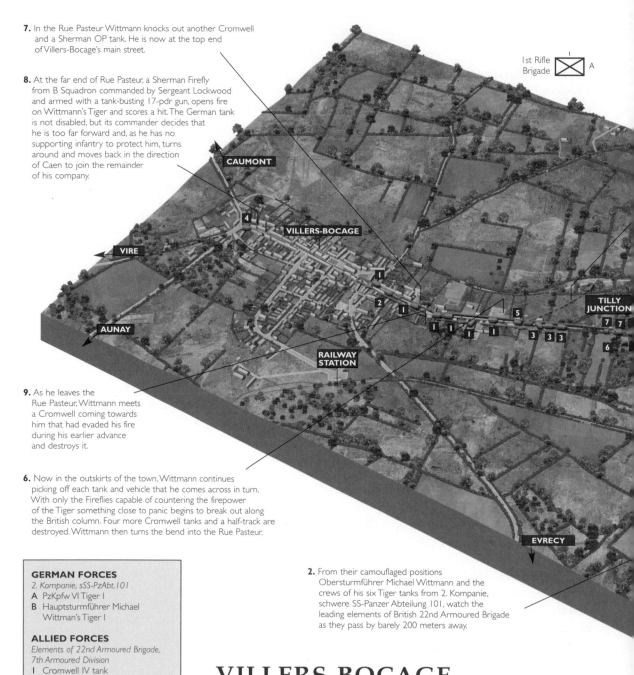

7. In the Rue Pasteur Wittmann knocks out another Cromwell and a Sherman OP tank. He is now at the top end of Villers-Bocage's main street.

8. At the far end of Rue Pasteur, a Sherman Firefly from B Squadron commanded by Sergeant Lockwood and armed with a tank-busting 17-pdr gun, opens fire on Wittmann's Tiger and scores a hit. The German tank is not disabled, but its commander decides that he is too far forward and, as he has no supporting infantry to protect him, turns around and moves back in the direction of Caen to join the remainder of his company.

1st Rifle Brigade — A

CAUMONT

VILLERS-BOCAGE

VIRE

TILLY JUNCTION

AUNAY

RAILWAY STATION

9. As he leaves the Rue Pasteur, Wittmann meets a Cromwell coming towards him that had evaded his fire during his earlier advance and destroys it.

EVRECY

6. Now in the outskirts of the town, Wittmann continues picking off each tank and vehicle that he comes across in turn. With only the Fireflies capable of countering the firepower of the Tiger something close to panic begins to break out along the British column. Four more Cromwell tanks and a half-track are destroyed. Wittmann then turns the bend into the Rue Pasteur.

GERMAN FORCES
2. Kompanie, sSS-PzAbt.101
A PzKpfw VI Tiger I
B Hauptsturmführer Michael Wittman's Tiger I

ALLIED FORCES
Elements of 22nd Armoured Brigade, 7th Armoured Division
1 Cromwell IV tank
2 M4 Sherman tank
3 Stuart light tank
4 Sherman Firefly (17-pdr)
5 Half-track
6 6-pdr anti-tank gun
7 Lloyd carrier

2. From their camouflaged positions Obersturmführer Michael Wittmann and the crews of his six Tiger tanks from 2. Kompanie, schwere SS-Panzer Abteilung 101, watch the leading elements of British 22nd Armoured Brigade as they pass by barely 200 meters away.

VILLERS-BOCAGE

June 12, 1944, 8:55a.m.–9:10a.m., viewed from the southeast showing 2. Kompanie, schwere SS-Panzer Abteilung 101's devastating attack on the leading elements of 22nd Armoured Brigade, around the small market town of Villers-Bocage.

10. Near the junction with the road to Tilly, men of the 1st Rifle Brigade have got one of their 6-pdr anti-tank guns working and fire a shot at Wittmann's Panzer. The shell hits the Tiger's running gear and immobilizes it, forcing Wittmann and his crew to abandon the tank. They make off to the north towards the Panzer Lehr Division's positions near Orbois.

5. Wittmann's Tiger reaches the junction with the road to Tilly after devastating the line of transport vehicles backed up along the highway. His tank's high explosive shells have smashed through eight half-tracks, four personnel carriers and two 6-pdr anti-tank guns. Near the junction he goes on to attack and destroy three Stuart light tanks.

1. Tanks from A Squadron, 4th County of London Yeomanry, and mobile infantry from 'A' Company, 1st Rifle Brigade, advance towards Point 213 along the Villers-Bocage–Caen road.

4. Wittmann knocks out a Sherman Firefly and a Cromwell tank and then turns south, driving down the road attacking a line of infantry transport as he goes.

Y SUR SEULLES

4th
CLY [I / ⬭] A Sqn.

11. Around Point 213, the remaining Tigers from Wittmann's company deal with the tanks and men of 4th County of London Yeomanry, knocking out five Cromwells and a Sherman Firefly and capturing 30 men. A Squadron has been completely wiped out.

5 5 5

POINT 213

B

I

4

I

4

I

CAEN

A

A

A A B

LES HAUTS VENTS

A

LA CIDERIE

3. 9:00a.m., Wittmann decides to attack and breaks cover, heading for the vehicles on the main road while four other Tigers from his company attack the British around Point 213. One Tiger remains immobile with engine trouble.

sSSPzAbt [I / ⬭] 2
101
WITTMANN

N

This Tiger tank lies knocked out in Villers-Bocage. (IWM B8635)

Panzer Lehr, the attack shifted to the right in an attempt to gain control of the vital crossroads town of Villers-Bocage. British control there would effectively envelop the German line and make it untenable. The attack caught the Germans completely by surprise and the British armored column rolled into the town encountering no German resistance. The decisive moment was at hand.

This early success at Villers-Bocage might have produced a spectacular victory had it not been for the brilliant tactics of one German commander acting on his own initiative without waiting for orders from higher authorities. His small force was all that stood between the British armor and German encirclement. *Obersturmführer* Michael Wittmann, commanding five Tiger tanks and one Mark IV, was entrusted to protect the exposed left flank and rear of Panzer Lehr. Wittmann's small command was the only force plugging the enormous gap on the German left flank. He was in position on June 13 to observe the column of 25 British tanks and half-tracks exit Villers-Bocage after its capture. The British column, however, stopped for further reconnaissance by the infantry, and while stationary, the tankers surprisingly dismounted from their vehicles during the lull.

Wittmann sensed the opportunity and went into action. Without trying to gather his other five tanks, he attacked, roaring down on the leading British vehicles firing his 88mm main gun. To the British, the first evidence of Wittmann's presence was the ear-splitting *crack* of his solid shot smashing into the armored side of the lead personnel carrier. It twisted sideways across the road and burst into flames. Wittmann raced his 60-ton Tiger alongside the parked column, literally firing broadsides into the unmanned vehicles leaving them crushed and burning. At the end of the column, he swung onto the main road and roared into Villers-Bocage, with his head and shoulders out of the turret, and continued his destruction on the idled tanks. Within five minutes the devastating attack was over.

But Wittmann was not finished and the German captain raced back to rearm and gather his remaining tanks. In the early afternoon he returned to the head of the column with his full force to crush the remainder of the outgunned British column. Pressing his attack on, he was finally defeated by British reinforcing armor, and Wittmann lost four of his tanks. He managed to escape on foot, but his attack had destroyed 30 tanks and armored vehicles and had halted the attempted breakthrough to Caen. Although the road to Caen and an encirclement of the German Army was now open, the British column was badly damaged and, not knowing the strength of forces to their front, withdrew.

The opportunity to envelop the German flank was gone. General Dempsey, commanding Second Army, lamented that: "Caen can be taken only by a set piece assault, and we do not have the men or ammunition for that at this time."[9]

OPERATION GOODWOOD

The failed breakthrough at Villers-Bocage was bad news, but there was more to come for the British. Early on the morning of June 13, Hitler unleashed his secret weapon. Ten V-1 rocket bombs were fired toward England. Only four of the two-ton rockets managed to reach the mainland, and only one landed in London, killing six people, but in the next 90 days Germany launched over 8,000 V-1s causing massive damage and civilian casualties.

On June 14, General Montgomery realized that he had lost the initiative and abandoned the offensive. "When the panzer division suddenly appeared in the Villers-Bocage … area, it plugged the hole through which I had broken," he said. "I had to think again not to get off balance."[10]

General Montgomery's rethink led him to the proper conclusion. He was not strong enough to break through in the east around Caen so he revised his plan. He would hold at Caen hoping to draw the German armor to his sector, and attempt to break through in the west with the American First Army. Caen would be a great hinge on which to swing the American Army.

For some reason, after having made this proper modification to his original Normandy plan, Montgomery denied that he had changed anything, steadfastly insisting that he had always planned to attack that way. Perhaps it was ego, but it drew criticism from even his supporters, strained Anglo-American relations, and forever diminished the sound thinking of his new tactic.

"Monty's talk of his original intention to hinge on Caen is absolutely balls,"[11] huffed Captain J. Hughes-Hallett of the Royal Navy, an original planner of the Normandy attack.

"It is true that he helped the attack to the west and he deserves credit for that," said Group Captain T. P. Cleave, another of the original planners. "But when he says that was his plan, he is stating his second reconsideration…The original plan was to run out great armored fingers around Caen."[12]

Regardless of when Montgomery made the decision to go on the defensive, Major Hans von Luck, commanding Panzer Grenadier Regiment 125 of the 21st Panzer Division, observed that the British had lost the initiative:

"The British began to mine themselves inside the lines they had reached. This was a sure sign … they had no intention of launching further attacks."[13] Major Luck was correct that the British Second Army had assumed a defensive strategy, but he was wrong about their tactics.

They did not sit in a defensive posture. On June 25, General Montgomery launched Operation EPSOM in yet another attempt to capture Caen. Like the previous attacks, EPSOM failed with severe losses to both sides. The 4,000 British casualties during the five-day operation were alarming, and the War Office warned that it would not be able to make up such losses past the end of July. At that point, they would have to begin cannibalizing existing divisions to fill manpower demands. Despite this dire shortage, the specter of stalemate in Normandy drove Montgomery to launch Operation CHARNWOOD, a frontal assault preceded by heavy bombing of the approaches to Caen and the city itself. Six thousand bombs pulverized the target, and the British infantry secured the northern half of the city only to be stopped with more heavy casualties by a new German line holding the southern half. As CHARNWOOD ended one day later, July 9, the Allied Army was no closer to breaking out of their lodgement than they were in mid-June.

In an effort to break the stalemate, the two Allied Army commanders, General Miles Dempsey of the British Second Army, and General Omar Bradley of the First US Army, each devised a new plan. Dempsey's plan was Operation GOODWOOD; Bradley's was Operation COBRA.

GOODWOOD would employ massive saturation bombing followed by an armored attack of 750 tanks to break the German line, outflank Caen from the east, and move into the good tank country south of the city.

"My whole eastern flank will burst into flames…"[14] Montgomery wrote enthusiastically to General Eisenhower. The Supreme Commander seemed enthusiastic about the boldness of the plan, especially since it promised something other than indecisive action leading to a dreaded stalemate. In the back of his mind was a replay of the trenches of World War I. On top of that, the press was getting impatient. Many criticized Montgomery. Others questioned when Eisenhower would move to Normandy and take over running the attack. But GOODWOOD had some serious flaws. First were the defensive minefields that von Luck had observed. Instead of being an obstacle to the Germans, they now forced the entire British armored force to single-file through a few cleared lanes, thus delaying a concentrated arrival to the attack line. Second, and most importantly, the Germans had stiffened their defenses beyond the detection of the Allies.

"We thus set up a graduated defense about 15 kilometers in depth," said Luck, "which would be able, sooner or later, to bring any enemy attack to a standstill." Allied intelligence had estimated a defensive depth only half that size.

On the morning of July 18, the attack began. Allied air crushed a narrow lane two miles wide and three miles deep. The German forces were smashed. Even some of the 60-ton tanks were turned upside down. British armor poured through the gap. The feeling of the tankers who rode unopposed through the shattered German lines was that nothing could have survived the inferno. They would soon open the way to Paris. The infantry busied itself with the task of clearing small towns on the flanks of the armored thrust. The tanks rolled forward alone. It was a bad tactic and defied the principles of mutual tank–infantry support.

"As almost always with the British," said Hans von Luck, "they carried out their tank attacks without accompanying infantry; as a result they were unable to eliminate at once any little anti-tank nests that were lying well camouflaged in woodland or behind hedges."[15]

Perhaps this squeamishness to use infantry with tanks is to be found in the terrible manpower shortage the British Army faced. General Miles Dempsey summed it up: "I was prepared to lose a couple of hundred tanks. So long as I didn't lose men."[16]

As the British juggernaut smashed forward, 32 tanks in a line, German survivors of the devastating bombing staggered from their holes. 3rd Royal Tank Regiment passed between small villages along the axis of attack.

"Very dazed and shaken infantrymen came out of the cornfields and attempted to give themselves up," said Major William H. Close commanding A Squadron. "Tank commanders waved them to the rear."[17]

The British tankers pressed on, but the further they went, the less dazed were the Germans. One Mark IV German tank suddenly appeared and was immediately knocked out, but in the distance other German vehicles scurried into position.

"Our orders were to press on," said Major Close. "The only thing we could do was fire on the move and hope to keep the enemy's heads down."[18]

The Normandy countryside now opened enough to allow the tanks of Fife and Forfar to join the leading tanks of 3rd Royal Tank Regiment, forming a formidable phalanx. Just ahead was the limit of the preparatory artillery barrage. Also to the front, standing like a signpost, was the village of Cagny. The plan of attack had designated this village as the demarcation line for the three armored divisions. 11th Armoured Division was to drive straight through, Guards Armoured Division would pass to the left, while 7th Armoured Division passed to the right. Once past Cagny, the three divisions would re-form into a massive armored "V" to smash forward. Facing this British juggernaut was Battle Group Luck commanded by Major Hans von Luck, who at that very moment was frantically riding along the forward edge of his defensive line, shocked at the sight of the approaching British armor.

"The whole area was dotted with British tanks which were slowly rolling south against no opposition," he said. "How could I plug the gap?"[19]

Major Luck raced his vehicle past the church in Cagny and skidded to a halt when he observed an 88mm Luftwaffe anti-aircraft artillery battery with its guns aimed skyward. He ran to the young captain who informed the major that he was part of the anti-aircraft ring protecting

Caen. He was now waiting for the next aircraft attack. With British tanks in full view, Luck was incredulous that the captain had not engaged the enemy armor. Luck ordered him to move to the northern edge of Cagny and attack the advancing tanks.

"Hit the enemy from the flank. In that way you'll force the advance to a halt," ordered the German major. The captain's answer was astounding. "Major, my concern is enemy planes, fighting tanks is your job. I'm Luftwaffe."

As the captain started to turn away, Luck drew his pistol and aimed it at him and said, "Either you're a dead man or you can earn yourself a medal."[20]

The captain placed his four guns in an apple orchard. The surrounding corn in the fields was so high that it offered good concealment. The barrels just cleared the leafy tops. Most of the armor of Battle Group Luck had been destroyed or damaged by the bombing, but the force still had three anti-tank sections ready for action on the right flank and the four Luftwaffe guns in Cagny. Luck's only hope was to hold with those meager forces until reserves could be brought up.

Wireless operator Werner Kortenhaus, 21st Panzer Division, best described the British attack: "When the enemy tanks came rolling at us, wave after wave, we knew there was no more hope here. A short struggle, and four of our tanks were destroyed, five simply overrun, the crews taken prisoner."[21]

3rd Royal Tank Regiment was the first to come into the range of Luck's anti-tank guns. The British tankers could observe movement in the orchards and German gunners frantically getting into position.

"Opening fire at almost point blank range, they hit three of my tanks which burst into flames; and I could see the squadron on my left also had several tanks burning furiously,"[22] said Major W. H. Close.

On the left, the tanks of Fife and Forfar went off the air. Thirty-four of its tanks were aflame. A follow-up squadron immediately came under devastating fire forcing the remainder to withdraw.

"The whole area was ablaze," said wireless operator G. H. Marstan of the Grenadier Guards, "tanks on fire and abandoned, carriers, half-tracks, motor vehicles, all knocked out."[23]

In Cagny, the Luftwaffe flak battery engaged the British tanks. "The 8.8cm cannons were firing one salvo after another," said Major Luck. "One could see the shots flying through the corn like torpedoes. In the extensive cornfields to the north of the village stood at least 40 British tanks, on fire or shot up."[24]

The armored attack stopped. During the afternoon of July 19, German reinforcements plugged the line. General Montgomery terminated

Operation GOODWOOD on July 20, having failed to break through. Dempsey had lost over 400 tanks and had not minimized his human losses, suffering over 5,000 casualties. On that same day, an assassin's bomb failed to kill Adolf Hitler at his headquarters in Rastenburg in East Prussia.

OPERATION COBRA

Operation COBRA was General Omar Bradley's attempt to break the German line. COBRA would be the culmination of the series of American attacks that had begun with the beach invasion followed by the attack to cut the Cotentin Peninsula, and the attack on Cherbourg. Until Cherbourg was captured, the American lines facing the German defenses to the south had remained static. Now General Omar Bradley's First Army prepared to attack to the south and gain maneuver room to launch COBRA.

The problem was that the land in front of the army had been flooded in many places by the Germans during their occupation, to prevent possible enemy maneuver. The Vire River and its associated Taute–Vire Canal, running generally north to south, formed natural obstacles requiring any attack to be confined between those two bodies of water. Numerous drainage canals also criss-crossed the area. But the major obstacle confronting First Army was the maze of hedgerows enclosing the hundreds of tiny farm fields in the French countryside. A close analysis of aerial photographs revealed a staggering 4,000 hedges in an area two miles deep and less than four miles wide.

Because of these obstacles, General Bradley had no room to maneuver and very limited use of his armor. His soldiers would have to conduct frontal assaults, giving the advantage to the German defense. Offsetting these severe restrictions was total Allied air supremacy. Like prowling falcons, the P-47 fighter-bombers attacked all German movement. Supplies and reinforcements could approach only at night.

"We drove only at night to get into the battle," said Corporal Friedrich Bertenrath, 2nd SS Panzer Division. "The vehicles had small light slits at the front. We could not use the headlights, so someone stood on the front of the vehicle to tell the driver where to go. On the back of the vehicle hung a white handkerchief so that the car behind could get an idea where the car ahead was going."[25]

During daylight hours, tiny spotting aircraft called down thunderous artillery and naval gunfire on enemy concentrations and muzzle flashes. It rained down in such profusion that the German soldiers called it "steel weather."

A Panzer Lehr Panther tank, badly damaged by the carpet-bombing that preceded Operation COBRA.

"The American weapons superiority was so great," said Captain Gunter Materne, commanding a battery of Artillery Regiment 363, "that I told my second-in-command that we'd be knocked back to the Siegfried Line."[26]

The German term for the American fighter-bomber was *Jager-bomber*. The German soldiers shortened the plural to *Jabos* and the *Jabos* were their scourge. Eighteen-year-old Gunther Behr, a radioman with Artillery Regiment 363, was 12 miles from the coast:

"We arrived at our position," he said. "We were attacked by *Jabos*, then by artillery. A shell landed in front of the horses. The first two deaths I saw were horses. That was our welcome to battle. That was my first contact with the war – a *Jabo* attack."[27]

The American First Army began its attack with three corps abreast. VIII Corps was to the west, VII Corps in the center, and XIX Corps to the east. On July 3, VIII Corps attacked. For three days, the soldiers slugged it out with determined Germans for little gain. On July 4, VII Corps attacked on land virtually surrounded by flooded fields. The Germans had organized a strong defense across the narrow dry land between the flooded areas and after three days of hard fighting, VII Corps also reported little gain. On July 7, XIX Corps tested the German line. Its objective was the crossroads town of St-Lô, 12 miles south of Carentan. Although the German line was substantial, the main enemies were mud and hedgerows. But by July 10, the German Panzer Lehr Division had moved to confront XIX Corps and attacked the following day. The initial onslaught broke the American lines and German forces were suddenly a mile deep. The German success was, however, short lived and American tank destroyers and Allied air forces counterattacked to seal off the breaks forced by the Tiger and Panther tanks.

"Twelve Panthers were caught out there when the gun destroyed the first few and the last one," said Major Helmut Ritgen commanding 2nd Battalion, Panzer Lehr Regiment 130. "The Americans proceeded to destroy practically a fourth of our fighting power."[28]

Artillery and air prevented German exploitation of the original success. The attack failed and Panzer Lehr was forced onto the defense. The Americans quickly continued their relentless attack, pushing the weakened German forces slowly backward. The renewed offensive

A modified tank with "teeth," for destroying hedgerows. (NARA)

was on a 10-mile front into the heart of the hedgerow country. The Americans planned to use newly discovered tactics to deal with the hedgerows. Infantry, tanks, and engineers combined to attack these natural defensive positions. Engineers modified tanks, welding two long iron prongs to the front. The infantry first seized the front face of the hedgerow and the tank penetrated its prongs into the earthen base. Upon retraction, the engineers packed the holes with explosives and detonated them. The Germans also had tactics to defend in the hedgerows. In the beginning, the American tanks had to climb the hedge embankments, thus exposing the underbelly to anti-tank fire. Now the tank could blast through to enter the enclosed field.

"We had two pairs of machine guns on either side," said PFC Adolf Rogosch. "We let them come forward and cross the hedge, then we blew them apart."[29]

"The tiny dirt roads and the large hedges everywhere provided good cover from air attacks,"[30] added Corporal Friedrich Bertenrath.

The tank–infantry–engineer teams began to attack the hedgerows on July 11. Explosives blasted a gap in the hedgerow, the Sherman tank roared through and fired its 75mm gun into each of the far corners of the field, and its .30 caliber machine gun sprayed the rest of the enclosure. The infantry poured in and cleared and secured the small field, and the engineers came forward to select the next spot to blast. And on it went, one after another. The hedgerows became killing fields.

Each was different. Some were not defended, but the infantryman didn't know that until he entered it. Most of the fields were attacked by infantry without tanks. That meant hacking through the hedge and entering one man at a time. No-one wanted to be first through.

Such was the fighting of First Army in its drive for St-Lô. The infantry inched forward through the mazes. The artillery bludgeoned the next series of fields, and the infantry again attacked. *Jabos* pounced on the retreating enemy targets. The German commander futilely requested that German air attack: "particularly obnoxious artillery observation planes, and the heavy bombers and the light bombers, at least once in a while."[31] He said that it was sure to boost morale.

On July 19, XIX Corps forced the German defenders to retreat to a new defensive line south of the city of St-Lô. The hedgerows and close combat finally came to an end. It had cost the Corps 11,000 casualties for the five miles gained in the two-week attack, but it gave General Bradley the room he needed to launch Operation COBRA.

COBRA began badly on July 25, with the massive bombardment by bombers of the Eight and Ninth Air Forces dropping 3,400 tons of bombs on enemies and friendlies alike. There were 600 American casualties.

American troops move through a hole punched in the hedgerow by a dozer tank on July 25, 1944.

"It was hell," said General Bayerlein, commanding Panzer Lehr. "The planes kept coming overhead like a conveyor belt, and the bomb carpets came down, now ahead, now on the right, now on the left."[32]

Reporter Ernie Pyle described the bombers. "Their march across the sky was slow and studied. I've never known anything that had about it the aura of such a ghastly relentlessness."[33]

Following the bombing, 50,000 artillery rounds smashed into the German defensive line. "When the banging and smashing finally stopped, I looked out of the bunker," said Major Joachim Barth, commanding Anti-Tank Battalion 130. "The world had changed. There were no leaves on the trees. In some cases, our tanks were stuck in holes; in others, the big guns had tipped over."[34]

"My front lines looked like a landscape on the moon, and at least 70 percent of my personnel were out of action – dead, wounded, crazed, or numbed," said General Bayerlein. "All my front line tanks were knocked out."[35]

Six days later, on July 31, the American First Army broke out of its Normandy confinement.

Chapter 11

"With unbelieving eyes"

(Franz Gockel, 726th Infantry Regiment, German 716th Infantry Division)
*"With unbelieving eyes we could recognize individual landing craft.
The hail of shells falling on us grew heavier, sending fountains of sand
and debris into the air."*

The German experience

Professor Russell Hart

D-Day represented one of the most titanic military confrontations in human history, and the experience left an indelible impression on the German soldiers that survived the Allied invasion on June 6, 1944. The experiences of these *landser* differed enormously depending on location, branch of service, rank, and assigned mission. For many of the German conscripts stationed in Normandy, D-Day represented their first real experience of combat. For most of the *Ostkämpfer* – the experienced Eastern Front veterans – this was their first encounter with the Western Allies. For months the German Army in the West – the *Westheer* – had been expecting this day. But no amount of training could prepare grenadiers, gunners, panzer commanders, pilots, sailors, and officers alike for the shocking awe that accompanied their first encounters with the fully arrayed military might of the Western Allies.

THE ABWEHR PREDICTS THE INVASION

During the evening of June 5, 1944, a group of German military intelligence officers in Paris were sitting huddled around a radio listening to messages being broadcast by the BBC. There was an expectant tension in the air: the officers were waiting for lines from the poem "Autumn Song" by French poet Paul Verlaine. German military intelligence – the Abwehr – had recently interrogated a Maquis leader who knew how the Allies intended to alert the French Resistance to the impending invasion. Under torture he had revealed the truth: the alert would come in the guise of a two-part coded message contained in the lines of the Verlaine poem. Since then the radio intercept officers had learned the poem's opening lines by heart. They had gasped when the BBC had broadcast the first line of the verse – "*Les sanglots longs des violins de l'automne*" – on June 1, indicating that the invasion was imminent. When they heard the second line "*Blessent mon Coeur d'une langueur monotone*" at 11:15p.m. on June 5, they exulted, since they believed that this information would help the Germans to defeat the Allied landings. Unfortunately, the Abwehr did not know precisely when and most importantly, where, the Allies would land.

The Abwehr headquarters immediately alerted all army, navy, and air force high commands in the West before midnight that the invasion was at hand. But at the palatial headquarters of Army Group B (tasked with defending northern and western France) at La Roche-Guyon, the information was received with derision. The notion that the Allies would announce the invasion on the BBC seemed preposterous to senior German commanders, and the warning was discounted as enemy disinformation. Only in the Pas de Calais – deemed the most likely invasion

OPPOSITE German Army prisoners of war. (Public Archives of Canada)

site by the German High Command – did the defending German Fifteenth Army go on high alert on the initiative of its commander, *Generaloberst* von Salmuth. Unknowingly, the Germans had already wasted the single most important piece of intelligence that confirmed the imminence of the Allied landings. The Germans threw away this early advantage, and no one in Normandy received the alert.

SOMETHING IS AFOOT...

Thus, it was not until the early hours of June 6 that the first tangible signs that an invasion was afoot began to emerge. Around 1:00a.m June 6, Colonel Paul Frank, a regimental commander in the 346th Infantry Division stationed south-west of Le Havre, received an alert from the LXXXI Corps headquartered at Rouen. Corps informed Frank that enemy parachutists were landing in the sector of its left neighbor, the 711th Infantry Division, which defended the coast between the Orne and Touques Rivers in eastern Normandy. Reports of massive air activity and parachute landings led Colonel Frank to conclude that the invasion was underway. However, where was the enemy going to land? Frank, like so many other German officers, got this crucial answer wrong. He continued to believe that the enemy would land astride Le Havre in order to capture quickly a port – a strategic imperative for a successful landing, as Frank logically perceived. He thus concluded that the paratroop drops were intended to provide flank protection for the invasion. In this regard he was right, but the flank those British airborne troops were trying to protect faced the other direction – west, not east as Frank assumed. The port the Allies sought was not the strongly defended Le Havre, but the less well-defended Cherbourg on the northern tip of the Cotentin Peninsula. At no time did Frank think that the Allies would land on the beaches of the Baie de Caen, since it had no major port.

Frank informed corps headquarters in Rouen of his premonitions. But the corps commander – *General der Panzertruppen* Adolf Küntzen – scoffed at the idea that the invasion was on. The corps believed that what they were experiencing were diversionary landings intended to deflect German attention from a major attack that would follow in the Pas de Calais, where the Channel was much narrower and the distance to the Reich much shorter. If the Allies landed in Normandy, they would have to fight their way across the whole of France – a landing in Normandy made no strategic sense. Küntzen would be one of many who would make that same mistake that day. Instead, Küntzen ordered Frank to mount local counterattacks where necessary to mop up the enemy but not to get embroiled in pitched battles, so that the division could be rapidly committed against the real landing soon to materialize in the Pas de Calais. Thus another opportunity for rapid, vigorous countermeasures slipped through German hands.

IS NORMANDY THE TARGET?

During those same early morning hours, a dozen miles further east, *Generalleutnant* Joseph Reichert of the neighboring 711th Infantry Division probably became the first German officer to discern correctly the Allied intent to invade Normandy. The divisional commander and his

The main landing zone of the glider elements of the 6th Airborne Division near Ranville, east of the Orne River. It was scattered elements of this formation that unsuccessfully attacked *Generalleutnant* Reichert's 711th Infantry Division headquarters in the early morning hours of D-Day. (IWM CL 59)

staff were enjoying a relaxing drink of Norman calvados – a strong apple brandy that many German occupation troops had come to appreciate – in the Officers' Mess after a long day of anti-invasion training and fortification work, when a flight of planes flew very low over the command bunker. These planes were silhouetted intermittently against the full moon during breaks in the dark storm clouds that shrouded the coastline. Reichert immediately returned to the command bunker and grabbed his pistol. Dashing back outside he saw enemy paratroopers landing just outside the strongpoint that was home to his divisional headquarters. It was just after 12:30a.m. on the morning of June 6. The garrison opened fire with their heaviest weapon – a 20mm anti-aircraft gun designed to provide close-range defense against low-level air attack.

Reichert immediately alerted his staff and the clerks, messengers, drivers, and orderlies hastily dressed, donned helmets and webbing, grabbed rifles and carbines, and jumped into the trenches and foxholes of the strongpoint that encompassed the divisional headquarters. Reichert now regretted his recent decision to disband the division's guard company. If ever he needed that unit it was now. But offense was the best form of defense, as Reichert, a highly experienced officer, knew full well. He quickly ordered fighting patrols to probe the enemy strength and intentions. Within a short period of time, the first patrols returned with two captured British paratroopers from the 6th Airborne Division who had inadvertently landed within the strongpoint perimeter. But, the elite British paratroopers revealed nothing more than the obligatory name, rank, and serial number mandated by international law.

Reichert initially thought that the British were seeking to neutralize his divisional headquarters by *coup de main*. Consequently, he frantically called the nearest unit – the 3rd Company, 711th Engineer Battalion, located several miles away near St-Arnoult – to relieve the headquarters. As the fog of war began to clear, Reichert realized that the headquarters could not possibly be the target of the enemy, for the British attack was too poorly coordinated and too weak to achieve such a mission. Gradually, he came to appreciate that it was only stragglers who had drifted from their units and original targets in the vicinity that had attacked his staff. Dispersion, Reichert registered, was an occupational hazard that attended combat airborne drops. Nevertheless, despite his demands for restraint, his nervous troops – many of them in their first ever combat – repeatedly fired in the darkness upon their own returning patrols. Fortunately for them, their edginess made them lousy shots and no friendly fire accidents materialized.

Some time after 3:00a.m., the engineer company fought its way through to the headquarters. As information slowly trickled in of enemy drops throughout his divisional zone, Reichert presciently concluded that the enemy was about to land on the Cotentin Peninsula and the Baie de Caen, and that the airborne landings were designed to seize the high ground between the Touques and Orne Rivers so as to secure the eastern flank of an impending seaborne assault. He was probably the first German officer on the ground to discern Allied intentions on D-Day.

THE HIGH COMMAND THINKS IT IS A BLUFF

Higher headquarters proved much slower in accepting what Reichert already knew: the invasion was on and the Allies planned to land on the Normandy coast. As Generalfeldmarschall von Rundstedt's suspicions grew during those early morning hours, one of his first responses was to alert Rommel – then on leave in Germany visiting his wife – by telephone. Rommel immediately raced back toward France. He travelled through the night, but would miss the crucial early hours when the fate of the invasion was decided. As reports came in of Allied airborne forces dropping as far afield as Carentan in the west and Lisieux in the east, von Rundstedt finally ordered the highest state of alert for Army Group B at 3:00a.m., and gave preparation to move orders to the Armed Forces High Command (OKW) strategic reserves – the 12th SS Panzer Division Hitlerjügend, and the Panzer Lehr Division – on his own authority. Von Rundstedt dispatched a request for the release of these two divisions, but the OKW peremptorily rejected the request, since, they claimed, Hitler was asleep and no one dared wake him.

At 5:00a.m., von Rundstedt, again on his own authority, advanced two battle groups from the 12th SS and Panzer Lehr Divisions toward Lisieux and Falaise. Von Rundstedt made a second round of requests as dawn approached for the release of these two divisions to his control, but these were again rejected. Additional requests were sent throughout the morning and early afternoon of D-Day but it was not until 4:00p.m. that approval finally came through from Hitler – far too late. Both divisions received orders to advance on the coast and throw the Allies back into the sea. In the meantime, Rommel finally arrived back at La Roche-Guyon around 6:00p.m. He had missed the single most important day in his military career. Consequently, the German defenders of the Normandy coastline faced the brunt of the Allied landings unsupported. The panzers of the strategic reserves would not arrive in sufficient strength to throw the enemy back into sea. Only stubborn defense by the coastal forces stood between the invaders and the establishment of a bridgehead.

US troops secure a German coastal defense casemate on the eastern shore of the Cotentin Peninsula. Such casemates were designed to provide enfilade fire along beaches and were heavily reinforced on their seaward flanks to withstand naval fire.

THE LANDINGS

Leutnant Arthur Jahnke of the 709th Infantry Division, the commander of coastal strongpoint W5 on the eastern coast of the Cotentin Peninsula, could not sleep on the night of June 5. A decorated 23-year-old Eastern Front veteran with a Knight's Cross, Jahnke had been transferred to France during spring 1944 to help "stiffen" the defenses after convalescing from a wound. The constant stream of Allied aircraft overhead that night had made him nervous and he left the stone building that passed for the strongpoint command bunker and looked warily into the sky. He commanded a platoon-strength garrison from the 3d Company, 919th Grenadier Regiment. He was not unduly alarmed by this air activity, however, as it was low tide and the reassuring words of *Generalfeldmarschall* Rommel that "the enemy would never come at low tide" filled his head. His strongpoint was well defended: an 88mm anti-aircraft gun, a 75mm anti-tank gun, several 50mm tank guns, flamethrowers, even some Goliath radio-controlled tankettes filled with explosives and a WWI vintage 75mm field gun. The enemy would never attack such a position – at least not without softening it up first, he thought soberly.

During the early morning hours, Jahnke received an alert from the neighboring strongpoint about enemy paratroopers. He quickly mobilized the garrison, doubled the sentries, and sent out a fighting patrol to ascertain the situation. The patrol soon returned with 19 US paratroopers who, caught in the middle of the swamps behind the strongpoint, had no choice but to surrender. Jahnke immediately reported the capture of troops from the elite 101st US Airborne Division to headquarters, but the line went down – the French Resistance had cut the trunk cable. Now Jahnke retained contact only with the neighboring strongpoints. The battle for strongpoint W5 had begun.

Soon, continuous waves of bombers droned overhead. A concerned Jahnke moved into his grandiosely labeled combat command post – a foxhole shored up with planks and protected by the sea wall. Concerned about his nervous, inexperienced troops, Jahnke ordered extra rations distributed – soldiers always fought better with some food in their stomachs. He watched as a flight of bombers made a beeline for the strongpoint. He dropped his binoculars and pressed his face into the ground. A nearby bomb hit and its force threw him hard against his dugout wall. A cartload of sand descended, burying him completely. He immediately dug himself free, staggered into a shallow bomb crater, and then raced for the shelter of the large concrete anti-tank obstacles that blocked the road. Loud crackling and popping sounds told him that the strongpoint's ammunition bunkers had been

Throughout spring 1944 the German defenders erected powerful coastal defenses. The inherent strength of these fortifications is illustrated by the numerous hits this coastal gun bunker withstood. (Imperial War Museum B6381)

American Martin B-26 Marauders of 9th USAAF bomber command returning from an attack on enemy installations. Medium bombers like these dropped hundreds of tons of bombs on *Leutnant* Arthur Jahnke's strongpoint W5 to soften it up on the morning of June 6, 1944. (IWM EA 25486)

hit. Then silence descended, punctuated only by the cries of wounded and dying men. Dust and smoke shrouded the strongpoint. The fortifications they had laboriously dug had been leveled. The 75mm anti-tank gun was a heap of metal, shrapnel had hit the flak gun, and the foxholes and machine-gun nests had been buried under tons of sand. Panic began to rise among his green troops. Jahnke was well acquainted with panic – he had seen it before on the Eastern Front. He quickly fell the men in, and ordered them to begin digging out the positions. Keeping the troops busy was often the best tonic for fear. But more was to come. No sooner had the troops begun the herculean task of digging out, than smaller planes – fighter-bombers – soon appeared and shot up with rockets the strongpoint's two flanking 50mm turreted guns and demolished them, annihilating their crews.

When the smoke finally cleared from the rockets, Jahnke saw an amazing sight – the innumerable ships of the invasion fleet. Jahnke was shocked – he could not believe there were that many ships in the world. Momentarily, the armada opened up and laid fire all along the frontage of the strongpoint. Jahnke observed a destroyer racing toward the shallows, reducing the distance before turning to present a full broadside. Jahnke ordered the old field gun to return fire. It was an unequal fight, and on the third salvo the US naval gunners found their range and obliterated the field gun and its crew. But this was only the beginning, as heavy caliber shells from battleships and cruisers pounded the strongpoint, leveling trenches, shredding barbed wire, detonating mines, and burying bunkers. Even the stone building housing the communications center collapsed after receiving a direct hit.

Uppermost in Jahnke's mind was that Rommel had blundered. The enemy was coming at low tide and the endless and painful toil he and his men had put into laying foreshore obstacles had all been in vain. The enemy was prepared to cross half a mile of open beach to get ashore – and strongpoint W5 had been so pulverised they would probably succeed. Jahnke realized he needed fire support and quickly, and thus sent a dispatch rider to alert the nearby coastal artillery battery for fire support. But the rider never got through.

At 5:20a.m. enemy landing craft approached the beach, ran aground, and disgorged their troops. These were engineers who immediately set about dismantling the foreshore obstacles. Combat experience told Jahnke to wait for the enemy to close to 500 yards before opening fire, but he did not have that luxury as wave after wave of landing craft approached the beach. He gave the order to open fire. *Gefreiter* Friedrich manned an obsolete WWI French Renault FT-17 tank that had been dug into the strongpoint. He laid a deadly fire with his machine gun. But a strange specter now confronted Jahnke – peculiar small landing vessels approached the shore. As they waded ashore Jahnke finally recognized them for what they were – amphibious tanks. They advanced up the beach toward the anti-tank ditch. Frantic efforts had returned the 88mm flak to serviceability and it opened fire. Its first shot disabled the leading tank. But it did not fire a second shot: the first round proved to be the last for the damaged gun. The tanks moved up to the sea wall and began firing into the strongpoint at point blank range. One by one they eliminated the remaining bunkers. A tank scored a direct hit on the Renault turret – it sounded like a church bell being rung, Jahnke remembered. With all his heavy weapons destroyed, Jahnke turned to his last resort – the Goliath explosive charge layers, the "pocket wonder-weapon" the troops had sardonically called them. Under remote control the Goliaths inched toward their targets carrying their explosive charges. But the bombardment had damaged the delicate radio control circuits and they could not be properly controlled – they wandered around aimlessly and erratically

This was the scene that *Leutnant* Jahnke witnessed on UTAH Beach after strongpoint W5 had fallen and its survivors were marched down to be shipped back to England. Already, US forces were consolidating their beachhead and preparing to bring in heavier weapons. (IWM EA 26008)

before finally grinding to a halt. Only later would one of them claim a deadly toll, when a GI threw a hand grenade at one, detonating it and wiping out a nearby American infantry squad.

Jahnke grimly held, waiting for relief – for the counterattack that would drive the enemy back into the sea – but none came. Near noon, "resistance" had dwindled to sporadic and scattered rifle fire against the tanks that now stood all along the sea wall. Finally, a shell impacted at the edge of Jahnke's dugout – he saw the flash out of the corner of his eye. He was smacked in the back and buried in sand, losing consciousness. When he regained consciousness he realised the strongpoint had fallen. A US officer showed Jahnke a silk scarf with accurate details of strongpoint W5 and "UTAH Beach" written across the top. *Leutnant* Arthur Jahnke thus became the first German officer to know the codename for the newly established US bridgehead on the eastern shore of the Cotentin Peninsula.

Suddenly, as Jahnke was being questioned, he heard a loud bang and walls of sand flew through the air – artillery fire, he realized. German guns were shelling the beach. It must be the 10th Battery, 1261st Army Coastal Artillery Regiment at Quineville, Jahnke thought. Typical, he thought – trust the gunners to be too late as usual (a typical infantryman's bias against gunners). In fact, army coastal artillery played an important role in the German plan to repulse the invasion. On the eastern flank of the Cotentin Peninsula it was *Oberst* Gerhard Triepel's 1261st Army Coastal Artillery Regiment that was responsible for providing the fire support to stop an invasion; a rather tall order for a single regiment. His headquarters was a camouflaged command bunker on the gorse-covered slopes of the Quineville ridge. Just behind the command post his 10th Battery, equipped with powerful high-elevation 170mm guns, was dug into camouflaged field positions. It was this unit that now fired on UTAH Beach. The shells flew directly over Triepel's command post as he calmly watched the invasion fleet discharging its cargo of troops and equipment. Shell after shell smacked into the closely packed vehicles inching their way up the beach, through the narrow lanes cleared by the engineers between the foreshore obstacles, and through the gaps that engineers had blown in the seawall. It was an inviting target for the German gunners; their guns, long ago pre-registered on the beach, hit home with deadly accuracy. With horror, Jahnke saw some of his own troops hit by friendly fire. Then, he too was hit again; a shell splinter tore into the side of his body and a red patch quickly spread across his tunic. Fear coursed through him – a deadly stomach wound – he knew that if he was not operated upon within 24 hours he would die. He had survived the might of the enemy only to succumb to a shell splinter from one of his own guns. He pushed his hand under his uniform and cautiously probed the wound. Despite the excruciating pain, with relief Jahnke realized that he had suffered only a flesh wound. He unbuttoned his field tunic and placed a lint bandage on his wound. Then he saw a senior American officer – no less than Brigadier General Theodore Roosevelt, Junior – standing before him. Jahnke formally saluted the general, placing his fingertips to his bare head. The general lifted his hand to return the salute but then evidently had second thoughts and dropped his arm and moved away and barked orders demanding the immediate evacuation of Jahnke and the other German POWs to the relative safety of ships at sea. Jahnke was shipped out to a destroyer that set sail for a British port; the coast of the Cotentin Peninsula faded away through the haze. For Jahnke, D-Day spelled the end of his military career as he faced a lengthy period as an Allied prisoner of war.

DUEL WITH THE NAVY

The German High Command placed great importance on the navy's heavy coastal artillery batteries to thwart the invasion. These comprised statically emplaced long-range naval batteries to buttress the more prevalent but less powerful army coastal artillery. The former tasked with engaging and destroying an approaching invasion fleet, the latter with engaging and annihilating the disembarking enemy, as Triepel's 10th Battery had done on UTAH Beach. But nowhere did the Germans have sufficient heavy coastal artillery to repulse the Allied landings. The experiences of *Oberleutnant* Ohmsen's heavy naval artillery battery at St-Marcouf on the east coast of the Cotentin Peninsula are a case in point. The battery fielded a formidable three 210mm guns, a solitary 150mm gun, and six 75mm anti-aircraft guns. The battery had been constructed that spring, waging a constant battle with Allied air power, which repeatedly attacked the battery site. They came again on the night of June 5, and dropped some 600 tons of ordnance on the battery. All six flak guns were destroyed, but the reinforced roofs of the gun casemates held, and the erected interior netting caught the cones of concrete blasted off the ceiling by the force of direct hits above.

But Ohmsen's agony had only just begun. Soon, the battery came under sporadic small arms fire from US paratroopers. His second in command, *Leutnant* Grieg, led a fighting patrol out into the surrounding swamps. The night air filled with the sound of frog croaks. Grieg noted that he had never heard so many frogs before. Soon the patrol captured an American paratrooper equipped with a snapper that croaked – evidently a recognition signal. The patrol stalked through the swamp pressing the snapper. "Croak" came back the reply. One by one, the patrol rounded up all the croaking "frogs" in the swamp. Twenty

The Germans emplaced a wide variety of heavy coastal artillery pieces in reinforced casemates, like this one, at strategic locations along the French coast. The heavy naval battery emplaced at St-Marcouf under the command of *Oberleutnant* Ohmsen was built in the late spring of 1944 to help protect the eastern Cotentin Peninsula. (US National Archives)

prisoners were brought in from the 502nd Parachute Regiment. Disorganised by their hazardous drop, St-Marcouf did not fall to airborne assault as the invaders had planned. At 5:00a.m. Ohmsen observed the invasion fleet through his trench scissor telescope and called *Admiral* Hennecke in Cherbourg for permission to open fire. "Use ammunition sparingly" came back the reply. Ohmsen opened fire with his three heavy guns. His second salvo straddled an enemy destroyer at long range, and he hit it amidships on his next salvo, breaking its back, its bow and stern rising before sinking beneath the waters. Around 8:00a.m. a shell from the US battleship *Nevada* hit just in front of one of Ohmsen's guns. The heavy caliber round excavated the foundations of the bunker and caused its front to collapse. A little later Ohmsen's gunners hit a second destroyer, immobilizing its rudder. Now Ohmsen concentrated his fire on the target, hitting it again and again as it turned helplessly in circles, then listed to port, and sank beneath the waves. But shortly after 9:00a.m. the *Nevada* scored a lucky hit – straight through the open loophole of the battery's No. 2 gun, obliterating the gun and crew.

US troops explore a knocked-out naval gun. The St-Marcouf battery proved a major thorn in the side of the US landings on the eastern shore of the Cotentin Peninsula. (IWM AP 26881)

The armoured loophole plate that should have protected the gun from this unlikely calamity had never arrived – it was sitting on a bombed-out train somewhere in France, the victim of an Allied air attack. With his last heavy gun, Ohmsen fired on UTAH Beach, bringing it under accurate fire during the midday hours. To make matters worse, that morning the 4th US Infantry Division attacked the battery. Having been plowed over by air and naval bombardment, it was vulnerable to such an attack. "Alarm – all round defence", Ohmsen shouted out. The attackers fought their way into the disorganized defences. Ohmsen was pinned in his command bunker, shot through his left hand. The enemy climbed atop the fire control bunker and prepared to thrust Bangalore torpedoes down through the apertures to roast the defenders alive. In desperation, Ohmsen called the neighboring army artillery battery at Azeville, and calmly requested fire on his position. Shell after German shell fell within the battery position, sweeping away the US assault troops. The US infantry mistakenly thought that they were being shelled by their own naval guns and fled in panic from the battery position, leaving valuable equipment behind. Ohmsen's gambit had worked. In fury, the American naval gunners pounded the battery position and fighter-bombers swept down. But as twilight arrived on D-Day, *Oberleutnant* Ohmsen and his naval gunners grimly held on to St-Marcouf battery, which was rapidly becoming a thorn in the side of the Allies. Ohmsen, like so many desperate German defenders, anxiously looked skyward hoping to see German planes – there were none.

WHERE ARE OUR AIRMEN?

But what of Göring's vaunted Luftwaffe? *Generalfeldmarschall* Sperrle had only 319 aircraft in total and fewer than 100 fighters. Trained pilots were in scarce supply too. The Luftwaffe flew just 309 sorties on D-Day, most of which the Allies immediately intercepted. No more than a dozen fighter-bombers reached the landing beaches. Among them was "Pips" Priller, a seasoned Focke-Wulf FW 190 fighter ace and commander of the 26th *Jagdgeschwader*. At 8:00a.m. Priller took off with his long-time wingman, Heinz Wodarczyk, and headed toward Normandy while hugging the terrain to avoid the Spitfires overhead. Above Le Havre they climbed into cloud cover and when they emerged the entire Allied invasion fleet was laid out below before them. Surprised British soldiers dived for cover as Priller and Wodarczyk appeared out of the cloud at over 400mph to strafe SWORD Beach on the very eastern end of the Allied lodgement. An enormous flak barrage filled the sky, as hundreds of anti-aircraft guns on the invasion fleet attacked the two planes. But masked by the coastline,

A Focke-Wulf FW 190-A8 fighter-bomber of the 26th *Jagdgeschwader* wrecked or abandoned on the retreat from Normandy. It was this type of plane that "Pips" Priller and Heinz Wodarczyk sortied with over SWORD Beach on D-Day. (Imperial War Museum)

they were not easy to pick out among the pall of smoke that hung over the beach. After their pass, both pilots climbed for cloud cover and headed back to base – a second run, they both knew, would be suicide. Military honor had been satisfied, yet the cold reality was apparent – that the Luftwaffe was a broken arm that could not stop the invasion.

A SORTIE BY E-BOATS

Woefully weak, the German Navy could only disrupt the Allied landings. At 1:50a.m. on June 6, Naval Group West alerted Kapitänleutnant Heinrich Hoffmann's 5th E-Boat Flotilla based at Le Havre. The first reports of sighting enemy ships in the Channel provoked a sortie by the flotilla. At 3:30a.m. Hoffman set sail with T28, Jaguar and Löwe and sped up the Channel at high speed. An hour later they came across a gigantic smoke screen. At top speed the three E-boats soared through the smoke. "It's impossible," a shocked Heinrich Frömke stammered as the boats emerged from the smoke and saw myriad ships of the invasion fleet before them. All business, Hoffmann immediately ordered attack. In zigzag fashion, the boats maneuvered through the hail of fire unleashed toward them from defending escorts and loosed off 18 torpedoes before turning tail for the safety of the smoke screen. Though they heard the explosion that indicated a hit, they never saw their accomplishment – a Norwegian escort destroyer that was hit amidships, exploded, and sunk. Hoffman's "kill" was one of very few successes achieved by the German Navy on D-Day. But, like the entire German response, it reflected too little, too late.

Chapter 12

"Much the greatest thing we have ever attempted"

(Prime Minister Winston Churchill in a letter to President Franklin D Roosevelt)
"My dear friend, this is the much the greatest thing we have ever attempted."

OVERLORD and beyond

Dr David I Hall

When Winston Churchill enthusiastically described Operation OVERLORD and D-Day as being "much the greatest thing we have ever attempted" he was not exaggerating. The Anglo-American cross-Channel invasion of France in the summer of 1944 was the greatest joint and combined operation in the history of warfare. On D-Day itself, 6 June 1944, the Allies deployed more than 7,000 ships, 13,000 aircraft, and 155,000 men. News of the great invasion spread quickly throughout England, America, Europe and the rest of the world. Hiding in a secret first floor room in her house in Amsterdam, a young Dutch-Jewish girl, Anne Frank, listened on her wireless to the breaking news of the invasion. She recorded the events in her diary:

"'This is D-Day', came the announcement over the British radio. The invasion has begun! ... Great commotion in the 'Secret Annexe'! Would the long-awaited liberation that has been talked of so much but which still seems too wonderful, too much like a fairy-tale, ever come true? Could we be granted victory this year, 1944? We don't know yet, but hope is revived within us; it gives us fresh courage, and makes us strong again."

In London, Churchill addressed the House of Commons at midday on the progress of the invasion. He told his parliamentary colleagues of the extraordinary effort being made by American, British and Canadian sailors, soldiers and airmen, about the immense armada crossing the Channel, about parachute troops and airborne landings, and amphibious forces storming the beaches and overcoming German seafront obstacles. "Reports are coming in in rapid succession", he said, further noting "that everything is proceeding according to plan. And what a plan!" D-Day was the culmination of more than two years of detailed planning, preparations and training. Hard lessons had been learned in earlier amphibious operations at Dieppe, in North Africa, Sicily and Italy. Four difficult years of war had also taught the Western Allies to respect the superb fighting ability of their German adversaries. As a result, the Allies' strategy for Operation OVERLORD was based on superior administration, organisation and overwhelming material superiority. The aim was to win the build-up race in the lodgement area and break out into Normandy before the German Army massed sufficient forces to mount a decisive counter-attack. Irresistible force would overcome German operational and tactical skill.

Earlier chapters have described the planning and build-up to the invasion, the vast naval effort (Operation NEPTUNE), the role of air power, the elaborate deception plans (Operation FORTITUDE), the amphibious landings and the desperate fighting on the beaches, and the

OPPOSITE General Sir Bernard Montgomery addressing Canadian troops preparing for the Normandy invasion. (Department of National Defence/National Archives of Canada)

British and American aircraft of the
Expeditionary Air Forces that
provided essential direct support
for Allied armies in Normandy,
operating from an Advanced
Airfield a few miles inland from the
Normandy coast. (Courtesy of the
Wilfrid Laurier Centre for Military
Strategic and Disarmament Studies,
Wilfrid Laurier University, Canada)

costly battles of attrition inland in the *bocage* and around Caen, Cherbourg and St-Lô. This chapter looks above the details of the planning and the fighting and examines the impact of Operation OVERLORD in a broader, more strategic way. It considers what happened as a result of D-Day, and explains why the success of D-Day and OVERLORD sealed Germany's fate.

FROM BRIDGEHEAD TO STALEMATE

The Allied D-Day plan had worked. Deception, tactical surprise, and concentration of overwhelming force all contributed to the establishment of a sizeable bridgehead within the first 24 hours of the invasion. Hitler's vaunted Atlantic Wall had been breached. There was nothing fancy about the Allied land commander's strategy. General Sir Bernard Montgomery, commander of 21st Army Group, opted for a frontal assault of unprecedented violence that would 'shock and shatter' the German defenders. And, just as it was planned, a series of precisely timed air, naval and amphibious attacks in echelon overwhelmed the static German coastal divisions. Both physically and psychologically, the very effect that Montgomery had intended had been achieved.

Once ashore, the Allies planned to consolidate their positions at the same time that they advanced inland. This approach enabled the Allies to proceed with their build-up according to plan and to safeguard the lodgement areas from the anticipated German counter-attacks. Priority, not surprisingly, was given to joining up the five landing beaches rather than exploiting any local successes through a strategy of deep thrusts inland, for the latter was deemed too risky given the Germans' proven abilities in manoeuvre warfare. The three British and Canadian beaches were joined together on 7 June and a day later a link was established between GOLD Beach and OMAHA, the most easterly of the two

American beaches. By 12 June, following the fall of Carentan, UTAH Beach was incorporated within a 50-mile front. The Allies continued to edge forward in what looked like a series of concentric lines emanating from the beaches, as the German defenders re-discovered their nerve and started offering stiffer resistance.

Paradoxically, the Allies' plan and initial success in the assault phase sowed the seeds for the subsequent stalemate. As in many of the earlier amphibious operations, there was a tendency to concentrate so intensely on the landings themselves that the subsequent follow-on operations became almost an afterthought. This shortcoming was compounded by the sheer physical difficulties faced by the forward troops. Many had been seasick during the crossing, and few had had much sleep for several days while they waited onboard their ships and landing craft until the invasion commenced. The searing experience of the initial assault also left many of the survivors with a feeling that they had done their bit for the war. For some, fear and debilitating tiredness made the shelter of a quiet barn or a cellar stocked with strong Calvados a brief respite before their next terrifying encounter with the enemy.

The Allied breakout was also delayed by a number of unexpected environmental, physical and technical conditions that affected both attackers and defenders alike. Difficult terrain, inappropriate ratios of armour and infantry units, and outdated tactical concepts all conspired against a rapid breakout. Fearful of a major counter-attack by German panzers, the Allies concentrated on getting their own armour ashore first. Tanks, rather than infantry and artillery employing their own anti-tank weapons, were the preferred Allied method for dealing with the panzer threat. This decision led to an inappropriate balance of ground forces for the character of fighting that developed. Tanks were not suited to the difficulties of close fighting in either the Norman *bocage* and its maze of hedgerows, or the numerous villages dominating the vital ground that needed to be secured to achieve a breakout. Without infantry support, Allied tanks became easy victims for dug-in German armour, anti-tank gunners, and infantry using the effective and much feared *panzerfaust*. At the end of the war, a senior American staff officer said candidly: "We simply did not expect to remain in the *bocage* long enough to justify studying it as a major tactical problem." Supreme Headquarters Allied Expeditionary Force (SHAEF) was aware of the topographical features in Normandy, but it was unable to decide if the unique features of the area favoured the defender or the attacker.

When the Allies did use infantry to spearhead an attack, the results were not much better. British, Canadian and American infantry knew very little of the infiltration tactics that were so skilfully employed by German infantry. Instead, Allied infantry pinned their hopes on a simple open order advance with two companies forward. Such attacks had more in common with the futile and costly advances between the trenches in World War I than with modern infantry tactics in this war. As 'managers' gave way to 'leaders', the tactical performance of the Allied forces diminished.

Lacking an effective tactical doctrine and short of new ideas, the Allies were unable to maintain momentum in the attack. The Allied breakout had stalled, but the Germans were having their share of problems too. Counter-attacks aimed at driving the invaders back into the sea were costly in terms of casualties, and ineffective. The Germans were short of mobile infantry at the front and they could not concentrate sufficient armoured forces for a decisive attack. The 21st Panzer Division deployed most of its tanks forward in static anti-tank positions. Whilst effective against Allied ground forces, they were exposed and vulnerable to naval gunfire and air attack. Panzer Lehr was also used to fulfil infantry tasks. Eleven days after the landing, this elite German tank division had been reduced in strength from 8,635 men to 1,531.

Damaged German PzKfW V 'Panther' tank, Bretteville, Normandy, 20 June 1944. (National Archives of Canada)

RAF Spitfire MK IV with invasion recognition stripes. (Wilfrid Laurier Centre for Military, Strategic and Disarmament Studies, Wilfrid Laurier University, Canada)

Many of the Germans' problems were a direct result of Allied air supremacy. Pre-invasion air and naval bombardment, and from D-Day onwards the relentless efforts of the RAF's Second Tactical Air Force and the USAAF Ninth Air Force, severely damaged the rail and road networks throughout most of France and Belgium. Air attacks also disrupted the German Army's command arrangements, its communications, and its logistics chain, key points to be developed later.

Once the initial shock of the invasion had passed, both sides soon found themselves bogged down in a costly battle of attrition. Casualties suffered by inexperienced Allied troops did impose a psychological check on taking unnecessary risks. By 8 June the Allies had suffered 15,000 casualties and with them came a discernible decline in offensive spirit. The defensive nature of the plan – to secure a bridgehead first – also encouraged the troops to dig in rather than push forward inland. Moreover, it was beyond the tactical ability and experience of the Allies to conduct a blitzkrieg-style campaign. Against an increasingly determined German defence, what Allied progress there was tended to be limited and slow.

CRISES IN THE GERMAN HIGH COMMAND

Three days into the invasion, awkward questions were already being asked by the Supreme Command (OKW). Hitler wanted to know why the seaward defences were overrun so quickly on D-Day. In his report to the Führer, Major General Wilhelm Richter, commander of the 716th Infantry Division, blamed Allied air power and "the total absence of support from the Luftwaffe" for his division's inability to hold their coastal positions. By the end of the first week of fighting, Richter's division had been completely destroyed. Unknown to Hitler and the German General Staff was the staggering scale of violence delivered by the Allied assault. The paucity of German survivors meant that the answers Hitler sought were neither accurate nor forthcoming.

Lacking reliable intelligence, both before and after D-Day, meant that the German High Command operated in the dark. The Germans also lacked adequate air and naval forces to challenge the Allies' command in the air and at sea. Conscious of these weaknesses, the Germans were compelled to seek a single-service army solution to the complex problems of defence in the West against an amphibious invasion fully supported by Allied air power. Hitler laid down the foundations of this strategy in early November 1943 with his Directive Number 51. He ordered the construction of major fortifications all along the coast. Vulnerable areas, such as beaches and coastal ports, were to be heavily

Hitler's 'first paladin', Reichs-marschall Hermann Göring, greets his Führer at a Nazi Party rally. (United States Holocaust Museum)

defended by stationary artillery and static infantry formations. These front line defences were to hold the invading forces in the lodgement area until mobile armoured forces could mount a major counter-attack. Once unleashed, Hitler predicted, the full fury of the counter-attack would "prevent the enlargement of the beachhead, and throw the enemy back into the sea".

Two experienced field marshals were responsible for turning Hitler's ideas into the actual defence of the West. Gerd von Rundstedt was Commander-in-Chief West and Erwin Rommel was Commander Army Group B, with specific instructions to strengthen the coastal defences of the Atlantic Wall. Rommel set about his tasks with great determination and energy. Giant concrete casements were constructed to protect coastal artillery and shore-defence guns, immobile tanks were dug in, and the seashore was blanketed with mines and all sorts of passive obstacles. In addition, Rommel wanted to base the panzer divisions just a few miles from the beaches. His experience of Allied air power in North Africa convinced him that it would be impossible to assemble an effective armoured counter-attack from reserve positions located deep behind the front. He also believed that the invasion "must be destroyed within the first 24 hours amid the coastal fortifications" if it was to be defeated at all.

Both von Rundstedt and General Leo Geyr von Schweppenburg, commander of Panzer Group West, disagreed with Rommel. They preferred a defence based on the classic German doctrine of a massed counter-attack by armoured forces at the earliest moment once the enemy's true intentions had been determined. The coast they had to defend was long and the principal target of an invasion force was uncertain. Mobility would be the key to a successful defence, so they did not want to spread their vital panzer forces too thinly along the coast. Moreover, almost all the German generals believed that the Pas de Calais was the most likely site for the anticipated Allied invasion. Intuition led Hitler to think Normandy was where the invasion would come, but he, too, believed that the Pas de Calais was the principal target. Hitler therefore settled the disagreement between his commanders with a compromise. Some armour was deployed forward in support of Rommel's plan but most of it was held in reserve. Hitler also reserved for himself the crucial decision on how and when the armour was to be deployed. Despite differing views on how best to defend against an invasion, the Germans did have supreme confidence in their ability to blunt an assault and to "throw the enemy back into the sea".

D-Day caught the Germans completely by surprise. Confusion and indecision bedevilled the ordered defence they had planned. Other than at OMAHA Beach, where the Germans were ready, commanders were not at their headquarters and many soldiers were still in their beds when the first waves of the invasion crashed upon them. Rommel was in Germany for his wife's birthday, and von Rundstedt was reluctant to commit his panzers until he was sure of the Allies' intentions and had Hitler's authorisation. Permission to release the panzers did not come until 4:00p.m. News of the invasion first reached OKW early in the morning on 6 June, but Colonel-General Alfred Jodl, chief of operations, rejected von Rundstedt's requests to deploy the armoured reserve. Jodl took this important decision on his own initiative and, inexplicably, without informing Hitler. Later in the morning, when Hitler was appraised of the events taking place in Normandy, he also hesitated. Was this the main effort of the Allied invasion – the *schwerpunkt* – or was it a diversion preceding the main attack at the Pas de Calais? By default the Germans settled on a passive defence of containment in Normandy, dependent on the forces that were already there. The opportunity to defeat the invaders had passed.

Earlier confidence gave way to deepening depression. The field marshals had no answers and were lost for ideas. Allied air superiority could not be countered and the invasion forces could not be stopped. On 16 June, Hitler and Jodl went to France to discuss with von Rundstedt and Rommel the growing crisis in the West. They met at W2, a specially designed battle headquarters at Margival near Soissons. Hitler impressed upon his commanders the need to contain the bridgehead and then crush the Allied forces within through a decisive counter-attack. The field marshals equivocated. Under a storm of Allied gunfire and air attack their diminishing forces struggled to contain the gradually expanding Allied beachhead. Reinforcements were not arriving either fast enough or in sufficient strength. Allied air power made movement by day extremely dangerous. What could they do? The next most immediate concern was how to avert the imminent threat that the Cotentin Peninsula, and with it the port and fortress at Cherbourg, would be cut off from the rest of Normandy. Hitler attempted to stiffen the resolve of his faltering commanders. He demanded that Cherbourg be held to the last man, and that every effort should be made to counter-attack the enemy at every opportunity.

Cherbourg fell on 28 June. On the same day, General Dollman, commander of Seventh Army, died suddenly. It was reported that he died of a heart attack but it is quite likely that he committed suicide. Earlier in the week, the Russians began their major summer offensive. Some 2.5 million men, 5,200 tanks and 5,300 aircraft attacked along a 35-mile front in the direction of Minsk. This was the start of the Red

Army's offensive into Belorussia, and the destruction of German Army Group Centre. Shaken by the recent setbacks, on 1 July Field Marshal Wilhelm Keitel, Hitler's chief of staff at OKW, telephoned von Rundstedt to seek his advice on what to do. "The writing was on the wall", replied von Rundstedt, "make peace you fools".

Gerd von Rundstedt resigned the following day. On 4 July, Field Marshal Hans Günther von Kluge, a long-experienced veteran of the Eastern Front, succeeded him. Kluge had never faced the devastating effects of Allied air power. Boastfully, he assured Hitler that "all would be well". Kluge, however, kept all his options open. He was a leading member of an Army-led conspiracy to remove Hitler and seek an armistice with the Western Allies.

ALLIED AIR SUPERIORITY

The contribution made by the Allied air forces to the success of D-Day and the Normandy campaign cannot be over-emphasised. They fought for, won, and maintained air supremacy over England, the surrounding seas, the battlefields in France and even over much of Germany. Anglo-American bombers dropped some 71,000 tons of bombs in pre-invasion operations that isolated Normandy from German reinforcement. On D-Day morning, Allied aircraft delivered a devastating attack on German coastal positions, communications and military depots behind the front. Once the invasion was underway, the air forces switched their attention to the panzer reserves. 17th SS Panzer Grenadier Division needed five days to drive 200 miles from Thouars, south of the Loire, to Périers, at the bottom of the Cotentin Peninsula. 2nd Panzer Division took nine days to reach the front from Abbeville, losing one third of its tanks in the process. Air attacks were equally effective against German communications, command and control. By 7 June Panzer Group West had lost 75 per cent of its radio equipment. On 9 June its headquarters were destroyed by RAF bombers. General von Schweppenburg was injured and many of his officers were killed. Panzer Group West HQ remained out of action until the last week of June.

Fuel convoys, tanks and troops on the move, and even spare temporary headquarters also came under relentless air attack. The Germans were totally unprepared for the savagery of the Allied air assault. Ubiquitous and effective, Allied tactical and strategic air power was a determining factor between victory and defeat. In support of the land battles of the Allied armies, Allied air power was a triple threat to the Germans – destroying or disrupting troop deployments, command centres, and the logistics chain. The Anglo-American air forces kept the German defences off-balanced while at the same time they enabled the

Allied armies to maintain the offensive initiative throughout the campaign. Between 6 June and 31 August, Allied aircraft flew just under half a million sorties in direct support of the battle for France. General Richter was merely one of many German survivors from the Normandy campaign to cite Allied air superiority as the main reason for the Allied victory.

Having experienced the devastating impact of Allied air power before, Rommel knew that the battle was as good as lost. His army had lost 2,360 officers and over 94,000 men, while he had received only 6,000 replacements. He had also lost 225 tanks and received 17, in addition to the new formations reaching the front. By mid-July he believed that the entire Normandy front would collapse in less than a month. He advised von Kluge accordingly, reporting that "our troops are fighting heroically but the unequal struggle is drawing to its close". On 15 July, Rommel, acting on his field marshal's prerogative, met with Hitler and implored him to negotiate an end to the war. The Führer

A Halifax bomber of No. 6 Group RCAF on a mission against transportation targets in France. Allied medium and heavy bombers played a vital role in isolating Normandy from German reinforcements. (Courtesy of the Wilfrid Laurier Centre for Military Strategic and Disarmament Studies, Wilfrid Laurier University, Canada)

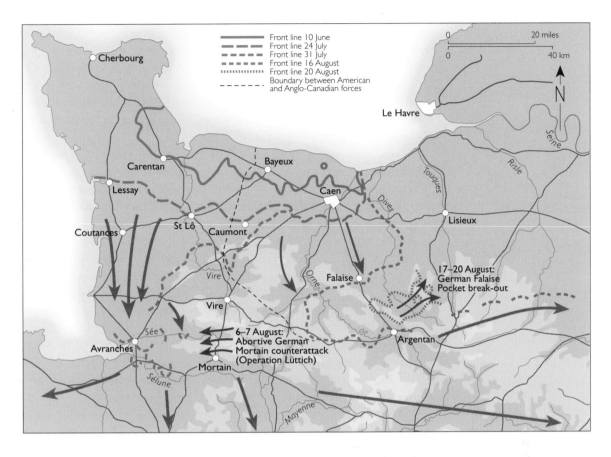

Front line 10 June
Front line 24 July
Front line 31 July
Front line 16 August
Front line 20 August
Boundary between American
and Anglo-Canadian forces

0 ___ 20 miles
0 ___ 40 km

Cherbourg
Le Havre
Carentan
Bayeux
Lessay
Caen
Lisieux
St Lô
Coutances
Caumont
Vire
Falaise
Vire
6–7 August:
Abortive German
Mortain counterattack
(Operation Lüttich)
Argentan
Avranches
Mortain
17–20 August:
German Falaise
Pocket break-out
Sée
Sélune
Mayenne
Dives
Orne
Touques
Risle
Seine

The Normandy campaign,
6 June–20 August 1944.

abruptly rejected the advice of his favourite general. Two days later, while en route to his headquarters, Rommel suffered serious head injuries when his car crashed following an RAF Typhoon attack near Vimoutiers. Rommel's career as a battlefield commander was over.

THE JULY PLOT

Defeatist talk and depression swept through the German officer corps throughout July. German forces were in retreat on every front and the prospects of a reversal in fortune looked bleak. Few officers were willing to renege on their oath of allegiance to Hitler, but a small group, led by General Beck, Colonel von Stauffenberg and Field Marshal von Kluge, decided that they must assassinate Hitler before the Normandy front collapsed and the Russians arrived in Poland and East Prussia. The conspirators considered Rommel to be a suitable figurehead, who, along with von Kluge, would negotiate an armistice with the Western Allies. Their opportunity came when von Stauffenberg was invited to attend the Führer's daily commanders' conference. On three occasions between

6 and 15 July, von Stauffenberg took a bomb with him, in his briefcase, into the conference. But the conspirators wanted to kill Hitler, Göring and Himmler at the same time, and all three had not been present. On 20 July, Stauffenberg decided to explode the bomb regardless. In the event, neither Göring nor Himmler were there and Hitler survived. Severely shaken but not seriously injured, Hitler spoke on German radio just before midnight to confirm his survival.

The planned assassination and *putsch* had failed. Hitler, with Jodl and Keitel's concurrence, responded by taking draconian powers over the army and exacting terrible revenge on those suspected of complicity. The failed plot also had a direct impact on German military operations. Hitler viewed his survival as an act of providence. Moreover, he was certain that he and he alone could snatch victory out of the jaws of defeat. Turning to the problems in Normandy, Hitler rejected the passive strategy of containment and ordered more offensive operations. He demanded a decisive counter-offensive to drive a wedge between the American and British sectors. The British were still bogged down west of Caen, but the Americans had won a bitter battle of attrition around St-Lô. On 25 July, the Americans launched another offensive, Operation COBRA. It began with a devastating air attack on Panzer Lehr, and created a sizeable gap in the German front. The First US Army broke through towards Avranches, which they took on 30 July. Hitler believed the time was right for his masterstroke. Codenamed Operation LUTTICH, a newly formed panzer army constructed around XLVII Panzer Corps headquarters was to destroy the American spearhead and drive to the sea at Avranches. It was an ill-advised and impetuous decision that backfired with dire consequences.

WINNING IN NORMANDY

The German counter-offensive at Mortain was just the sort of orthodox armoured attack that Rommel had declared impossible against Allied air power. Only Hitler thought it would work. The attack began on the night of 6 August. Mortain was captured, but the Germans were unable to secure the high ground east of the town, Hill 317. A reinforced battalion of the US 30th Infantry Division held out against repeated attacks. From this ideal vantage point, the Americans were able to direct Allied tactical air forces against the German panzers. Hitler's gamble had failed. On 9 August, German commanders pleaded with Hitler to order a withdrawal. He refused, ordering them to hold their ground while a second panzer army concentrated for another attack.

Through ULTRA (the special intelligence obtained from breaking the German code and reading German signals communications), the Allies knew that the Germans would not retreat. Montgomery and US general Omar Bradley also recognised the possibility of a double envelopment. After conferring with each other, they issued their respective orders: the British and Canadians would advance towards Falaise, while the Americans would first drive south and then turn east in behind Argentan. Allied progress was slow, but the Germans were driven back onto Falaise where a pocket began forming around the remnants of the Fifth Panzer Army and the Seventh Army. The fighting around Falaise and Argentan was some of the fiercest in Normandy. While the Allied armies slowly collapsed the pocket, Allied air forces bombed and strafed the retreating Germans. Between 16 and 19 August some 240,000 men escaped the Allies' grasp, but they left behind their tanks, artillery and vehicles, 50,000 dead, and another 200,000 men taken prisoner. On 15 August, the Allies executed Operation DRAGOON, landing additional armies in southern France. Hitler called these few days in August the worst days in his life. The battle of Normandy was over.

Shattered German armies streamed westward across the River Seine and four Allied armies followed them in full pursuit. Elements of General Patton's Third US Army crossed the Seine on 19 August. By 25 August all of the Allied armies were crossing the Seine. On the same day, French General Jacques Philippe Leclerc's 2nd Armoured Division triumphantly drove down the Champs Elysées. After four years of Nazi occupation Paris was free.

Churchill, Roosevelt, Hitler, and even Stalin, all knew that the events unfolding in Normandy from D-Day onwards would determine the outcome of the war. There are many reasons that account for the Allies' success – overwhelming air and naval supremacy, the brilliant deception plan, bountiful resources, and the ever-improving fighting abilities of the American, British, Canadian and Polish soldiers. Many Allied soldiers were inexperienced when they landed in France, but they learned quickly how to fight and defeat their German opponents.

Germany's defeat was made certain through the beaches of Normandy. By losing France, Germany lost not only armies and territory but also material resources and labour, seaports that had sheltered the dreaded U-boats, radar sites that had afforded early warning of the Allied bomber attacks, and most of the V-weapons launch sites. Moreover, France provided the Allies with a secure continental base from which to launch their final offensive into Nazi Germany. As Field Marshal Rommel told his son, during their final days together at home in Herrlingen before his enforced suicide, the future was clear: "the war is lost, there is no longer anything we can do".

Chapter 13

"The eyes of the world"

(General Dwight D. Eisenhower in his address to Allied forces, June 6, 1944)
"The eyes of the world are upon you.
The hopes and prayers of liberty-loving people everywhere are with you."

Commemoration and memorial

Carlo D'Este

When the Allies invaded Normandy on June 6, 1944, France was entering its 1,453rd day of German occupation. D-Day marked the launch of the Allied campaigns that not only liberated France, but also led to the defeat of one of the most odious dictatorships in history. The significance of D-Day cannot be overestimated, both in military terms and in its impact upon morale throughout the free world. It was not only an historic day militarily – one that signaled a significant new phase of the war – but for the weary populace of the Allied nations, and elsewhere throughout the world, it meant that at long last the struggle was being taken directly to Nazi Germany, and that the liberation of Europe was at hand.

D-Day was also the ultimate example of Allied cooperation. The soldiers, sailors, airmen, and civilians who gave their lives did so for a truly Allied cause. From the planning, to the training, and the massive logistical effort to mount Operation OVERLORD, it was Allies pulling together to prepare for the largest and most dangerous amphibious undertaking in military history. American, British, Canadian, Free Polish, Free French, Dutch and Belgian soldiers, sailors and airmen all made the invasion of Normandy succeed, in an unprecedented international venture.

On D-Day, almost nothing went right, as exemplified by bloody OMAHA Beach. Moreover, important as it was, D-Day was only the vital first step toward liberating France and ending the war. The battle of Normandy lasted 80 days before the German Army was defeated and the Allies reached the Seine River. Although the campaign took longer than the false expectations of some, it was, in fact, a masterful military achievement. Indeed, the Allied logisticians based their plans on reaching the Seine by May 1945. Along the way there were serious disagreements among the senior Allied commanders over strategy.

Yet, in the end, it was Allied patience and perseverance that won the day on June 6, 1944, and the entire Normandy campaign. Too often lost in the post-war controversies was the fact that the strategic objectives of the Allies were fully met. Eisenhower's mission was to successfully land a large Allied force and eliminate the German Army defending Normandy. By the end of August 1944, the German Army had been shattered, with the loss of an estimated 200,000 killed or wounded, and another 200,000 captured.

THE CONSEQUENCES OF FAILURE

Looking at history with hindsight can often be misleading. Such is the case with D-Day. It is tempting to believe in retrospect that the success of the Allied landings was a given. Such was never the case.

OPPOSITE Large numbers of German prisoners of war became a common sight walking along the country roads of Normandy. This photograph shows some of the 2,000 prisoners of war captured at Avranches which was taken on July 31, 1944. (IWM KY 32191)

Almost every bridge over the Loire and Seine Rivers had been bombed by the Allies in the weeks prior to D-Day. When the Allies came to cross the Seine in August 1944, they were forced to rely on pontoon bridges. (IWM B9748)

Eisenhower fully understood OVERLORD's potential for failure, and went so far as to write a note (later found crumpled in his shirt pocket and preserved by his naval aide, Captain Harry C. Butcher) accepting full responsibility in the event the Allies were obliged to withdraw from Normandy.

Had the D-Day landings failed, the outcome of the war would have been very different. The English Channel is one the most unpredictable and deadly bodies of water in the world, and the graveyard of more ships than any other place. Only brief periods were available during the late spring and summer during which Operation OVERLORD could have been carried out with both a combination of low tide and a full moon. As historian Alistair Horne has noted: "On re-opening the files on OVERLORD, 1944, one's immediate reaction is: what a staggering risk! Across the years, it now comes across as a much nearer-run thing, to use Wellington's famous dictum, than one had previously realised. There was absolutely no margin for error, and penalties for failure would have been inestimable."[1] Historian Ian Kershaw points out that, "The advantage, other than in sheer numbers, lay plainly with the defenders. OMAHA gave a horrifying taste of what the landings could have faced elsewhere had the German defense been properly prepared and waiting."[2]

The most serious repercussion of failure is that the Allies would have lost their precious initiative and the element of surprise, and to re-mount OVERLORD before late spring or early summer of 1945 would have been virtually impossible. For better or worse, OVERLORD was a one-time proposition. Britain's military manpower was already at a desperately low level, particularly in the infantry arm, and during the Normandy campaign a number of front line units had to be disbanded, including the entire 59th Division, in order to provide replacements to other units. Casualties within the infantry arm ran well beyond War Office estimates and were as high as 80 percent in British units and 76 percent in Canadian formations. Faulty projections, and the fact that Britain was now in its fifth year of war, combined to produce irreplaceable shortages in the summer of 1944 that were projected to reach 35,000 by September. To reconstitute a British force for a second landing might well have proved impossible.

Other scenarios had the D-Day landings failed are chilling, and include enormous casualties against greatly strengthened Normandy defenses, and replacement of virtually the entire fleet of landing craft which the Allies were chronically short of throughout the war. Had the war been extended into 1946, it is entirely plausible that the Red Army might have advanced as far west as the Rhine River and thus redrawn the landscape of post-war Europe.

REACTIONS TO THE D-DAY LANDINGS.

In Germany on the morning of June 6 no one dared awaken the notoriously late-sleeping Führer until the day (and the Allied invasion) was already well advanced.[3] A group of American airmen in an Allied POW camp in nearby Austria learned of the invasion before the German dictator, via a clandestine homemade wireless set. Hitler's response to the landings was pure bluster and a prime example of why Germany lost the war. Hitler boasted that the weather favored his army: "The news couldn't be better … Now we have them where we can destroy them." The reality was that Hitler had repeatedly spurned Rommel's warnings that to defeat an invasion of Normandy required the presence of the panzer reserves (Panzer Group West) at the front, under his operational control and available for immediate commitment. Hitler's visceral distrust of his generals and his unwillingness to entrust Rommel with the precious panzer reserves guaranteed that the German defense of Normandy would ultimately fail, and that Rommel's grim prediction

Military personnel at La Guardia Field in New York gather around a radio and listen intently as President Franklin D Roosevelt prays for the Allied invaders of Normandy on June 6, 1944. (Corbis BE002765 © Bettmann/Corbis)

would come true. The penalty incurred by Hitler's paranoia was paid on June 6.

The effect of Eisenhower's speech to the troops, broadcast to the rest of the world the morning of June 6 was nothing short of stunning. "The eyes of the world are upon you. The hopes and prayers of liberty-loving people everywhere march with you," he said, as the Allies embarked on the "great crusade."

The BBC interrupted its regular broadcasts to air the news. The British seemed to breathe a national collective sigh of relief. Workers in war plants stopped work and sang "God Save the King", and throughout Britain people flocked to churches to pray. Strangers who merely wanted to shake their hand stopped American military personnel on the streets.

In the United States, June 6 was one of the most extraordinary days in American history, and an unofficial national day of prayer. Word of the invasion spread like a wildfire through the night and early morning hours. Church bells tolled, stores closed, Broadway shows and sporting events were called off as Americans, like the British, flocked to churches in record numbers.[4] US President Franklin D. Roosevelt hailed the invasion of Normandy on June 6, 1944 "a mighty endeavor to preserve … our civilization and to set free a suffering humanity."[5] Churchill made no public pronouncement to the British people. In the House of Commons at noon on June 6 he merely remarked that, "This vast operation is undoubtedly the most complicated and difficult that has ever taken place."

That same night, Roosevelt went on national radio to deliver a prayer for "our sons, pride of our Nation," asking that God would "Give strength to their arms, stoutness to their hearts, steadfastness in their faith … in our united crusade."[6] In Canada, there was a similar reaction to the long-awaited news of the Allied invasion, but in Germany, however, there was no reaction because the propaganda machine of Joseph Goebbels suppressed Eisenhower's announcement and German citizens remained in ignorance of the historic events occurring in Normandy.

THE CONTRIBUTION OF THE FRENCH RESISTANCE

A vital but relatively unknown aspect of D-Day was the contribution of the French Resistance, which was extremely active in the Caen–Bayeux region of Normandy. The men and women of the Bayeux section toiled in obscurity and extreme danger to provide valuable intelligence to the Allies about German dispositions in Normandy, for which they paid a terrible price. The Gestapo vigorously hunted them and a significant number were eventually caught, tortured, imprisoned, and killed. After the war, SHAEF chief of staff, Lieutenant General Walter Bedell Smith, wrote to the French Minister of Information: "Without the networks of the French Resistance, the invasion would not have been possible." Eisenhower later said the work of the Resistance was worth 15 Allied divisions.

One of Eisenhower's gravest concerns was the German coastal battery of six 155mm guns that Allied intelligence had located atop the Pointe-du-Hoc. With a range of 12 miles, these guns had the potential to engulf both OMAHA Beach and UTAH Beach with deadly fire. Allied consternation ran so deep that an important part of the OVERLORD landing plan was an assault of the cliffs of the Pointe-du-Hoc by Lieutenant Colonel James Rudder's Second Ranger Battalion to eliminate the gun battery.

Georges Mercader, chief of the Bayeux Resistance, had been a professional cyclist prior to the war and possessed a precious permit that granted him access to the "Forbidden Zone" that the Germans had created along the Normandy coast. Concealing his true purpose under the guise of training, Mercader daily risked his life to reconnoiter the Forbidden Zone: to learn about and map the German defenses, and to report German naval activity. In the spring of 1944 his primary focus was the Pointe-du-Hoc.

Shortly before D-Day, Mercader discovered that the Pointe-du-Hoc battery had inexplicably been moved inland and abandoned, and thus would not menace the invasion force. An urgent signal sent to London by the Resistance in early June was apparently lost in the bureaucracy of SOE or SHAEF. On D-Day the Allies landed fully expecting to encounter deadly fire from these guns.

France later honored Mercader with the *Croix de Guerre*. In 1991 he received another unexpected honor from a group of visiting American generals touring the Normandy battlefields. Present as an honored guest at a ceremony hosted by the Lord Mayor of Bayeux was Georges Mercader. Through a translator, Mercader modestly recounted to three of the generals how he had discovered the secret of the guns of the Pointe-du-Hoc. The generals were all Ranger-trained, and the senior officer was so impressed that he decided on the spot that Mercader would be honored in the US Army Ranger Hall of Fame at Fort Bragg, North Carolina – very special distinction from a tight-knit fraternity that rarely embraces outsiders. One of the other generals wore an expensive sterling silver US Army Ranger emblem in the lapel of his

French Forces of the Interior join in a Nazi sniper hunt in Normandy woods. Their local knowledge meant they provided valuable assistance to Allied troops.
(IWM KY 31947)

suit. Abruptly, he removed the emblem and fastened it to Mercader's lapel in an impromptu ceremony. The aura of dignity about this gallant Frenchman, and the pride in his face at this unexpected accolade, must have mirrored the occasion when Charles de Gaulle honored him for his service to France. Afterwards, a colleague asked the general why he had just given away one of his prized possessions. The general replied simply: "Because he deserves it more than I do."

Parisians celebrate the liberation of Paris on August 25, 1944, by Allied troops. This event is still commemorated in the city. (IWM KY 35196)

THE RETURN OF GERMAN TOURISTS AND VETERANS

By the 1960s, German citizens and war veterans had begun returning to France as tourists. The sight of German license plates on automobiles in Paris and elsewhere became commonplace. An exception occurred in August 1969 when the author was in Paris during the 25th anniversary celebrations of the liberation of Paris. French tricolors decorated the city; flowers and wreaths were placed at spots along the quays around Boulevard St-Michel and sometimes in cracks in walls to commemorate where resistance fighters were killed during the city's liberation. It was

The German war cemetery at La Cambe. The bodies of 21,500 German soldiers who died in 1944 lie here. (Ken Ford)

both a solemn and festive time marked by the utter absence of German tourists. During the entire week not one single German license plate was noted. With French sensitivities still raw even after a quarter century, it was as if any German presence would not only have been unwelcome but very likely an object of derision.

Over time, German war veterans began returning to Normandy to recall their days in the line of fire, and to pay homage to their dead. Given that its citizens were subjected to severe deprivations during four years of occupation, it is a measure of French magnanimity that the Germans were permitted to erect military cemeteries for their dead. The stark black crosses of a German military cemetery are in marked contrast to the traditional white crosses of the British, American, Canadian, and Polish cemeteries.

Among the grimmest is the German ossuary located at Huisnes-sur-Mer, within sight of Mont-St-Michel. Inside its walls are the remains of over 11,956 German soldiers killed during the Battle of Normandy. In all, there are six German cemeteries in Normandy where 77,976 soldiers are buried.

REMEMBERING D-DAY

Although it was not the bloodiest battle of the war on the Western Front (that dubious distinction belongs to the Battle of the Bulge), Normandy has become the symbol of World War II in Europe. Its sheer magnitude and overall importance have placed it in the forefront of the remembrances.

Interest in D-Day after the war, while the subject of many books, was never quite as high as it was commencing with the 40th and 50th anniversaries in 1984 and 1994. Public consciousness in Britain, Europe, and the United States gained new heights through extensive television coverage. Attendance at D-Day ceremonies in 1984 by President Ronald Reagan, and in 1994 by President Bill Clinton, drew the attention of the world. Since he assumed office in 2001, President George W. Bush has also made a ceremonial pilgrimage to Normandy on Memorial Day.

Other outside factors have drawn attention to D-Day, among them Steven Spielberg's film *Saving Private Ryan* (1998) which portrayed the event in the starkest terms ever filmed. The first 30 minutes of the film, which depicts the landings on the beaches, were so horrific that many World War II veterans left the film, some in tears, and others utterly distraught by the memories. For many, particularly younger generations of Europeans and Americans, the film was a harsh reminder that the events of June 1944 were far more than pages in the history books. As the *New York Times* noted, the film depicts "the fury of combat, the essence of spontaneous courage, the craving for solace, the bizarre routines of wartime existence, the deep loneliness of life on the brink … This film simply looks at war as if war had not been looked at before."[7]

RETURNING TO NORMANDY

Virtually every Allied soldier who landed on the beaches of Normandy on June 6, 1944, expected to die. A common expression among fighting men was that there were no atheists in a foxhole. These were young men who put aside their gut-wrenching fear to fight one of the most difficult battles of World War II. To this day, these veterans remember every detail of their experiences on the beaches of Normandy or in the bloody battles for Caen, Falaise, St-Lô, and for countless other nameless hills, towns, road junctions, and hedgerows. They remember, not to gloat, but as a continuing catharsis that they survived. Every survivor left behind comrades who did not, and those who revisit the sites of their battles do so to honor their fallen comrades.

Pulitzer Prize-winning cartoonist and World War II veteran, Bill Mauldin, who immortalized the combat soldier with his cartoons of the infantrymen Willie and Joe, had an equally skillful way with words. His post-war tribute to these men noted that: "They wish to hell they were someplace else, and they wish to hell they would get relief. They wish to hell the mud was dry and they wish to hell their coffee was hot. They want to go home. But they stay in their wet holes and fight, and then they climb out and crawl though the minefields and fight some more."[8]

Most survivors felt that God had given them their lives back and are to this day grateful beyond measure, but in a classic Catch-22 still experience guilt that they survived. A common trait among veterans of all nations returning to their former lives was that their families and friends back home had no concept of what they experienced. While there were, indeed, victory parades, the great majority of veterans merely returned to their former lives in quiet anonymity. Nor was this unique to World War II. Soldiers trained to kill and endure the horrors of combat suddenly found themselves thrust back into their former lives and jobs, and were expected to behave as if the war had never occurred. Thus, for most, their emotions are as raw today as they were on the beaches of Normandy 60 years ago.

Thousands of veterans have returned to Normandy in the past 60 years to honor their dead comrades. A visit to one of the many German, American, Polish, British, and Canadian military cemeteries that dot the Normandy landscape is often wrenching.

Most arrive in early June. An exception occurs in August, when the Free Polish veterans who fought in the First [Polish] Armored Division, in some of the bloodiest battles of the Normandy campaign during July and August 1944, return to Normandy. For many years they had no military cemetery of their own in Normandy. Eventually, the French Government set aside land for a Polish cemetery at Urville-Langannerie, located on the main highway (Route National 158) approximately halfway between Caen and Falaise, and the area where the Poles fought some of their bloodiest battles. Before that time, Polish soldiers killed in combat were buried by French citizens in local graveyards near where they fell. As a token of respect for the sacrifice of their Polish allies, ordinary French men and women lovingly tended these graves.

During the 50th anniversary ceremonies, the cameras of the world's news organizations recorded scenes of men and women releasing, many for the first time, a half century of repressed emotions. Such scenes will again be played out in 2004. In my own experience as a military historian, and in studies by social historians, it is not uncommon for veterans to have rarely, if ever, spoken to anyone, except a comrade-in-arms, of their wartime experiences. Untold numbers of veterans suffered from undiagnosed Post Traumatic Stress Disorder; others simply repressed their memories, some in the belief they were too painful to be shared, or in an effort to simply get on with their lives and not dwell on the past.

During the ceremonies at the American military cemetery on June 6, 1994, television cameras recorded the raw, emotional reaction that all but overwhelmed a friend – a hard-boiled infantry officer. His face tear-strewn, this veteran's feelings have been replicated a thousand times over. As their numbers daily grow fewer, a rate estimated at over 1,200 per day in the United States, such occasions will see fewer and fewer able to attend.

LEST WE FORGET

The passage of 60 years has produced new generations untouched by war. The large-scale commemorations held every ten years have served an important purpose, as a reminder that war demands payment of a very high price from which no one is exempt. As John Keegan has so thoughtfully pointed out in his landmark book, *The Second World War*, it was "the largest single event in human history, fought across six of the world's seven continents and all of its oceans. It killed fifty million human beings, left hundreds of millions of others wounded in mind or body and materially devastated much of the heartland of civilization."[9]

A British war cemetery in Normandy.
(Corbis PA 006847)

An American veteran holds the US flag at the 50th anniversary of D-Day at the American cemetery, Colleville-sur-Mer. (Corbis TL003013)

Scattered across the breadth of Europe are memorials and military cemeteries of the combatants. In Normandy alone, over 110,000 graves of the participants dot the landscape as grim reminders of the high cost of war. The tradition of placing military monuments and war memorials, as tokens of commemoration and remembrance, at places where battles were fought and men died dates to earlier wars. After World War I, hundreds appeared across France and Belgium. So, too, did the military cemeteries where the dead are buried. This practice was continued after World War II, and one can hardly pass through a city or village without coming across such memorials, large and small. For example, there are 70 monuments scattered across France, Belgium, the Netherlands, and Germany dedicated to the Free Polish First Armored Division that fought gallantly with the Allies from Normandy to the Baltic.[10] Museums, too, have been erected; two of the most important in Normandy are located in Bayeux and Caen. In the United States the late historian Stephen E. Ambrose founded the National D-Day Museum in New Orleans, Louisiana.

The military cemeteries themselves also play an important role. The smallest is British. Jerusalem Cemetery, near Bayeux, is one of 16 British cemeteries in Normandy, and consists of only 48 graves, most of them for those killed in the fighting shortly after D-Day. The American cemetery at Colleville-sur-Mer, overlooking OMAHA Beach, is one of the largest in Normandy and one of the most visited sites in Europe. Each year an average of one and a half million people visit there. American visitors rank about fifth or sixth in numbers, thus confirming that citizens of other countries feel strongly enough to visit the site and thereby honor the fallen.

Each of the 9,386 white crosses and Stars of David (307 of which are Unknowns bearing the inscription "Here Rests in Honored Glory an American Soldier Known but to God") faces west, toward the Atlantic Ocean and the United States. Each Memorial Day, and for special

The remains of MULBERRY B at Arromanches beach today. (Corbis SH005230)

occasions such as the anniversary of D-Day, every grave has planted next to it a miniature French tricolor and an American flag. It is a solemn place and few who visit leave unaffected.

The Allied Supreme Commander, General Dwight D. Eisenhower, was no exception. Eisenhower, who, more than any other participant, symbolized D-Day, did not return to Normandy until the 20th anniversary in 1964. After visiting his D-Day headquarters at Portsmouth, England, Eisenhower paid an emotional visit to OMAHA Beach and to the American military cemetery on the bluffs above the place so many had died to secure. His words were recorded by the Columbia Broadcasting System for a television documentary film. As he sat on the stone wall overlooking the beach, Eisenhower spoke eloquently for the dead when he said:

"These men came here – British and our allies, and Americans – to storm these beaches for one purpose only, not to gain anything for ourselves, not to fulfill any ambitions that America had for conquest, but just to preserve freedom ... Many thousands of men have died for such ideals as these ... but these young boys ... were cut off in their prime ... I devoutly hope that we will never again have to see such scenes as these. I think and hope, and pray, that humanity will have learned ... we must find some way ... to gain an eternal peace for this world."[11]

THE GREATEST GENERATION?

NBC television newsman Tom Brokaw has dubbed the men and women of World War II "the greatest generation," for their quiet heroism and exceptional patriotism. Others have rejected the designation as a slight to other generations that have fought other wars with equal honor. What is more certain is that those who served do not think of themselves in such terms. Jack Murphy, an American veteran who returned to Normandy in 2003, may well have spoken for all veterans of every nation that fought there when he said: "They call us the 'greatest generation.' I don't know ... We were just a bunch of guys."[12]

In June 2004 the attention of the world will once again be focused on Normandy. It will be an occasion to re-affirm that the sacrifice of those who fought the battles and campaigns of the most devastating war in history will never go unremembered.

It was that common purpose, the spirit and grit shown on D-Day, that has permitted democracies to survive. This is what we celebrate on June 6, 2004.

Endnotes

Chapter 1

1 Although the German Navy's strength had been considerably reduced, D-Day planners could not ignore what happened at Slapton Sands. During a practice run for the US VIIth Corps on the night of April 27, German E-Boats slipped through the destroyer screen and sank two LSTs and damaged another six. Some 750 men were killed and 300 were wounded.

2 Great Britain's forces had also witnessed the resilience of the German Army in November 1943, when the Germans staged a seaborne and airborne attack and seized the Dodecanese island of Leros from a largely British garrison.

3 Russell Weigley. 1981. *Eisenhower's Lieutenants: The Campaign of France and Germany, 1944–1945*. Bloomington: Indiana University Press. p.77.

Chapter 3

1 Sun Tzu. *The Art of War*. trans. Samuel Griffith. 1963. London: Oxford University Press. p.66.

2 Although Clausewitz regarded deception as useful, he did not place the same emphasis on it as Sun Tzu. However, he did say that one of the products of deception, surprise, 'lies at the root of all operations without exception'. See C von Clausewitz. *On War*. trans. and ed. by Michael Howard and Peter Paret. 1976. Princeton: Princeton University Press. p.198 and Chapter 10.

3 M. Howard. 1990. *British Intelligence in the Second World War*. London: HMSO. Vol.5. pp.106–7.

4 Ibid. p.xii.

5 Howard. pp.34f, 224.

6 C.J.M. Goulter. 1998. "The Politicisation of Intelligence: the British Experience in Greece, 1941–44' in *Knowing Your Friends: Intelligence Inside Alliances and Coalitions from 1914 to the Cold War*. ed. Martin Alexander. London: Frank Cass. pp.176–7.

7   R. Hesketh. 1999. *Fortitude: The D-Day Deception Campaign*. London: St Ermin's Press. Chapter 3.

8   Howard. op. cit. p.ix.

9   Hesketh. op. cit. Chapters 3, 7, 9.

10 Howard. pp.5–11; Hesketh. p.46.

11 Hesketh. pp.46f.

12 Ibid. pp.64–5; Howard. p.115.

13 Howard. pp.16–17.

14 Hesketh. p.352.

15 Howard. pp.14–15.

16 Ibid. pp.130f.

17 Howard. pp.128f, 190–4.

18 Ibid. p.188.

19 Hesketh. pp.267–9, 271, 289f; Howard. pp.194–5.

20 Howard. p.125 and Chapter 7. See also Goulter. op. cit. esp. pp.176–90.

21 Howard. pp.150–2.

Chapter 8

1   Carlo D'Este. 1994. *Decision in Normandy*. New York: Konecky & Konecky. p.36.

2   Major General Pete Corlett. "Memoirs of his Military Career". Unpublished manuscript. Carlisle Barracks, PA: US Army Military History Institute.

3   Quoted in Stephen Ambrose. 1994. *D-Day, June 6, 1944. The Climactic Battle of World War II*. New York: Simon and Schuster. p.345.

4   Gunner Charles Wilson, 147th Field Regiment, quoted in Max Hastings. 1984. *Overlord, D-Day and the Battle for Normandy*. New York: Simon & Schuster. p.107.

Chapter 10

1   William B. Breuer. 1984. *Hitler's Fortress Cherbourg*. New York: Stein and Day. p.103.

2   Ken Cordry oral history, copy in National D-Day Museum in New Orleans (DDM).

3   Ibid.

4   Breuer. p.128

5   Hugh Ambrose interview with Adolf Rogosch, DDM.

6   Center for Military History. *Utah Beach to Cherbourg*. p.189.

7   Breuer. p.252.

8   Carlo D'Este. 1983. *Decision in Normandy*. New York: Dutton. p.164.

9   Chester Wilmot. 1952. *The Struggle for Europe*. London: Collins. p.340.

10 L. F. Ellis. 1968. *Victory in the West*. London: HMSO. p.261.

11 D'Este. p.206.

12 Ibid. p.209.

13 Hans von Luck. 1989. *Panzer Commander. The Memoirs of Colonel Hans von Luck*. New York: Dell Publishing.

14 Forrest C. Pogue. 1954. *The Supreme Command*. Washington DC: GPO. p.188.

15 von Luck. op cit. pp.188–9.

16 D'Este. p.370.

17 Alexander McKee. *2001. Caen: Anvil of Victory*. New York: Dorset Press. p.265.

18 Ibid.

19 von Luck. p.193.

20 Ibid.

21 McKee. p.268.

22 McKee. p.270.

23 McKee. p.273.

24 von Luck. p.197.

25 Hugh Ambrose interview with Friedrich Bertenrath, DDM.

26 Hugh Ambrose interview with Gunter Materne, DDM.

27 Hugh Ambrose interview with Gunther Behr, DDM.

28 Hugh Ambrose interview with Helmut Ritgen, DDM.

29 Rogosch interview.

30 Bertenrath interview.

31 Center for Military History. *St-Lô*. p.128.

32 D'Este. p.402.

33 Ernie Pyle. 1986. *Ernie's War: The Best of Ernie Pyle's World War II Dispatches*. New York: Touchstone/Simon & Schuster. p.332.

34 Hugh Ambrose interview with Joachim Barth, DDM.

35 D'Este. p.402.

Chapter 13

1   Alistair Horne, with David Montgomery. 1994. *Monty the Lonely Leader, 1944–1945*. New York: Pan Books Ltd. p.xix.

2   Ian Kershaw. 2000. *Hitler, 1936–1945, Nemesis*. New York: W.W. Norton & Company. p.640.

3   Kershaw. p.639. According to Kershaw, Hitler did not go to bed until 3:00 a.m. the morning of 6 June. "When Speer arrived next morning, seven hours later, Hitler had still not been wakened with the news of the invasion." Kershaw goes on to note that the

skepticism of the Wehrmacht Supreme Command that the invasion was a diversion was finally dispelled sometime between 8:15a.m. and 9:30a.m., June 6. "His adjutants now hesitated to waken him with mistaken information." Apparently Hitler was up in time for the lunchtime military conference and only then agreed to von Rundstedt's telegram to deploy and commit two panzer divisions held in reserve near Paris against the beachhead.

4   Stephen E. Ambrose. 1994. *D-Day*. New York: Simon & Schuster. pp.492–3.

5   Roosevelt quoted in "Normandy", US Army campaign pamphlet, US Army Center of Military History, 1994.

6   Doris Kearns Goodwin. 1994. *No Ordinary Time*. New York: Simon & Schuster. p.510.

7   Review by Janet Maslin, *The New York Times*, July 24, 1998.

8   Bill Mauldin quoted in Desmond Flower and James Reeves (eds.). 1997. *The War, 1939–1945*. New York: Da Capo Press. p.887.

9   John Keegan. 1990. *The Second World War*. New York: Viking. p.5.

10 Source: Zbigniew Mieczkowski (ed.). 1989. *Monuments and War Memorials on the Battlefields of the Polish Armoured Division*. London: Veritas Foundation.

11 *CBS Reports: Eisenhower and D-Day*. 1964.

12 Quoted in Richard P. Carpenter. "The Sands of Time," *Boston Sunday Globe*, August 3, 2003.

Bibliography

Ambrose, Stephen E., *Pegasus Bridge*. New York: Simon and Schuster, 1985.

Ambrose, Stephen E., *D-Day June 6, 1944: The Climactic Battle of World War II*. New York: Simon and Schuster, 1994.

Ambrose, Stephen E., *Citizen Soldiers: The U.S. Army from the Normandy Beaches to the Bulge to the Surrender of Germany, June 7, 1944–May 7, 1945*. New York: Simon & Schuster, 1997.

Badsey, Stephen, *Normandy 1944: Allied Landings and Breakout*. Campaign 1. Oxford: Osprey Publishing, 1990.

Barber, Neil, *The Day the Devils Dropped In: The Paras in the Battle of Normandy, June 1944*. London: Pen and Sword, 2002.

Blair, Clay, *Ridgway's Paratroopers: The American Airborne in World War II*. Garden City, N.Y.: Doubleday, 1985.

Blumenson, Martin, *The Battle of the Generals*. New York: Morrow, 1993.

Bradley, Omar, *A Soldier's Story*. New York: Rand McNally, 1951.

Breuer, William B., *Hitler's Fortress Cherbourg*. New York: Stein and Day, 1984.

Caldwell, D., *JG26: Top Guns of the Luftwaffe*. New York: Orion Books, 1991.

Carrell, P. (pseudonym), *Invasion: They're Coming!* New York: Dutton, 1963.

Carpenter, Richard P., "The Sands of Time," *Boston Sunday Globe*, August 3, 2003.

CBS Reports: Eisenhower and D-Day. 1964.

Center for Military History. *St-Lô*. Washington DC: GPO, CMH Pub 100–13, 1946.

Center for Military History. *Utah Beach to Cherbourg*. Washington, DC: GPO, CMH Pub 100–12, 1948.

Churchill, Winston S., *The Second World War* Vol. VI "Triumph and Tragedy". London: Cassell and Co. Ltd, 1954.

von Clausewitz, C., *On War*. trans. and ed. by Michael Howard and Peter Paret. Princeton: Princeton University Press, 1976.

Copp, Terry, *Fields of Fire. The Canadians in Normandy*. Toronto: University of Toronto Press, 2003.

Corlett, Major General Pete, "Memoirs of his Military Career". Unpublished manuscript. Carlisle Barracks, PA: US Army Military History Institute.

Detweiler, D., *German Military Studies*. New York: Garland Publishing, 1979.

D'Este, Carlo, *Decision in Normandy*. New York: Konecky & Konecky, 1994.

D' Este, Carlo, *Eisenhower: A Soldier's Life*. New York: Henry Holt and Company, 2002.

Eisenhower, Dwight D., *Crusade in Europe*. New York: Doubleday, 1984.

Ellis, L. F. and Warhurst, A. E., *History of the Second World War: Victory in the West*, 2 vols., Vol. I: *The Battle of Normandy*. London: HMSO, 1962.

Ellis, L. F., *Victory in the West*. London: HMSO, 1968.

Flower, Desmond and James Reeves (eds.), *The War, 1939–1945*. New York: Da Capo Press, 1997.

Fraser, D., *Knight's Cross: A Life of Field Marshal Erwin Rommel*. New York: HarperCollins, 1993.

Gale, R. N. (Lt Gen), *With the 6th Airborne in Normandy*. London: Sampson, Low, Marston & Co., Ltd., 1948.

Gavin, James M., *On to Berlin: Battles of an Airborne Commander, 1943–1946*. New York: Viking Press, 1978.

George, Robert H., "Normandy" in Craven, Wesley Frank and Cates, James Lea, eds. *The Army Air Forces in World War II*, 7 vols. Vol. III: *Europe: Argument to V-E Day, January 1944 to May 1945* (1951), pp. 185–227. Chicago: University of Chicago Press.

Goodwin, Doris Kearns, *No Ordinary Time*. New York: Simon & Schuster, 1994.

Goulter, C. J. M., "The Politicisation of Intelligence: the British Experience in Greece, 1941–44" in *Knowing Your Friends: Intelligence Inside Alliances and Coalitions from 1914 to the Cold War*. ed. Martin Alexander. London: Frank Cass, 1998.

Guderian, Heinz Gunther, *From Normandy to the Ruhr. With the 116th Panzer Division in World War II*. Tr U. Abele et al. Bedford, PA: Aberjona Press, 2001.

Hamlin, John F., *Support and Strike: A Concise History of the U.S. Ninth Air Force in Europe*. Peterborough, Great Britain: GMS Enterprises, 1991.

Harrison, Gordon A., *Cross Channel Attack in U.S. Army in World War II: European Theatre of Operations*. Washington: Government Printing Office, 1951 and *Omaha Beach* in *American Forces in Action* Series, 1945.

Hart, Russell A., *Clash of Arms. How the Allies Won in Normandy*. Boulder, Colorado: Lynne Rienner Publishers, Inc, 2001.

Hastings, Max, *Das Reich: The March of the 2nd Panzer Division Through France*. New York: Holt, Rinehart and Winston, 1981.

Hastings, Max, *Overlord, D-Day and the Battle for Normandy*. New York: Simon & Schuster, 1984.

Hesketh, R., *Fortitude: The D-Day Deception Campaign*. London: St Ermin's Press, 1999.

Horne, Alistair with David Montgomery, *Monty the Lonely Leader, 1944–1945*. New York: Pan Books Ltd, 1994.

Houston, James A., *Out of the Blue: U.S. Army Airborne Operations in World War II*. West Lafayette, Ind.: Purdue University Studies, 1972.

Howard, M., *British Intelligence in the Second World War*. London: HMSO, 1990. Vol.5.

Isby, D., *Fighting the Invasion*. London: Greenhill Books, 2000.

Keegan, John, *The Second World War*. New York: Viking, 1990.

Kershaw, Ian, *Hitler, 1936–1945, Nemesis*. New York: W.W. Norton & Company, 2000.

Kershaw, Robert J., *D-Day. Piercing the Atlantic Wall*. London: Ian Allan Publishing, 1993.

Kirkpatrick, Charles E., *An Unknown Future and a Doubtful Present: Writing the Victory Plan of 1941*. Washington DC: US Center of Military History, 1990.

Klöss, E., *Die Invasion 1944*. Munich: Deutscher Taschenbuch, 1984.

Kuhn, V., *Schnellboote im Einsatz*, Stuttgart: Motorbuch, 1986.

Lewis, Adrian, *Omaha Beach*. Chapel Hill, N. C.: University of North Carolina Press, 2002.

von Luck, Hans, *Panzer Commander: The Memoirs of Colonel Hans von Luck*. New York: Dell Publishing, 1989.

Marshall, S. L. A., *Night Drop: The American Airborne Invasionof Normandy*. Boston: Little Brown, 1962.

McKee, Alexander, *Caen: Anvil of Victory*. New York: St. Martin's Press, 1964.

Messenger, Charles, *The Last Prussian*. London: Brassey's, 1991.

Mieczkowski, Zbigniew (ed.), *Monuments and War Memorials on the Battlefields of the Polish Armoured Division*. London: Veritas Foundation, 1989.

Murray, Williamson and Allan R. Millett, *A War to Be Won: Fighting the Second World War*. Cambridge, Mass: Bellknapp Press of Harvard University Press, 2001.

Ose, D., *Entscheidung im Westen 1944*. Stuttgart: Deutsche Verlags-Anstalt, 1982.

Pogue, Forrest C., *The Supreme Command*. Washington DC: GPO, 1954.

Pyle, Ernie, *Ernie's War: The Best of Ernie Pyle's World War II Dispatches*. New York: Touchstone/Simon & Schuster, 1986.

Rapport, Leonard and Arthur Norwood, Jr., *Rendezvous with Destiny: History of the 101st Airborne Division*, reprint. Old Saybrook, Conn: Konecky & Konecky, 2001.

Reynolds, Michael, *Steel Inferno. I SS Panzer Corps in Normandy*. New York: Sarpedon, 1997.

Ropp, Theodore, *War in the Modern World*. New York: The MacMillan Company, 1962.

Ruge, F., *Rommel in Normandy*. London: MacDonald and Jane's, 1979.

Ruppenthal, R. G., *Utah Beach to Cherbourg* in U.S. War Department, Historical Division, *American Forces in Action*. Washington: Government Printing Office, 1947.

Ryan, Cornelius, *The Longest Day: June 6, 1944*. New York: Popular Library, 1959.

Salmaggi, Cesare and Alfredo Pallavisini , *2194 Days of War*. New York: Gallery Books, 1979.

Simpson, Keith, "A Close Run Thing? D-Day, 6 June 1944: The German Perspective". *RUSI Journal* 139 (June) 60–71, 1994.

Speidel, H., *Invasion 1944*. Chicago: Henry Regnery Company, 1950.

Sullivan, John J., *Overlord's Eagles: Operations of the United States Army Air Forces in the Invasion of Normandy in World War II*. Jefferson, N.C.: McFarland, 1997

Sun Tzu. *The Art of War*. trans. Samuel Griffith, London: Oxford University Press, 1963.

Warlimont, Walter, *Inside Hitler's Headquarters 1939–45*. London: Weidenfeld and Nicolson, 1964.

Wegemüller, H., *Die Abwehr der Invasion*. Freiburg: Rombach, 1979.

Weigley, Russell F., *Eisenhower's Lieutenants: The Campaign of France and Germany, 1944–1945*. Bloomington: Indiana University Press, 1981.

Westphal, S., *The German Army in the West*. London: Cassell, 1950.

Wilmot, Chester, *The Struggle for Europe*. London: Collins, 1952.

Wilt, Alan F., *The Atlantic Wall. Hitler's Defenses in the West, 1941–1944*. Ames: Iowa State University Press, 1975.

Zimmerman, R., *Der Atlantikwall von Dünkirchen bis Cherbourg*. Munich: Schild-Verlag, 1982.

Index

Related titles

Find out more about D-Day and the Second World War

in the following related titles, also available from Osprey:

Essential Histories series
The Second World War – A world in flames (ESSPE 3)
by Paul Collier, Alastair Finlan, Mark J Grove, Philip D Grove, Russell Hart, Stephen A Hart, Robin Havers, David Horner, Geoffrey Jukes With a foreword by Sir Max Hastings

Campaign series
D-Day 1944 (1) Omaha Beach (CAM 100)
by Steven Zaloga

D-Day 1944 (2) Utah Beach & the US Airborne
Landings (CAM 104)
by Steven Zaloga

D-Day 1944 (3) Sword Beach & the British
Airborne Landings (CAM 105)
by Ken Ford

D-Day 1944 (4) Gold & Juno Beaches (CAM 112)
by Ken Ford

Visit **www.ospreypublishing.com** *for details*

of over 1,000 military history books published by Osprey

First published in Great Britain in 2004 by Osprey Publishing,
Midland House, West Way, Botley, Oxford OX2 0PH, United Kingdom.
Email: info@ospreypublishing.com

A CIP catalogue record for this book is available from the British Library

ISBN 0 681 56691 4

The authors, Duncan Anderson, Ronald J Drez, Carlo D'Este, Andrew Gordon, Christina
J M Goulter, David I Hall, Russell Hart, Stephen A Hart, Allan R Millett, Williamson
Murray, Samuel J Newland, Dennis Showalter and Major Richard Winters have asserted
their rights under the Copyright, Designs and Patents Act, 1988, to be identified as the
Authors of this Work

Editor: Jane Penrose
Design: Ken Vail Graphic Design, Cambridge, UK
Index by Alan Thatcher
Maps by The Map Studio
3D bird's-eye views by The Black Spot
Originated by Grasmere Digital Imaging, Leeds, UK
Printed and bound in China through Bookbuilders

06 07 08 09 10   10 9 8 7 6 5 4 3 2 1

FOR A CATALOG OF ALL BOOKS PUBLISHED BY OSPREY MILITARY AND AVIATION PLEASE CONTACT:

NORTH AMERICA
Osprey Direct, c/o Random House Distribution Center,
400 Hahn Road, Westminster, MD 21157
Email: info@ospreydirect.com

ALL OTHER REGIONS
Osprey Direct UK, P.O. Box 140, Wellingborough, Northants,
NN8 2FA, UK
E-mail: info@ospreydirect.co.uk

www.ospreypublishing.com

Publisher's Note
Please note that spelling reflects the nationality of the author of the chapter.